Making the Carry

Making the Carry

The Lives of John and Tchi-Ki-Wis Linklater

TIMOTHY COCHRANE

University of Minnesota Press
Minneapolis
London

The University of Minnesota Press gratefully acknowledges the generous support provided for the publication of this book by the National Parks of Lake Superior Foundation.

NATIONAL PARKS OF
LAKE SUPERIOR
FOUNDATION

Frontispiece: Tchi-Ki-Wis and John Linklater at Birch Island, Isle Royale, during the Macdonald–Massee Expedition, 1928. Photograph by George Fox. C-809-H-93. Courtesy of the Milwaukee Public Museum.

Maps on pages xi–xvi by Rhys Davies

Published by the University of Minnesota Press
111 Third Avenue South, Suite 290
Minneapolis, MN 55401-2520
http://www.upress.umn.edu

ISBN 978-1-5179-1388-5 (pb)

A Cataloging-in-Publication record for this book is available from the Library of Congress.

Printed in the United States of America on acid-free paper

The University of Minnesota is an equal-opportunity educator and employer.

30 29 28 27 26 25 24   10 9 8 7 6 5 4 3 2

CONTENTS

I FIRST LEARNED of John Linklater in 1976 on a ten-minute foray into the Isle Royale National Park Library. Hired as a fire lookout, with time on my hands, I wanted to learn everything I could about the island. But I rarely had a chance to visit park headquarters and the compact library wedged into the attic of a warehouse building. When I did, I glanced at a black-and-white slide of an Indian man, John Linklater, clowning around wearing a top hat at a fishery. I was unintentionally searching for evidence of Native American history on Isle Royale.[1] At that time, in the 1970s, the park story included a distinguished prehistory of aboriginal copper miners but no mention of a historic Indigenous presence. But then there was John Linklater, fooling around for the camera. It turned out he was given the top hat and a hundred dollar bill in 1928 for guiding prominent industrialists on an archaeological expedition to the island. The lighthearted photograph challenged the park narrative, as he clearly was Native.

So began my "hunt" for "things Linklater." Through an off-and-on effort, incrementally, one discovery led to the next; for example, I learned of Linklater's connection to the fabled Hudson's Bay Company. Thus, he must have been an extraordinary canoeist. His wife, Tchi-Ki-Wis, was Anishinaabe, literally of the canoe country at Lac La Croix. My pursuit of the Linklaters' story fit two of my inclinations: biographies and bioregionalism. In my training as a folklorist, I was drawn to biographies, particularly of nonelites, as a humanizing endeavor. As I naively understood bioregionalism, I wanted to learn more about the people of a particular place and ideally about the Indigenous people of the North Country.[2] The Linklaters fit these affinities.

The Linklater research also paralleled my recognition that the Canadian Shield and Lake Superior landscape and people created a place where I felt deeply at home. I had already canoed in the far north, on

Lake St. Joseph in Ontario. And I had illegally built log cabins on Lac Seul; it was illegal at the time for an American to work in northwestern Ontario. Only later would I learn that these two large and daunting lakes were home places for the Linklater family and Hudson's Bay Company posts. Escaping college one winter, I tried fur trapping, apprenticing with an older French Canadian, Ebenezer Bouge, on his trap line south of Lac Seul. Graduate school followed, and a grant provided me the opportunity to locate and chat with Ellen Hanson, Tchi-Ki-Wis's White friend and admirer with a razor-sharp memory.[3] Eventually I was hired as the park historian at Isle Royale and, ironically, became keeper of the park library and Tchi-Ki-Wis's extraordinary cedar mats.

The Linklaters were well remembered by island old-timers, mostly commercial fishermen—further spurring me on. My career with the National Park Service intervened, and I worked at Isle Royale, in Alaska, and at Grand Portage, but the desire to focus again on the Linklaters remained. In 2009 *Minong—the Good Place: Ojibwe and Isle Royale* was published, including what I knew about the Linklaters at that time. But I always knew there was more. When I was near retirement, I began earnestly researching their lives again, with assistance from Linklater family members, who encouraged me. Writing this book has been both rewarding and daunting—daunting in the sense that the Linklaters' story is so good, so compelling that I worried I might blow it, not tell it well. But their remarkable story carries this work as their lives were epically lived during difficult times, in a beguiling country of canoes, dog teams, lakes, rivers, and the homeland of Anishinaabeg.

Author's note: Whenever possible, I tried to use Anishinaabemowin words and phrases reflecting the Border Lakes dialect of the Ojibwe language. This dialect is now threatened: there are fewer and fewer speakers, making it difficult to accurately transcribe that dialect into a written format. Anishinaabe people who live along the U.S.–Canadian border from Lake of the Woods to Lac La Croix, and eastward to Grand Portage, conversed in this dialect, including Tchi-Ki-Wis and John Linklater.

The Families of John and Tchi-Ki-Wis Linklater

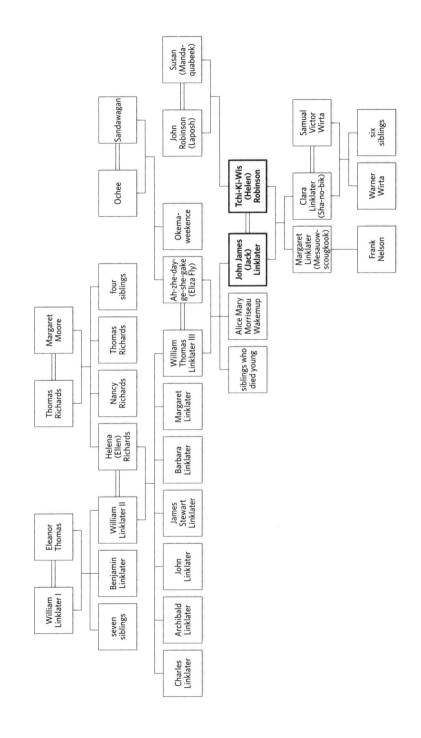

Linklaters' Home Region

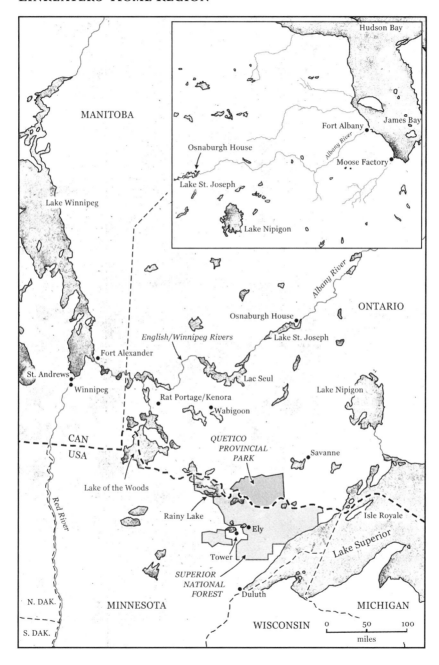

Linklaters' Canoe Country

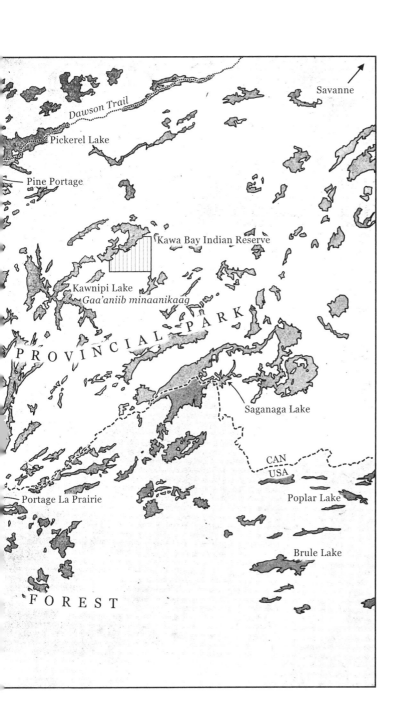

BASSWOOD LAKE ANISHINAABEG, CIRCA 1910

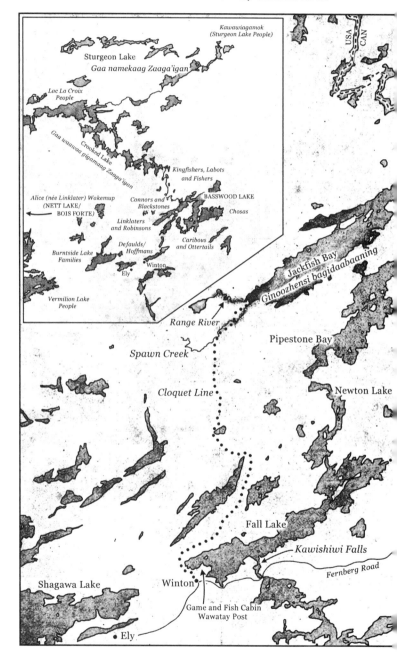

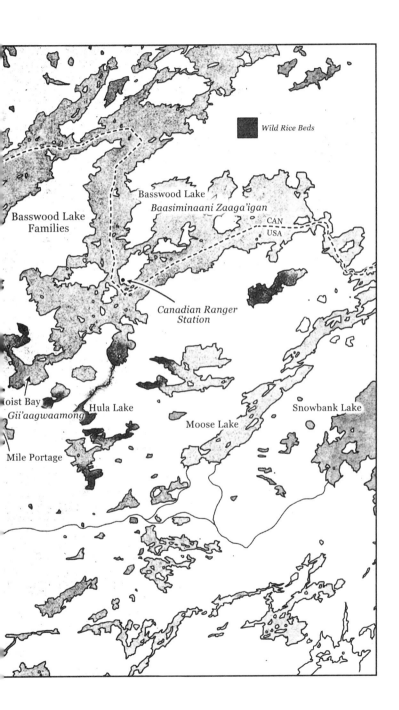

Wild Rice Beds

Basswood Lake
Baasiminaani Zaaga'igan

Basswood Lake
Families

CAN
USA

Canadian Ranger
Station

oist Bay
Gii'aagwaamong

Hula Lake

Moose Lake

Snowbank Lake

Mile Portage

Linklaters' Isle Royale, circa 1930

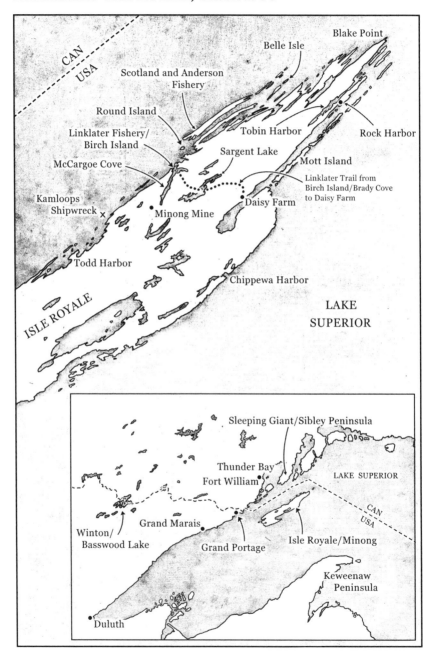

Introduction

JOHN LINKLATER COULD "make a canoe do everything but talk."[1] John and Tchi-Ki-Wis were canoe people; they made, used, and, when necessary, repaired canoes—the old way. There is movie footage from the 1920s of John repairing a canoe with a flaming birch-bark torch melting pitch into a gouge, making it waterproof again. Tchi-Ki-Wis made "portage collars," or tumplines, out of strips of tanned moose hide to haul loads. John (also called Jack, especially by his friends) grew up in canoes; he used them to travel, fish, hunt, harvest wild rice, trade, move, and visit. When guiding, he would let clients walk the portages and then shoot the rapids alone. Even in his midsixties, he was still adept in a canoe and had planned a canoe trip to Hudson Bay, likely following the routes of his ancestors. His untimely death cut this trip short.[2] He grew up along a major Canadian river system used by both First Nation peoples and fur traders. While trapping and trading along the border canoe route, he met a young woman from the Lac La Croix First Nation, Tchi-Ki-Wis. Most records in English name her Helen Robinson. Sometime circa 1889, the young couple moved eastward along the border route and made their home on Jackfish Bay, Basswood Lake, in what is now the Boundary Waters Canoe Area Wilderness in northeastern Minnesota.

When Sigurd Olson wrote his essay "Wilderness Music," he recalled remarkable experiences he had had with Jack Linklater and purposefully talked of Indians and voyageurs "making the carry."[3] Traditional canoe guides knew and would use the phrase, *carry* being an alternative word for *portage.*[4] Many languages have words to express the primal act of carrying burdens overland from one body of water to another, indicating a near universal experience. *Portage* is, of course, a French word, likely attempting to capture the essence of the Anishinaabemowin *gabadoo,* translated as "he or she goes over a portage," or *gakiiwenige,* meaning "he or she carries things on the shoulder over a portage."[5] As used here, "making the carry" is not just a descriptor of hauling things: it metaphorically captures much of the Linklater story. It is a de facto participation in the past, using a portage made by others long ago. It was likely first a game trail; hence one is following the ancient tracks of caribou, moose, or waddling beavers. Like Linklater, a portage adeptly follows the lay of the land, the best route between waters. It became a pathway for subsistence, to move to harvest food, to survive. Linklater's ancestors might have neatly hung a gillnet in a sheltered tree off a portage so the next Indigenous traveler could pause and conveniently catch and eat fish along the way.[6]

John and Tchi-Ki-Wis Linklater prepare a meal while guiding the Warren family on Isle Royale, circa 1929. Frank M. Warren photograph. Courtesy of University of Minnesota Duluth, Archives and Special Collections.

Linklater knew each portage, each "carry," was different. Each has its own character and history. Making the carry describes the Linklaters' penchant for bringing the expert past into the present (as readers will see in Anishinaabeg cedar mats, canoes, story, and traditional ecological knowledge). Their wide base of knowledge and experience was a carry across time, an accumulation of learning from their Indigenous forebears that they were deeply committed to passing along to others. The Link-laters could also make the carry across cultures, people, and worldviews. They were teachers reaching across different languages, customs, and ways of seeing and being in the world. And making the carry is a fitting description of their resilience amid adversity and tumult. They made the carry across hardship—discrimination, ignorance, and the loss of a twenty-year-old daughter under suspicious circumstances. And yet they remained productive and kind. Rarely stumbling, they made the carry in a humble manner that inspired those from a different station in life—the well-off, professors, scientists, and game wardens. All the while they remained devoted to their Anishinaabeg and Métis family roots and their homeland.

The Linklaters' place on Jackfish Bay was smartly situated. The cabin, made of vertical cedar logs, and *wiigwaasigamig* (birch-bark lodges) faced south, with a rocky ridge behind them blocking out cold north winds and reflecting heat in the summer. Niche-like, the site's warmer microclimate today is dotted with rare oaks and sugar maples. Perched fifteen feet above the lake, the site has an expansive view.[7] The buildings and small garden are obliterated today, and the site is located in designated wilderness, as are other Anishinaabeg homesites in the Boundary Waters Canoe Area Wilderness. There was no dock or dock cribbing to denote the location, and at the waterline only a couple of flat, black ledge rocks are convenient for pulling a canoe out of the water. Nearby are rich wild rice beds and two stream mouths as well as deep lake water perfect for the spawning grounds where plentiful fish could be harvested. To catch fresh fish in the winter months, the Linklaters and others used setlines to jig for large pike. Jackfish Bay, or Ginoozhensi bagidaabaaning, is named for the many setlines with flags, which would sway above the ice when a jackfish, or northern pike, took the bait.[8]

The Linklater home was also opportunely situated for cultural purposes. Tchi-Ki-Wis's relations lived nearby, forming what one mapmaker called a "village." Before there were reserves in Canada and reservations in the United States, the Anishinaabeg lived in settlements dispersed throughout their territory, throughout canoe country. Living in a small encampment—as did the Linklaters, Robinsons, and Hoffmans—was common, and the encampment was where "villagers" assisted one another and shared harvested plants and food, such as moose meat. The home was also situated on a crossroads of canoe routes, one following the border, and another running from Basswood Lake through Mud Lake to Lake Vermilion, linking together distant Anishinaabeg bands.[9]

Tchi-Ki-Wis's family were Lac La Croix First Nation tribal members. Lac La Croix is situated in the heart of the vast home territory of Anishinaabeg (also named Chippewa or Ojibwe). Anishinaabeg bands, or nations, lived in an area that extended from Michigan to Montana in the south, and from central Ontario to Manitoba in the north. The Lac La Croix people speak a "border lakes dialect" along with nearby bands such as Bois Forte, Seine River, Grand Portage, and the many Rainy River bands.[10] Speaking the same dialect is predicated on dwelling nearby for a far stretch of time, long-standing relationships, frequent marriages between neighboring Anishinaabeg, and infusing a landscape with rich collective memories. The home territory was a storied landscape, where places were remembered because of remarkable concentrations of fish, special plants, or the rare birch tree bearing large sheets of smooth and tough canoe bark. It was a place of important events, gatherings, and ceremonies. The Lac La Croix people lived along an ancient route, what is now known as the border route, or "Voyageur's Highway," used by early people moving east or west to trade Isle Royale copper, and later to trade pemmican. The border route is a riverine system that flows westward until Lake of the Woods and then turns northwest and runs wholly into Canada and Lake Winnipeg. It runs from the shade of pines and boreal

Painting by David I. Bushnell of birch-bark lodges on Basswood Lake, 1899. Note the cedar-bark mat on its frame on the far right. Photograph courtesy of Bureau of American Ethnology, GN 00472, National Anthropological Archives, Smithsonian Institution, Washington, D.C.

forest to the openings of savanna and prairie lands of the Red River and Lake Winnipeg.

The Anishinaabemowin name of Lac La Croix, the large lake where the village is situated, is Zhingwaako/Ningwaakwaani Zaaga'igan, meaning: "big pine trees hanging or bowing over the lake."[11] Tchi-Ki-Wis's parents, "Laposh," or alternately John Robinson, and his wife, Mandaquabeek, or Susan Robinson, lived in Lac La Croix during the treaty years (1870s) and the era of Magatewasin, or Chief Blackstone.[12] Known for his successful resistance to Euro-Canadians' incursions to mine gold, he was a strong and widely acclaimed ogimaa. Lac La Croix was and is a traditional community, and during the time of John and Susan Robinson's young adulthood, missionaries had made little inroads in converting community members. In 1881, the Indian agent of the Department of Indian Affairs recorded eighty-four "heathens," three Catholics, eighteen canoes, and thirty-six dogs living on the reserve.[13]

John James Linklater's family roots are also along water—shorelines, rivers, islands, Hudson Bay, and the Atlantic Ocean around the Orkney Islands, northeast of Scotland.[14] For most of the first half of the nineteenth century, John Linklater's parents, grandparents, and great grandparents lived where great inland rivers meet James Bay, at Fort Albany and Moose Factory.[15] William Linklater (the first, as there are three) came to the New World from Flotta Island, a relatively small, flat, and windy Orkney Island.[16] He was, like so many of his fellow Hudson's Bay Company (HBC) servants and clerks at the time, a poor Orcadian.[17] He and others of John Linklater's forebears married Cree women and started families along the lowlands while working for the HBC. Because of family trauma, the Linklaters moved to the Red River (Winnipeg) area, joining relations already there. For all of John's adult life, most of his paternal uncles, aunts, and cousins lived in parishes and villages away from the Red River or northward along Lake Winnipeg or its major tributary from the east, the Winnipeg River.

The Linklater family story, lost to memory, is literally set along two major east–west riverine systems. To the north, the Albany, English, and Winnipeg Rivers run from James Bay on the east across a height of land into waters running to the west, eventually into Lake Winnipeg. Southward was the east–west border route along which John and Tchi-Ki-Wis lived. They knew the geography first by sight and experience (such as knowing where caribou frequently lived or where there were thick blueberry patches) rather than by maps. Both east–west routes converge at Lake Winnipeg and the once Métis capital of Red River. The northern supply route (Albany–English–Winnipeg Rivers) would eventually lose favor with the HBC after the Linklaters moved to Red River, supplanted by a more northerly route from Red River to York Factory on Hudson Bay. There is a height of land on the Albany–English River route, and John's grandfather worked for the HBC at the headwaters of the Albany on Lake St. Joseph. Family members would deliver the summer mail packets by canoe and winter mail by dog team to James Bay. The eastward flowing river is more than six hundred miles in length. John's father, William Thomas Linklater, began his HBC career and married his wife, Ah-zhe-day-ge-she-gake (alternately named Eliza Fly), at Lac Seul, also at the headwaters of the westward flowing English–Winnipeg River system.[18]

JOHN LINKLATER was a wiry man, not quite 150 pounds and shy of five feet ten inches tall. But he was remarkably strong, able to easily carry heavy loads. His stamina, even into his sixties, was well known. He had a neatly trimmed moustache, preferred to wear wool in summer and winter, and always wore a brimmed hat while outdoors. Linklater

John Linklater wears a shirt sewn by Tchi-Ki-Wis, circa 1922. Frank M. Warren photograph. Courtesy of University of Minnesota Duluth, Archives and Special Collections.

walked on his toes and walked fast, keeping one teenager sweating on a hot day on a hike into town. In photographs he is often looking away from the camera and is usually caught doing something, his hands busy cooking pancakes, holding a stringer of fish, or setting up camp. Linklater was notably observant and kind. One of his Ely contemporaries said he was "friendly—always willing to help you." People were comfortable around him, and he mixed easily with Whites and Indians. His friendship with the well-off is testified to by the many Christmas cards he received. His fellow game wardens fondly called him "Link."[19] He was a renowned Indian game warden. Being even-tempered and "pleasant of speech" served him well. He was, in the eyes of one supervisory game warden, "the personification of honesty and courtesy." The same man wrote he was "the most qualified and unpretentious outdoors man I have ever known." After he died, a well-to-do friend wrote, "he loved wild creatures. In the later years of his life, he used a Kodak much more than he did a gun." Known for his loyalty and discretion, he was widely liked and respected. While he was memorably patient on the job, he was not to be trifled with. "He didn't like to be insulted. He stood up for himself, others would back down."[20]

Both Tchi-Ki-Wis and John loved to laugh. John had "lots of humor about him . . . and a mischievous grin on his face sometimes." John once told a university veterinarian who requested his help, we "are living in the North country where a man's vacation has not been spoiled by a plumber." John and Tchi-Ki-Wis were careful about their personal appearance, and Tchi-Ki-Wis kept a neat house.[21] Both were generous with berries, fish, use of handmade parkas, and doing someone a favor, this being an esteemed and common Anishinaabeg trait.

Tchi-Ki-Wis was a few inches shorter than John and heavier. She wore her hair long, parted in the middle, but often in a bun at the back. She sewed expertly but preferred wearing plain cotton dresses and made her own moose tanned moccasins (and made them for many others). She was notably reticent when among non-Natives, another customary trait for Anishinaabeg women. Her daughter, Clara, also was "quiet, didn't talk much. [Her husband] did all the talking."[22] Their reticence to talk served a purpose: it deflected the conversation and thus attention away from them. Tchi-Ki-Wis was a traditionalist and lived on Basswood Lake most of her life. She took care of the family grave houses nearby, attentive to any spirits lingering there.[23] Since Tchi-Ki-Wis did not publicly speak English, friends openly wondered how much she understood. Ellen Hanson, her White friend, thought Tchi-Ki-Wis knew more English than people thought.[24] Her father, John Robinson, spoke French fluently as well as some English. John Linklater had limited schooling but wrote clearly with a crisp script. He wrote well and descriptively. He was a reader, too, as he had a subscription to *Sports Afield* and wrote letters, always reluctantly except to his granddaughter and sister.[25]

A rare portrait of Tchi-Ki-Wis, perhaps taken while she was gathering plants, 1920s. Unusual for her, she is wearing gloves and boots, rather than moccasins. Frank M. Warren photograph. Courtesy of University of Minnesota Duluth, Archives and Special Collections.

For all his life, John Linklater was called a "half-breed."[26] In Canada, closely associated names included "mixed bloods," "freemen," "Canadians," *bois brules* (French), and Métis. Later they were more respectfully called of "mixed ancestry" or "mixed descent families." "Half-breed" came to mean different things in the United States than in Canada. In both countries it meant a child of European and Indigenous parents, most typically a father of European and a mother of Aboriginal descent. In Linklater's case he was of Anishinaabeg, Cree, Orkney, and Welsh heritage. In Canada, the Linklaters were eventually called "Scotch breeds" in documents such as census and marriage certificates. By 1814 in Red River, the term *Métis* came to denote a separate group.[27] Begrudgingly the Canadian government recognized "Métis." The name Métis signified to both outsiders and insiders that they were a distinct group. They had their own language, art, and identity. For example, John's uncle, Archie, was a renowned fiddle player who introduced Métis music to the Gwitch'in in the Yukon.[28] A seminal event for many Métis was the summer buffalo hunt west of Red River in which the meat was dried and mixed with berries and fat to make pemmican. Red River was the largest Métis community, and Linklater family members would live in the greater region for all of John's life. But movement too was a Métis characteristic of which John's family is a prime example. Indeed, after the second Métis rebellion in 1885, countless Métis made themselves "invisible" by moving away, by becoming non-Indigenous or Indigenous, or by becoming Americans.[29]

Linklater was a common Métis and Orcadian name. A John Linklater, a distant relation to Jack, was one of the first Métis to sign the 1875 "Half breed Adhesion" to Canadian Treaty 3. Coincidentally, the older John Linklater's wife was named Tchi-Ki-Wis. The elder John Linklater had been in the Rainy Lake area for more than twenty years before the younger John was born. While it is likely the two John Linklaters knew of each other, there are no records that suggest they were close.[30]

In reality there were two Métis groups. The members of one were of French and often Anishinaabeg descent, were commonly Catholic, and frequently had family roots working for the North West Company.[31] The

Linklaters are exemplars of the second Métis group, who were "Scotch" or English, often of Orkney and Cree descent, typically of Anglican faith, and long associated with the Hudson's Bay Company. This later group created its own language called Bungee, literally mixing elements and syntax of Cree and Orcadian English. It was spoken primarily in Manitoba in the Red River area where the Linklaters have roots. We do not know if John spoke Bungee, but he likely did. Thus, he might have known the Bungee word *apeechequanee* used to describe an overturned canoe.[32] We do know that John was multilingual and could speak English, Cree, Anishinaabemowin, and some French and write English. John was careful with language, once advising an archaeologist on the proper ways of pronouncing and thus spelling *siskowit*—or fatty lake trout—with a long "o" sound "used abruptly."[33] A newspaper friend wrote that John "thinks in it [English]."[34]

THE STORY OF THE MÉTIS is the story of the birth of a new people through what anthropologists call "ethnogenesis." They were more than people of mixed ancestry as they developed a self-identification with a flag of their own and had been perfecting self-authority on a small scale with canoe brigades "rules" for more than a century. But later they established provisional governments in Manitoba and Saskatchewan and fought two wars against the fledgling Canadian government to protect their rights. A long painful history eventually resulted in the inclusion of Métis in Section 35 of the Canadian Constitution, recognizing the Métis as one of Canada's Aboriginal groups.[35] It is only of late, in a few academic documents, that Americans have written of the Métis, but they are not recognized as an Aboriginal group in the United States.

One of the most intriguing parts of researching the Linklaters and the borderlands is the comparative perspective it provides. The life of John Linklater's older sister, Alice Linklater Morrisseau Wakemup, illustrates how different the American and Canadian race-based categories were (and are still). In Canada, she was officially recognized as Métis as a young woman, receiving Métis scrip from the Canadian government.[36] To do this, she had to have witnesses testify she was of "half-breed" parentage and she had not received treaty payments. She had not. Later, after being widowed, she married an American Anishinaabe man, and after years of effort to be recognized as an American Indian, she received a treaty allotment, recognizing her as a Bois Forte band member. "Indian" in the United States, she was Métis in Canada.

There has been a groundswell of Canadian Métis research, based, in part, on Métis "scrip," a Canadian government certificate document theoretically redeemable for land or money. The scrip were a belated, inadequate (in terms of land or money), and bureaucratically hidebound attempt to recognized Métis presence and possession of land largely in the Prairie Provinces. However derisory the scrip was in the late 1800s, it is a marvelous documentary record to explore today because the individual completing the scrip had to name his or her parents and where they lived.[37] The scrip documentation not only provides clarity on family relations but also fills in gaping holes of what is known about where the family lived. They are a revealing primary source born out of the Métis heartbreak of losing control over their provincial government and becoming marginalized in the years to come. Using the scrip as a key source, drawn from Linklater family members, we can identify the Linklater family line and their Métis heritage in northwestern Ontario and Manitoba.

John was normally reserved with strangers but grew animated and conversant when someone was truly listening. He was particularly reserved about his personal life.[38] Only a few reliable tidbits were then known, such as his family's time at Rat Portage—Kenora today. He would mention his father's HBC roots (but not the extent of those roots, which were unknown by his friends). Some of the more common stories about John's father, William Linklater, were quite misleading. But John (and others such as friend and boss Bill Hanson) seemed to let these false leads persist, such as John's birthplace, which was said to be in North Dakota. Better to let those inaccuracies go than to draw attention to his story by correcting them. For example, after John's death a story cropped up that his father had returned to the old country, to Scotland, and that he had left his wife when he crossed the Atlantic. In truth, his great-grandfather did return to Orkney but brought his Métis wife and three daughters with him. Knowledge that some traders "turned off" their wives and left them at posts got grafted onto the Linklater legend. Only a few people, such as Bill and Ellen Hanson, knew accurate but still fragments of Linklater family history.

Tchi-Ki-Wis was characteristically quiet among strangers, but she "spoke" eloquently with her craft and actions.[39] She was extremely generous, gifting beautiful handmade objects to those who needed or voiced interest in them.[40] The breadth of what she made—bead and quill work, birch-bark baskets, moose-hide moccasins, family clothes such as John's wool shirts, tanned hides, dogsled traces, canoes, paddles, parkas—is astounding. And what she made, like most Anishinaabeg crafts, married a utilitarian need with beauty. Her cedar-bark mats, with root-dyed geometric patterns, are gorgeous. They were once called "Ojibwe linoleum" and used to insulate from the cold ground but were beautiful enough that Whites purchased them and hung them on walls. Even more remarkable, several of her creations survive. This book considers many of them as it examines her family history on the border lakes, as well as the stinging changes—treaties and reserves, mining, the Dawson Trail, settlement by Whites, forced assimilation, the creation and administration of the Quetico–Superior conservation area—that engulfed her traditional village, homeland, and waters.

RECOUNTING THE LINKLATERS' early lives together is unfortunately hampered by the existence of only a few records. We do not know, for example, much about their formal marriage, as those records appear to have been lost. We know, without many details, that John trapped and traded furs in Minnesota and Ontario. He moved around in both his youth and young adulthood, though the country he roamed in was expansive—northwest Ontario, northern Minnesota, and eastern Manitoba. Later, after he married Tchi-Ki-Wis and they had two daughters, they increasingly returned to Jackfish Bay, Basswood Lake. There he worked in dangerous logging jobs during the cutting of massive stands of white and red pines in northern Minnesota.

After the logging companies pulled out, Linklater worked as a game warden for the State of Minnesota. He started in this position before Indians were formally recognized as citizens and when state game wardens were often an instrument of Indian oppression by restricting their hunting, fishing, and gathering rights. Perhaps most stirring is Linklater's impact on many area conservationists, writers, and wildlife biologists of the day. He collected scientific samples, including porcupine parasites and rare plants, and noted the dying out of woodland caribou in Minnesota and on Isle Royale. Ultimately, he was a teacher to university professors, fellow game wardens, Boy Scouts, and others he guided in canoe country.

He was also a remarkably observant individual, who linked his observations and biological knowledge to come to interesting ecological conclusions. Fourteen years after his death, a Minneapolis conservationist remembered an example of this:

Kaupy and the late John Linklater, a Scotch-Chippewa game warden, were trekking along the Ely-Buyck road.

They came across a porcupine that had been clubbed to death. Said John: "I see the forest rangers have gotten another porky. Come along and I'll show you something."

They walked along until they came to a small stand of cedars and spruce.

"Last winter," John said, "we had about six-foot of snow on the level. The deer would concentrate in this area, and I spent a lot of time watching for poachers. The deer in this area would have starved to death had it not been for the twigs dropped by the porkies. They had eaten everything up as far as they could reach."

He went on: "You know, our greatest deer killer is the bobcat, and the bobcat has only one enemy and that enemy is the porcupine.

"The cat likes nothing better than to follow the lines of least resistance, with the result he kills a porky for food. That's the end of the bobcat; the quills kill him."[41]

Linklater put his knowledge to work in ingenious ways. In Darragh Aldrich's novel *Earth Never Tires* (1936), she describes how the young city-raised couple wanted Christmas candles for their remote cabin but had few candles to spare. In response, Linklater made candles out of a bit of cloth (for wicks) weighted down with buttons in mason jar tops and floating in bear fat (that had been saved for boot grease). The lit candles were placed in the frosty windows to lovely effect.[42] Linklater's ingenuity while guiding clients on canoe trips was frequently noted, particularly if his party had lost or forgotten their fishing gear. "A good mess of fish" were often caught with Linklater's impromptu lure made of "old nails and pieces of wire" to the surprise and satisfaction of astounded campers.[43]

Linklater had a significant impact on area conservationists, writers, and certainly his close friends. For many summers, he worked as a guide and handyman for Frank and Alice Warren on Isle Royale.[44] Linklater's guiding on Isle Royale was part of an effort to establish Isle Royale National Park. Even while commercial fishing there, Linklater continued to guide and teach tourists and those willing to listen, including professors, doctors, and museum personnel. Linklater was a mentor, role model, and inspiration to noted conservationist author Sigurd Olson, as is evident in Olson's writings. Linklater's outdoor skills and knowledge were much praised to the degree that Olson, recommending a guide to renowned conservationist Aldo Leopold, wrote, "do everything in your power to have Jack Linklater guide you."[45]

The Linklaters lived a hard life. It was a long run of grueling work and devotion to one another, and punctuated by change and tragedy. Much of the tragedy was wrapped up in great part with being an Indian, or Métis, in a world increasingly dominated by non-Indigenous people. Settler society functioned to disinherit Indigenous residents of the canoe country. In their childhoods the country was empty of Whites, but later in life they were surrounded by farms, small towns, and people owning nearby lands.

John Linklater and Frank Warren, close friends, take a "tea break" while photographing moose on Isle Royale, circa 1924. Warren family photograph. Courtesy of University of Minnesota Duluth, Archives and Special Collections.

And resource extraction industries (timbering and mining) escalated, instigating ecological change and often a boom-and-bust cycle as well as bringing a cash economy to the area. Treaty rights, though the Linklaters had none in the United States, were circumscribed by trespass laws.[46] The Linklaters inauspiciously came to Minnesota the same year the Nelson Act became law, further usurping Anishinaabeg of much of their lands within their reservations. And it was only with the passage of the Indian Citizenship Act in 1924 that all American-born "Indians" could become citizens. Discrimination was overt and pervasive but also nuanced. On the Canadian side in 1921, Indians were not allowed to "dance" in ceremonies and were officially dissuaded from leaving the reserve.[47] This and a similar "discouragement" on the American side led to the affront we still hear today of someone "going off the rez." Historically the phrase prescribed what an Indian might do. Indian agents had to permit them to leave the reservation or reserve, denying them self-determination. Its oppressive historical roots still evoke an ignorance of and contempt for Indian life and struggles. A 1912 newspaper account describes a fishing party, after discussing their fishing success, "joining" the powwow and dancing at Lac La Croix, and talking of "bucks," "maidens," "tom-tom," "chanting," and dirt.[48] At that time, Linklater was called "that Scotch–Indian breed in his canoe," or the half-breed, Indian, Nanabushu, Chief, "Buckshot," and a slur for a White man married to an Indian woman (and living among Indians). Friends called him "Link" or Jack. An overtly prejudiced 1916 State of Minnesota's Game and Fish Biennial Report ran photographs of two Anishinaabeg men on snowshoes with the caption: "Good Types of Indian Trappers and Hunters."[49] Even in an article complimentary of Linklater, an archaeologist felt compelled to add, he was "a very intelligent Indian."[50]

Indians also faced many discreet forms of discrimination, although these miseries are more difficult to trace. One trip led by game wardens Leo Chosa and Linklater uniquely illustrates stereotypes that entangled them, and their shrewd response. The purpose of a publicity trip across the Superior Game Refuge (a large part of the Superior National Forest) was to garner support for the understaffed wardens protecting game and fish subject to poaching and illegal activities. Chosa had the idea of a trip crossing the boundary waters, and Linklater was critical in the success of the trip with his skill with dog teams and noted ability guiding Whites. The trip was well documented in newspaper accounts, and a photograph from the trip was subsequently used in two other publications. The photograph in the official State of Minnesota publication *Fins, Feathers, and Furs* embodies Indian stereotypes of the time.[51]

The photograph is an exposé of these good and bad, or binary, stereotypes of Indians. Further, Linklater and Chosa's awareness and twist of these stereotypes are what one scholar has called a "hidden transcript." In other words, through playful disguise and humor Linklater and Chosa mock and reject Indian stereotypes.[52] This playful yet complex moment, really more like theater, could have simply been about two game wardens leading a group of VIPs across the boundary waters in winter. Linklater and Chosa were, in part, on display as Indian game wardens, and they clearly made the Whites comfortable enough to license the public play on stereotypes. Their theatrical performance was publicly acceptable to the VIPs.

Chosa and Linklater are "playing with" a suite of oppositional stereotypes: of being civilized and of being a "savage" or being deficient of White values.[53] Eating with a fork and plate, wearing a tie, eating after others were fed are emblematic of civilized behavior. Whereas eating fish heads—an anathema to well-off Whites—bringing a pistol to dinner, and eating with one's hands from a pail were deemed uncivilized and

BOILED FISH HEADS—OH, BOY!

There was always good-natured banter flying between the "savages" as Chosa and Linklater called each other. At this moment Chosa, at right, probably is saying: "Is that savage trying to highbrow me with a fork?"

—B. L. Brown Photo.

Game wardens John Linklater and Leo Chosa were photographed while leading VIPs on a trip across the boundary waters and Superior Game Refuge, 1924. Published in *Fins, Feathers, and Fur,* the magazine of the Minnesota Department of Conservation.

ungentlemanly behavior. But most important they are purposefully stirring the stereotypes together, much like the fish soup. They are toying with oppositional stereotypes, saying, in effect, none of them captures them. It is as if they are saying, life is a mix and is messy, and your stereotypes don't define us. Their "hidden transcript" rejects these polar stereotypes. Still the insulting stereotypes of Indians, either good or bad, are fundamental to this photograph, even while Chosa and Linklater artfully laugh at them. That this photograph was published is both evidence that Linklater and Chosa were successful in fostering a good time and got their message across in a nonthreatening way. The making of good spirits with the White VIPs created a temporary intimacy between Linklater, Chosa, and the other trippers. To do that, Linklater repeatedly overlooked the cultural gaffes, the unintended offensiveness of his friends, and the then current stereotypes that informed his White friends. To persevere, both Linklaters' often swallowed the hurt or offense (or Tchi-Ki-Wis might pretend to not understand the English words).

Invisible to all readers (and apparently most on the trip) was the relationship between Chosa and Linklater. Linklater was a work partner for many years with Chosa's father-in-law, Vincent Defauld. Further, Linklater was a distant relation of Chosa. Without an audience, Leo Chosa likely called Linklater uncle, out of customary respect and deference to him, not "savage." And the Chosas, like the Linklaters, were Basswood Lake people, though the Chosas lived at the other end of Basswood at Prairie Portage. Further, while the VIPs likely assumed themselves superior to Chosa and Linklater, they were essentially dependent on "the Indians" for their comfort, daily travel, and emotional support for the long days on snowshoes. Chosa and Linklater were the trip leaders, while the mayor of Minneapolis and businessmen were followers. So much of Linklater's and Chosa's lives remained undercover from Whites' understanding until they visibly played with known stereotypes. The photograph is ironic, too, in that teasing was a way of showing affection in both cultures. Still, the swirl of meanings implicit in the photograph is built upon stereotypes and biases impacting Indians and their assumed-to-be superiors at the time.

To write a biography of John and Tchi-Ki-Wis Linklater is to exam-ine the implicit and nuanced racism of their day, chronicling how they survived in this environment. They also persevered through trauma and setbacks. But the Linklaters were more than survivors: they were inspir-ing people who attracted interesting friends, such as Alice Warren, the first female regent of the University of Minnesota. Because they were so active, their lives so full, they invoked a sense that there was always more to learn, always more to their story than met the eye. As they inspired and enlivened others, some with a penchant to write took note of their lives, leaving scattered records of their doings and their influence. Undoubtedly, there are other poignant stories to uncover that are a measure of how often they captured quiet attention and respect.

Making the Carry takes readers into the North Country—north of the Minnesota–Ontario and Minnesota–Manitoba borders. For many, knowledge of this country is rudimentary. John grew up at Lac Seul, yet few Americans know of it despite it being considerably closer to Ely than are the Twin Cities. The Linklater story also involves Aboriginal, British-Canadian, Canadian, and American history played out mostly in the geography of the boreal forest. For example, the Linklater family history intersects the first Métis uprising in 1870 along the banks of the Red River (Winnipeg today). But it often takes some unusual twists. For instance, John's uncle Charlie fought "for the Queen," not the Louis Riel–led Métis, Blackfoot, and Cree making a stand for their sovereignty in the second uprising in 1885.[54] The family history is also deeply intertwined with the evolution of the Hudson's Bay Company, such as the company reorganiza-tion in the early 1890s when a number of employees, such as John's father and uncle, were let go. John himself lived in and experienced the creation of Superior National Forest and the Quetico Provincial Park, which give shape to this region today. This is a story sandwiched between the twilight of the golden age of the fur trade and today's era of Kevlar canoes and a wilderness made empty of residents and people with ancestral roots to these lands and waters.

The Linklaters lives wove together Canadian and American history.

Too often, Americans know little about seminal events in Canada such as the building of the Dawson Trail, an effort to construct an all-Canadian travel route to unite eastern Canada with what would become the Prairie Provinces. The route, through the Canadian Shield in what is now northwestern Ontario including the Quetico, made for rough and relatively slow traveling. For the young confederation, it was something of an Oregon Trail for boats rather than wagons. It also left improved portages, dams, hulks of steam engines, and "road houses," which were subsequently used by others after the Canadian railroads made the route obsolete. Among those using this route were the Linklaters and John's father, William, who was a clerk for the Hudson's Bay Company at Pine Portage, one of the way-stops along the Dawson Trail. The HBC post reused the buildings and the nearby clearing to plant potatoes where only a decade before potatoes had been grown for the travelers en route to the west. After the demise of the Dawson Trail and the closing of the HBC post, this area resumed its remoteness and was then reoccupied only by two Anishinaabeg bands—Lac La Croix and the smaller Kawawaigamok, or Sturgeon Lake Band.

The slide of Linklater clowning around wearing a top hat immediately piqued my interest (who was this guy?) but also begged the related question of what was going on here. I began to think more about the people he guided, such as these businessmen that gave him a one hundred dollar bill and the hat, both remarkably out of place on Isle Royale at the time. Increasingly, I thought more about the power differential between Linklater and the well-to-do people and groups he led, such as this private archaeological expedition on Isle Royale. In his guiding he learned what these wealthy men found amusing, and like most guides, he responded. He frequently worked in an environment of power discrepancy between him and his White friends and from a position of lower social status. That he maintained his integrity within this context made his story even more provocative.

An additional "early" hook for me was the question posed by a comment that Linklater made to a contemporary that his grandfather saw

John Linklater, Birch Island, Isle Royale, 1929. The top hat was a gift from polar explorer Commander Eugene MacDonald during the MacDonald–Massee Expedition to the island. Frank M. Warren photograph. Courtesy of University of Minnesota Duluth, Archives and Special Collections.

Thomas Richards, great-uncle to John Linklater and the last clerk at the HBC post at Fort William, mid-1880s. Richards witnessed Anishinaabeg paddling to and from Isle Royale in the 1880s, likely when Tchi-Ki-Wis and her grandmother made one lake crossing. Photograph courtesy of the Glenbow Museum, Calgary.

Indians off from the mainland to Isle Royale and that Tchi-Ki-Wis and her grandmother traveled there when she was a child.[55] Linklater was speaking of "grandfather" in an Anishinaabeg sense, namely an elder whom he respected and who may or may not have been directly related to him. His Métis great-uncle, Thomas Richards, the brother of his grandmother Ellen Richards Linklater, was the last clerk to work at the Fort William (now part of Thunder Bay) HBC post. Sometime during his tenure there from 1879 to 1883, Richards witnessed a group of Anishinaabeg setting out in canoes to paddle across Thunder Bay and out in the open for the last fifteen miles of waters of Lake Superior toward Minong (the Anishinaabeg name for Isle Royale).[56]

Tchi-Ki-Wis's statement of having gone to Minong as a child with her grandmother underscores all we don't know about her. Clearly her family had experience on Minong, strongly suggesting she was connected to the Grand Portage and Fort William Bands. And she did, as Tchi-Ki-Wis was "related" to the Caribou family of Grand Portage, though relations could be through blood or through clan or both. The late Walter Caribou knew Tchi-Ki-Wis from his time at Lac La Croix and thought she was a half-sister to his grandmother. One of the signatories to the "Isle Royale Compact" in 1844 was Attikonse, or Little Caribou, a generation or two older than Tchi-Ki-Wis. Here, as elsewhere, the Linklater story lifts a veil on regional events and illuminates patterns in regional cultural and political history.

John and Tchi-Ki-Wis lived through a momentous period of ecological change, the region-wide cutting of white and red pine (some estimates are as high as 92 percent).[57] John was born before the wholesale cutting began in the boundary waters, and hungry for work and cash for his family, he joined the lumbering effort. Further, unlike the majority who felled the trees or milled the lumber and then left, John stayed and lived in and traveled through the heavily altered landscape. In his day, he witnessed woodland caribou "leaving" the area northward. He liked to show newcomers places where they could still find caribou antlers, bones, and hair. He witnessed the opening of the pine forests, the deer that came into those openings, and even drew attention to some of the first cases of brainworm in moose, brought on in part by deer, the new host for the parasite. Ecological, economic, and political change, especially federal Indian policy, swept up the Linklaters as it did others living on reservations or reserves or in still-remote areas such as Basswood Lake.

Constructing a biography of the Linklaters is in many ways a serendipitous process. The documentary record of the Linklaters is both exceptionally rich in some subjects and then utterly lacking in others. Although a remarkable sampling of Tchi-Ki-Wis's masterful, geometrically designed cedar-bark mats survive, many objects she made are gone and were never photographed, and her life is much less documented than her spouse's. What "Indians" were doing was not often recorded unless it was not threatening, fit a stereotype, or was nearby someone with a special penchant to note it. If they were on a reservation or reserve (in Canada), they were "counted" every year in the treaty payment process. But those like the Linklaters, living on the borderlands away from census takers and Indian agents, were largely invisible to government officials and thus those who might document their presence.

There are also considerable gaps in the historical record about the Linklaters. For example, few friends or acquaintances could name Linklater's father, William, and no one could name his mother, Eliza. Most of the Linklater family history, far north of the border, had been lost. Working for the oldest and sometimes inflexible fur trade company, the HBC, was a family tradition.[58] But that tradition was broken when William's trail goes cold after 1893. We know that Pine Portage Post stayed open for a few more years, and perhaps William continued to work there. All we can say is that William must have continued to work in remote places, as he does not appear in later records. Consulting the many and varied genealogical, census, and immigration records now online, I found no record of William returning to Orkney. For those who enjoy intrigue, the idea he might have gone afar is refuted by the fact that John and his sister Alice told no such story. Nor is his death recorded beyond a "mystery sheet" listing Linklater family members and death dates as might have been done before a life insurance policy was taken out, which John did late in life. This sheet, written by someone whose handwriting is not identifiable, but clearly with John's input, says William died in 1906, at age sixty-one.[59] But there is no information about where and how he died, which would have been of interest to insurance underwriters then, and is now to us. William Linklater III's "disappearance" is a central mystery to his descendants, though it is quite likely that John and his sister Alice knew where he went, as John likely provided the information when he died. That information was not passed down in the family, a common, if sad, phenomenon.

Imperative for any biographer is to be careful about biases when reading the evidence about a subject, and to avoid filling in the gaps in the historical record with a hunch. One recurring bias in Linklater accounts is an ingrained cultural view of Linklater as an "ecological noble savage." Some idolized him so much that it is difficult to separate fact from fancy. Linklater was often portrayed as being inherently courageous and natural—a stoic woodsman with no parallel. So the task becomes to look beyond the cultural predispositions and to see Linklater in a non-stereotypical light. Indeed, the larger task is to see him as an individual, not as some emblem of "Indianness" and as either all good or all bad. A short sentence from Linklater's obituary brings this point home: "Like an Indian, he could go noiselessly through the forests."[60] This reads very much like a *Last of the Mohicans* moment, but why was it important to celebrate this? It may capture an essential truth of his remarkable woodcraft, of knowing his way around the woods. Even if Linklater was exceptional in the woods, we must be watchful about not overestimating his skills, knowledge, and personality. This is exemplified by friends arguing about whether he ever became lost in the North Country; most assumed no, a few said yes. We have to shift past cultural tropes that obscure one way Linklater understood animals, plants, and waters, that is, from a strong "rational" and intensely curious approach.

To the generation fortunate enough to know John Linklater, he was the real deal. Linklater became a living symbol of the North, of the wilds of Hudson Bay, where so many guides aspired to go. His geographic knowledge of the country north of the border lakes was unparalleled. And Linklater was much more than a canoeing or dog-mushing role model; he was a pioneering Indian game warden, given the difficult task of policing Whites who broke conservation laws in a time when racially construed differences in power were the order of the day. He was also extremely knowledgeable about the biological world of his homeland; in other words, he had what has come to be called "traditional ecological knowledge." He was part of a larger effort to understand and protect moose, Isle Royale, and canoe country all while honoring Indigenous heritage. He was, above all else, true to himself.

This book contains five chapters, loosely organized chronologically. Chapter 1 recovers much Linklater family history, from their roots on a small Orkney Island to immigration to Hudson Bay and their service with the Hudson's Bay Company. I describe their Métis heritage and movement in northwestern Ontario and Manitoba, particularly at Red River during the time of the first Métis rebellion. Chapter 2 begins by focusing on Tchi-Ki-Wis, her family, and their connections to the people of Lac La Croix and Basswood Lake. The second half of the chapter documents Tchi-Ki-Wis's myriad talents as a craftsperson who superbly married beauty, her identity, and aesthetics with her utilitarian creations. Chapter 3 recounts the Linklaters' early married life, their children, and the diversity of their efforts. John's mushing, lumbering, trapping, and guiding efforts for influential people are described. I also explain the unusual and largely unknown Native names of John and Tchi-Ki-Wis. Chapter 4 chronicles Linklater's later life as a game warden and as what we today would call a consultant or colleague to conservationists and professors, highlighting his penchant for communicating topics ranging from Indigenous heritage and beliefs to traditional ecological knowledge, which he shared with "students" such as Sigurd Olson. I detail how Linklater's role as a romantic figure served as an inspiration for understanding and protecting Isle Royale and his canoe country home. Chapter 5 draws together these various strands of what we know about the Linklaters' lives. I tell of their deaths and the subsequent family loss of their connection to Jackfish Bay, and I appraise their impacts on others. Like so many fellow Métis to the north and west, John did not center his life on ownership of land, yet he was profoundly part of special places. He used those remote places to buffer his family from overt and ever-present discrimination and, whenever possible, from crushing institutional forces. I conclude by assessing how others viewed and understood Linklater, how they befriended and trusted him yet knew so little about him, his resolute character defying facile stereotypes of him as an Indian or the more offensive "half-breed."

The book concludes with John Linklater's only published article, "An Old Indian Prophecy." It is eloquent for a person who had only a few years of schooling and for whom English may not have been his first language. It is vintage Linklater, taking a long view of biological phenomena and change, some of which he had witnessed. Linklater and the old friend he refers to in the article are bringing the Indigenous knowledge of the past into the future. As we read this today, it covers a great sweep of time, a time when Basswood Lake was exclusively Anishinaabeg *aki*—their land. Linklater is also culturally translating for a largely White sportsmen

readership, tying in Anishinaabeg belief and experience. While persua-
sively arguing that his old friend was right, he is also gentle in advocating
his friend's prophecy, respecting readers to make up their own minds.
Linklater favored this "carry," reaching across cultures to further understanding, one of the most universal of human experiences. This ability
and the many surprises of both of the Linklaters' lives—their creativity,
smarts, resilience, and kindness—are a hallmark of their story.

CHAPTER 1

Out of the North

THE LINKLATER FAMILY'S MÉTIS ROOTS

A GRIEVING ELLEN LINKLATER gathered her seven children together and set off in birch-bark canoes for Red River, almost five hundred miles away. Brave three-year-old Charlie stood in the front of the canoe, trying to keep up with the paddling rhythm of the others as the canoe set off from the sandy shore in front of Osnaburgh House.[1] They traveled with Hudson's Bay Company (HBC) men delivering the summer mail and goods to Red River. Days before, in July 1864, her husband, William Linklater, had drowned setting gillnets in the waters of Lake St. Joseph.[2] Drowning was one of the most common accidental deaths among HBC men.[3] But as experienced as he was on the water, his death was bewildering and shocking. Lurched from the routine of normal tasks, such as picking and drying blueberries, Ellen was thrust into making critical decisions that would transform her young family.

William had been the postmaster at Osnaburgh House, the highest position at the post. His years at "Oz" were profitable for the HBC, demonstrating his trading acumen.[4] But he never left Osnaburgh and was buried in a hastily constructed wooden coffin in the fenced "burying ground" on the hillock overlooking the post. He was likely buried alongside his grandmother Catherine Best Thomas, who had died there only a few years before. Ellen knew what hardships might fall upon an HBC widow, as she had nurtured William's grandmother, who had been reduced to hardship in Moose Factory as her annuity would not cover her basic needs.[5] Ellen had made her decision: she would take her family west to Red River to her sister's family place instead of paddling eastward to her parents at Moose Factory. She could not rely on William's parents, who had left Moose Factory for Flotta Island, Orkney, eight years before. Ellen must have felt a tug that she was further parting from both sets of parents.

It was forty-two portages and up to a month of paddling from Osnaburgh House to Red River. Ellen was thirty-nine years old with seven children, her youngest, Charlie, and her oldest, William, seventeen. Leaving Osnaburgh, they paddled westward to the end of the lake and the worst muddy and swampy portages of the trip. The streams shallowed as the family toiled toward the height of land between the Albany River watershed to the east and the English–Winnipeg Rivers watershed to the west. They passed familiar sights and portages at "Short's Falls," and later when they made Lac Seul, they passed the "Dancing Rocks." This was a storied passage to Red River, and the family had traveled it at least once before but with their father. Later, the lower stretches of the English River widened, prone to wind. On good days they might hoist one of their blankets or rolled birch barks (normally used to repair the canoe) to sail, or if it was rough, they might wait out the wind and waves on shore. At the mouth of the Winnipeg River entering Lake Winnipeg, at the HBC Fort Alexander post, they must have felt some relief.[6] This was the biggest post since leaving Osnaburgh, and they were likely treated kindly there. But they next had to ride the choppy waters of Lake Winnipeg. If the winds were calm, they would paddle quickly round the sandy Point du Grand Marais southward to the delta marking the mouth of the Red River. The delta was now filling up with the fall migration of ducks and snow geese, foretelling the changing seasons. From the marshland it was only a few miles upstream to St. Andrews, a parish mostly occupied by Scotch Métis, including Ellen's sister's family, the Browns. News of William's death spread upon their arrival.[7]

Tragedy and hardship did not relent for Ellen, John Linklater's paternal grandmother. But her trip, fleeing with her children, for Red River and family support did reorient her family to the area. She had left the cold

Osnaburgh House, Hudson's Bay Company post, 1886. This view looks east from a knoll on which the Anglican church and cemetery are located. Note both canoes and York boats for tripping up and down the Albany River. Courtesy of Library and Archives Canada.

tidal mudflats and marshlands of Moose Factory for Osnaburgh when she was six months pregnant, eight years earlier. Now she had left the boreal forest and the lengthy Lake St. Joseph for the prairie and oak savannas of the Red River country, her new home. She had relocated to the St. Andrews parish, with an imposing limestone church, the spire reaching into the sky. The Anglican church was the heart of the Scotch Métis settlement in St. Andrews. Many of Ellen's children stayed in the greater Red River area, including along the southern shores of Lake Winnipeg, and their children after them. But her eldest, William (the father of John Linklater), did not stay long. William returned off and on to St. Andrews, but like his father and grandfather, he began work with the Hudson's Bay Company, signing up at Fort Alexander as a laborer. Like others who were hired in a three-year contract, he received an HBC signing bonus of tea and sugar. Rather than working at Fort Alexander, he was sent upriver to the post at Lac Seul. Only four years after his father's death, one of William Thomas's tasks was to paddle and portage a mail packet eastward from Lac Seul over the height of land to Osnaburgh House. From there it would be combined with other letters, orders, and memos to be delivered downriver to Fort Albany on James Bay.[8] He was only twenty-one years old. He was born at Moose Factory, another, larger HBC post on James Bay, on February 14, 1847. All this was well-known territory of his youth, as his grandfather had been a captain on the bay, sailing the sloop between Albany and Moose, as they were called in HBC shorthand.

Three Cree women with unique beaded hoods in front of a Hudson's Bay Company sailboat, 1865. John Linklater's grandfather and great-grandfather captained a vessel like this one for runs to posts on James Bay and southern Hudson Bay. Courtesy of Library and Archives Canada.

There were, in fact, three successive William Linklaters, all forefathers to John, or Jack, Linklater. William Linklater I came from Flotta Island, Orkney, to Albany in 1816. Like so many Orkney Islanders, he was drawn to HBC wages that were three times what he might make at home.[9] He followed a traditional work path as Orkney Islanders were used to, shipping out for seasonal employment as fishermen, whalers, and seamen.[10] With this adventure he also escaped the dreary and dirty routine of harvesting and burning kelp (to make alkali shipped to England and used to make soap and glass). He certainly was "stout, able & active" as the HBC insisted. If he was frugal, he might save enough for a comfortable retirement back on Orkney. He is first mentioned in the Albany Post journals in fall 1816. Twenty-five-year-old William began his HBC work with menial jobs, cutting firewood, hauling supplies (often barrels packed with hundreds of salted geese) back to Albany from inland posts, digging a drain, "in the pit sawing planks for building a small vessel." Before the first year was out, he had repaired the rigging to the flagstaff, then repaired the rigging on the sloop, and prepared the sloop to be launched.[11] Having grown up on the sea, he was ready in 1823 when he was needed to navigate the sloop in James Bay and to the north into Hudson Bay proper.[12] Sometime prior to becoming a captain, he and a Métis woman, Eleanor Thomas, were married *á la façon du pays*, or in a common law marriage, as was customary in the fur trade. Other Orkney men were more casual in their relationships with Native women, but William and Eleanor were formally married decades after they began their relationship together.[13] This time lag between a country marriage and a minister-sanctioned marriage was often the result of too few clergymen to administer the wedding rites in remote areas than of any reluctance on the part of the individuals.

All three William Linklaters learned the strict three-tiered class system of the HBC employees. The highest in terms of rank (and smallest group in number) were the "gentlemen," including the governor, deputy governor, and stockholders in London. Officers, positions to which all the Linklaters must have aspired, were next in rank. Officers included surgeons, masters of major vessels, clerks, and postmasters. A postmaster was the man in charge at a remote post, essentially a clerk, often of some Native ancestry, but paid less than a clerk.[14] The majority of the workforce were "servants," or simply "men," lowest in pay and expected to follow the officers with absolute obedience. The largest number of HBC servants were "boatmen," or those who labored in canoes and York boats, such as up and down the Albany River. Orkney men were the dominant HBC servants before 1821, but their numbers and percentage of the HBC workforce diminished in the era of all three William Linklaters. At the same time, more and more Métis worked for the HBC, such as the latter two William Linklaters.[15]

A teenage William Thomas Linklater III was at Lac Seul, working what we would call casual labor before he entered into his first three-year contract. It was common for HBC children to apprentice as teenagers. Sometime before May 1869, he began a relationship with Ah-zhe-day-ge-she-gake of Lac Seul. Her name was rendered Eliza Fly in English, but her Anishinaabemowin name is better translated as Cross Sky Woman, or better yet, Going Across the Sky Woman.[16] Their marriage was "solemnized" at Lac Seul on May 7, 1869, meaning that on that date the Reverend Robert Phair passed through Lac Seul, paused at the HBC post, and married those he found worthy. Quite commonly these couples had already had their union memorialized by a contract drawn up by the post clerk or postmaster. When a minister came through a remote post, multiple marriages and baptisms tended to be the order of the day. Before long their first daughter was born, Alice Mary Linklater, and a little more than a year later, John James Linklater was born at Lac Seul on August 7, 1870.[17]

The Linklater family, Eliza, William, Alice, and John (or Jack), stayed at the post on the north side of Lac Seul for ten years. William and Eliza had other children there, but most of their children died very young. Two girls died as infants, another at a year and half. Charles Edward, born in 1876, lived at least five years before his death. Another brother, born later, died of scarlet fever. Only two of William and Eliza's children lived to adulthood, Alice and John.[18] And for an adult, like William, life could also be unrestrained (and involve a great deal of alcohol) at an HBC post such as Lac Seul, when William and other men were given the customary regale of "a quart of rum when the fish began spawning at Black Island."[19]

William rose through the HBC ranks beginning as a laborer, then bowsman (a position of midlevel responsibility in canoes), then employed as a steersman for the Lac La Pluie District (Rainy Lake) with the district headquarters at Rat Portage (Kenora). He likely paddled throughout the district as far east as Lac La Croix and perhaps farther. It was William's first time in the country that became so vital to his son and his family. But the family did not stay long; Eliza left sometime in 1881 to return closer to home. She and her children lived at Wabigoon Tank, or what is now close to Dryden, Ontario, and on a well-established canoe route to Lac Seul. The Canadian Pacific Railroad was completed through this area in 1881, and a town sprang up in addition to a small Indian reserve. Eliza received her treaty annuities at Wabigoon Tank in 1886, 1887, and 1888. Likely used to her husband being away on long canoe trips, delivering goods or hauling packs of fur, Eliza was no stranger to being the only adult in the home.

In 1883 William left the HBC service and became a "freeman," joining Eliza and their children in Lac Seul. Most likely he turned to trapping. Three years later, he returned to working for the HBC and was posted again to the Lac La Pluie District. His gambit away did not elevate him in the eyes of the company, and he returned to the lower ranks as a laborer. In 1891 he was working at the HBC post at Savanne, along the Canadian Pacific Railway line. In the eyes of an HBC inspector, he was "a very useful man at an Indian trading post under proper supervision."[20] The next year, he had risen to be a postmaster, the officer at Pine Portage, a postmaster being the highest rank a man of mixed ancestry could rise to in the hierarchical HBC at the time. Pine Portage is located off Pickerel Lake on the historic route through Sturgeon Lake in the center of the Quetico. Pine Portage was advantageous in a couple of ways; its relatively flat land with sandy soil was a productive potato ground, and there were buildings left standing from the old Dawson Trail. It was a customary camping ground for area Anishinaabeg traveling through. William was at Pine Portage until 1893 and perhaps later, then he disappeared from the historical record.

Hudson's Bay Company post at Pine Portage (in present-day Quetico Provincial Park), 1890. John Linklater's father was the man in charge there in the early 1890s. Courtesy of Hudson's Bay Company Archives, Winnipeg.

Eliza was not with William at Pine Portage. She had died a few years earlier, likely in 1889 or early 1890. She received (or in reality William received) her last treaty annuity in 1889.[21] Assuming she died in 1889, she died young, forty-two years old. She was a full member of the Lac Seul First Nation, making her son John half Anishinaabe.[22] Ironically, several of John's friends assumed his mother was "Cree." "Cree" had at least three different meanings to Minnesotans at the time. In a popular sense it meant his mother was Cree as we might understand it today; that is, she was a member of a distinct tribe living north of the Anishinaabe but speaking a language akin to Anishinaabemowin. Or "Cree" might hazily have meant only a "Canadian Indian." Or for those more knowledgeable about spoken Anishinaabemowin, "Cree" referred to "northerners" who spoke differently, a different dialect, or what today is called Oji-Cree. Calling them "Cree" did recognize the small linguistic and cultural differences from the Anishinaabeg in Minnesota.

John told few friends of his birthplace or exactly where his mother was from. He mentioned his mother was a traditionalist, with hopes that he would grow up with the mindset of an Indian, but offered few other details about her to his White friends—those who would hear and then recollect stories about him. Instead, those who recounted John's youth always spoke about his days at Rat Portage, stressing his father's HBC roots.

LAC SEUL IS A WIDENING of a long stretch of the English River and an Aboriginal homeplace. The family of Ochee, Ah-zhe-day-ge-she-gake's father, had long lived along the eastern reaches of Lac Seul. The family was heavily dependent on walleye, pike, and other fish. *Ochee* means "fly" in Anishinaabemowin, hence the name on her marriage certificate. But her father had died prior to the first treaty payment of 1875, or when Eliza was in her teens or early twenties. Thus, all the treaty payments to the family are to "Ochee's widow," who is eventually named in the historical record as "Sandawagan" or some rendition close to this.[23] Ah-zhe-day-she-gake's mother, Sandawagan, outlived her daughter, dying sometime after 1893. Alice and John had ample time to know their Lac Seul grandmother and their uncle, Okemaweekence, and likely stayed with one of them on their many visits to the area. Okemaweekence was likely an important teacher for John, as uncles often are to nephews in Anishinaabeg society. Unfortunately, we know little about Ah-zhe-day-she-gake's parents and brother. We do know Ah-zhe-day-ge-she-gake received treaty payments at Lac Seul on six occasions and received treaty payments at Wabigoon Tank for three more; hence she lived very near—only a couple days' paddle—from her kin in her adult life.[24]

Changes, such as the coming of the railroad south of Lac Seul, earmark much of Ah-zhe-day-she-gake's time.[25] Even before the HBC post at Lac Seul was built, the fur trade had impacted Aboriginal life for more than two centuries. The post was four decades old before Ah-zhe-day-she-gake was born. The establishment of the post and the residence of men and their families there brought lasting changes. As it did for William and Ah-zhe-day-she-gake, the trade resulted in marriages between First Nations people, Métis, and traders of European descent. Early on the Lac Seul post was impressive, including a "boat building shop" furnishing canoes for the downriver journeys to Lake Winnipeg.[26] The traders brought potatoes and other root crops, such as carrots and turnips. These crops did well and were adopted by the Lac Seul Anishinaabeg to the degree that eleven thousand bushels were harvested in 1884, the last year we know that Ah-zhe-day-she-gake was there. Indeed, potatoes were so integral to their way of life that they lamented to the Indian agent: "They had been planting potatoes introduced by the Hudson Bay Company a century ago, and wish potatoes of a better quality for seed."[27]

Later, the HBC post and then the establishment of the small reserve drove a centralizing of dispersed Anishinaabeg near Lac Seul. People living on Trout and Sturgeon Lakes began abandoning their homes and moving to Lac Seul, swelling the population to four hundred people in Ah-zhe-day-she-gake's day.[28] With the arrival of missionaries and the building of churches came exhortations for Anishinaabeg to convert and the assumption they would regularly attend services. Catholic and Anglican missionaries set up rival schools in the 1880s, but they were only lightly attended. Still tremendous change was occurring; in 1881, when Ah-zhe-day-she-gake returned to Lac Seul, 197 of her band members identified themselves as traditional, 158 as Catholic, and 51 as Episcopalian.[29]

Diseases, both new and returning, continued to sweep through the region. Nineteen Lac Seul Anishinaabeg died because of "relapses from exposure when recovering from measles." The return of measles reminded elders of the frightening winter of the 1819–20 measles epidemic that killed many Lac Seul Anishinaabeg. It was thought to have come up the Winnipeg River and then to the English River during the wild rice harvest.[30]

Much of traditional life continued, including the pattern of traveling nearby to harvest wild rice and to more distant locations to fish sturgeon and seek out better trading partners. Wild rice was a staple of their diet, though it became less so over time.[31] Lac Seul people regularly traveled to Lake of the Woods or Rainy Lake to harvest sturgeon, fish large enough that the return from harvesting them was worth the travel. They could also collect the sturgeon air bladders, dry them, and trade them as isinglass to HBC posts.[32] When dried, the rich sturgeon meat became more transportable and thus highly sought-after. By the early 1890s, however, sturgeon numbers declined because of increased fishing by both Indians and Whites.

Despite the more than 150 miles of lakes and portages between Osnaburgh House and Lac Seul, Eliza likely had met her father-in-law, William Linklater II, before her marriage. There were at least two HBC trips a year between Lac Seul and Osnaburgh House—one in winter by dog team and the other in summer by canoe. On special occasions there were others, such as the September 1857 trip when William II canoed to Lac Seul to bring back a "full calf." Eleven days later, William, "two servants and two Indians" returned to Osnaburgh with the bull calf.[33] It is a striking image: a bull calf in a birch-bark canoe with paddlers hurrying along, worrying about it kicking to rid itself of flies and punching a hole in the canoe, or having a smoke on a portage while the calf was munching wild hay. Despite the distance between Lac Seul and Osnaburgh House, the two sites were administratively tied together in the HBC Albany District. They were essentially at the "end of the line" for the district, and thus some exchange—for calves, seed potatoes, mail, trade goods, and sometimes food—was born of necessity. Because of these trips and the frequent movement of the Anishinaabeg, a young Eliza Fly likely met William II. And through these trips and given the HBC monopoly on trade in the area, she would have learned of his drowning and some family history, particularly that the Linklaters were an HBC family. She may have also laughed at their early attempts to speak fluent Anishinaabemowin, which were blended with Cree.

Eliza would have known that her future father-in-law was the postmaster at Osnaburgh House, the highest position at the post. He rose through the HBC ranks from "servant" to clerk class. Grandfather-in-law William Linklater I would live, marry, and stay on James Bay for four decades, then return to Flotta upon retirement. Eliza would not have met the Orkney man, William Linklater I, and yet he was still alive in Orkney when Eliza married William III.[34] From the Anishinaabeg perspective, the Linklater family appeared to be comprised of hardy and good providers.

William Linklater II's promotion and move to Osnaburgh House was one part of the geographic splintering of this Linklater family. Most of William I's male children stayed along James Bay, either at Moose Factory or Fort Albany, though three daughters returned to Orkney with William and his wife, Eleanor Linklater.[35] There is no evidence that William II ever saw his parents or most of his siblings again. When he did, it would have been a fleeting meeting with a brother making the 1,200-mile round-trip mail run in winter by dog team, or in summer during the annual canoe or York boat trip from Albany to Osnaburgh House and back.

William Linklater II was likely born at Fort Albany in the early 1820s, although his birth date is not recorded. He was the oldest child in the family, and his younger brothers, Benjamin, Archibald, and George, also worked for the HBC. Benjamin replaced his older brother on the HBC sloop that primarily ran from Albany to Moose Factory. The Linklaters were watermen. William II was, in turn, following the footsteps of his father, who had been a captain of the small sloop.[36] In retirement, William I returned to Flotta and resumed sailing and fishing in the North Sea to supplement his HBC annuity and savings. William II also inherited his strong Anglican faith from his father and mother, Eleanor Thomas, a Cree-Métis woman. When William II was in charge of Osnaburgh House, he regularly led prayers with the men on Sundays.[37] He also brought his grandmother, his mother's mother, along to Osnaburgh despite the HBC bureaucratic hurdles to having her there.[38] William II rose in the HBC ranks from sailor, to captain and master of the sale shop at Moose Factory to postmaster at Osnaburgh House. His salary increased with each promotion.

William II attended school at Fort Albany, the post being large enough that the HBC sponsored a school with a heavy Christian emphasis, common in that day. Because of this schooling, William II was literate.[39] His spelling sometimes failed him, owing to his meager education. He wrote on July 1857 while at Osnaburgh: "the country is on fire. . . . We cannot see across the Lack [Lac] for smook." He was, however, attentive to events happening at the post and precise in the census he took of area Anishinaabeg, including noting their clans, clan leaders, and relationships between leaders.[40] As was expected of a HBC clerk, he remained officious in his writings, though there were exceptions, such as when after dutifully noting the regular firewood cutting on November 18, 1857, he closed his entry with "and Mrs. Linklater was safely delivered of a son this morning at 7 A.M."[41] Rarely could an entry be described as ironic or funny except when they were unintentionally so: "one of the cows choked on fish called the Perch that she picked up along the waters edge."[42] But more important, his post journal entries demonstrate he could be relied on, persistent in looking out for the welfare of his men. When "John Smith and Ind lad drowned," he repeated his refrain of "poor man" in the next days, and he and his men looked for the body for months, even restarting the search with ice-out in the spring. Once the body was found, he had a coffin made and determined to bury John Smith where he was found as he was "not fit to bring in the house."[43]

William III grew up in the rhythms of life at the HBC post. He was nine when his family went inland to Osnaburgh, and he was seventeen when his father drowned. Like everyone at "Oz," he would have eagerly watched and anticipated the two (summer and winter) packets from Albany that brought letters, HBC gossip, maybe novel food, and the hubbub of supplies and goods to be distributed.[44] Similarly he would have watched his father and HBC men fish with gillnets and seines; like everyone else they lived primarily on fish and potatoes. They did not hunt moose or caribou in the country as there were none at this time.[45] Perhaps he helped cut hay for the cattle that had been laboriously brought up the six hundred miles from the coast. When young, he likely helped his mother snare rabbits when food was scarce, and with his father shot the first geese arriving in the spring. Later, when he was older, he might have joined one of the summer Albany boats, a monthlong journey back and forth. He grew up seeing birch bark being harvested and canoes being made and repaired. He grew up, too, around the post dogs that pulled the winter packet after New Year's and in early winter pulled birch sledges loaded with firewood. Accompanying his father, William III took snowshoe trips to Indian lodges to trade.

He observed the deference afforded officers of the HBC, like his father, who might, for example, stand in for a minister and issue a marriage "contract" to an Osnaburgh couple. As a boy, he witnessed and came to understand the inviolate class structure, or backbone, of the company that limited the jobs and salaries of "native"-born men. He probably already knew his father was also always indebted to the HBC for goods purchased. For example, while still at Moose Factory, one year his father purchased oatmeal, biscuit, flour, sugar, tea, coffee, soap, barley, rice, tobacco, blankets, blue cloth, cotton cloth, stroud, five men's cotton shirts, and more cloth. William III would have also learned his father was not alone—most servants and clerks were indebted to the HBC. His father's debt ran from one-half to three-quarters of a year's wages.[46]

Osnaburgh was a profitable post for the HBC. Six to eight servants along with their families made for almost twenty-five people total in residence. They lived mostly off the land. Linklater counted 181 Anishinaabeg at Osnaburgh in 1858.[47] Anishinaabeg from nearby and even from Cat Lake (north of Lake St. Joseph) regularly traded there. Its remoteness meant they had to travel great distances to find an independent trader with better rates. In 1860, William Linklater II traded for the following furs: 35 large, prime, small, and common black bears, 1 large brown bear; 276 large prime beaver, 169 small beaver, 34 common beaver, 14 small common beaver, 20 castoreum; 18 ermine; 111 prime fishers, 10 common fishers; 13 silver foxes, 7 common (all types of foxes 118); 96 prime and common lynx; 826 prime and common marten; 3,637 musquash (muskrat); 357 otters (all sizes/quality); isinglass 54 (pounds of air bladders from sturgeon); 7 skunks; and 14 wolverines.[48] The furs were carefully sorted and packed, and in the summer went with the "summer boats" (canoes and York boats) to Albany, and from there were loaded on HBC vessels and sailed to Europe for sale.

William II and Helena (Ellen Richards) were married in Moose Factory on October 23, 1845.[49] They both had lived in Moose Factory for years.

Both were Métis and of the same social class. Perhaps they were drawn together by their both being outwardly religious; Ellen had converted to Wesleyan Methodism at the age of fifteen, along with her older sister, Nancy.[50] Indeed, when Ellen's husband drowned, she must have thought of her devout older sister and her husband, who were doing well in Red River and could take her and her family in. The Browns were a successful Métis family that farmed a desirable river "lot," and they took in and adopted other orphans.[51] Ellen had also a younger sister, Mary, and her husband, James Corrigall, living in Red River. The thought of their homes in St. Andrews parish, a growing center of English Métis people and relatively well-off HBC retirees, must have brought the travel-weary Ellen some comfort. Upon arrival, she would learn much more about Red River, such as that to the south of her sister's farm were parishes dominated by French Métis.

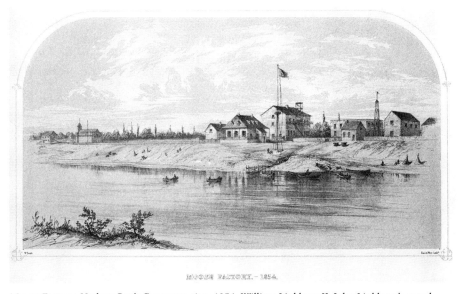

MOOSE FACTORY. – 1854.

Moose Factory, Hudson Bay's Company, circa 1854. William Linklater II, John Linklater's grandfather, was working there at the time. Courtesy of Archives of Ontario, Documentary Art Collection, I0003085.

Ellen and her children arrived in hard times. The drought and heat of summer 1864, when the thermometer topped 100 degrees Fahrenheit, had damaged crops. The grasshoppers then came and ate what was left. There was little farm food to spare.[52] A large delegation of Dakota came to nearby Fort Garry, further worrying the Red River residents. To ensure peace, the Dakota were treated generously, and the three thousand men, women, and children returned west to trade with HBC posts closer to their homes. The next summer, the grasshoppers came again, and the fall buffalo hunt on which the French Métis and indeed the settlement depended also was a failure. But with her sisters and their families nearby and a house to call home, Ellen might have felt some confidence about her future. Like all her neighbors', her family's beds were laid out and made snug with buffalo robes.[53] She even found a job as a nurse for a young doctor, Curtis J. Bird. Still, life was hard and involved tasks such as the two-day trek to cut firewood in the forests to the east and to haul it back across the prairie to their home. Red River was growing. In 1869 it was the home to 12,000 people, "5,757 French Half breeds, 4,086 English Half breeds, 1,565 Whites, and 558 Indians," most of whom lived along the Red or Assiniboine Rivers.[54]

Sometime during this period, Ellen and her family moved to a small house between river lots 116 and 117. Each lot had limited river frontage but ran from the river's edge almost two miles distant into rich prairie land. The stone Hawthorne Lodge owned by attorney and politician Alfred Boyd loomed nearby.[55] On the other side of them were James and Mary Gunn, a prominent Métis couple. Ellen and family did not own a river lot; instead, she likely did discrete domestic jobs for one or both families. There was a great deal of sympathy for her situation, as she settled in a community of retired or ex-HBC employees. She must have been quite friendly with the Gunns, as later two of her sons married two of their nieces. And perhaps she admired Mary Gunn, as Mary's life paralleled her own; Mary was once an HBC widow, who after eight years of raising five children alone had remarried at the relatively late age of forty-four.[56] Mary's marriage to James Gunn provided greater security for her and her children.

Ellen's sisters, friends, and even acquaintances must have hoped she would remarry. For a middle-aged woman then, a marriage would ensure better food, perhaps more reliable income, and perhaps even a prized river lot. As a spouse to an HBC retiree, she would have renewed status and help navigating the increasingly British Canadian systems and values that were challenging the Métis-dominant Red River life. Also diminishing was the status of Métis women among Red River society with the coming of British women, primarily as wives. "The officers of the Hudson's Bay Company fell into genuine rapture over the charms and accomplishments of the few British ladies who set foot in Rupert's Land."[57] But instead of greater stability or bolstered status, life took a turn for the worse.

In late 1865 Ellen became pregnant. With the stigma of being unmarried and pregnant, she attempted to hide the fact. But in early August 1866 she gave birth, alone, and perhaps outside while walking. The male child died. She wrapped the child in shawls and later confessed to her sister and neighbor. Ellen, like a few other Métis and Native women before her, was accused of infanticide. In court, in August, she pleaded not guilty and yet was not allowed to testify. She was convicted of a lesser offense, "concealment of the birth of a child," and sent to prison for three months. It is unclear from the existing record if the child died purposefully or not, whether she fainted after childbirth outside, or if she, indeed, let the child die of exposure.[58] What is remarkable and tragic in retrospect was that the court did not even inquire about the father, nor did Ellen name the father as part of this tragedy. This is unlike an infamous case a few years earlier when the father was named and was of a higher "station" than the mother.[59] What is very probable is that Ellen faced cruel rumors and innuendos for the rest of her life. It is not known how her young family coped with her being gone or where her children were. Her youngest, Charles, was five years old, and the oldest, William, nineteen.

The new year of 1867 may have brought Ellen some optimism. Her third born, Barbara, married another young Métis, Alexander Knott, whose family also came from Moose Factory. Later that year, Barbara bore Ellen's first grandchild. Barbara's older sister, Margaret, may have already been in a relationship or a "country marriage" to Pierre Swampy of Fort Alexander First Nation. A few years later they would formally marry.[60] William III was working for the HBC as a boatman. Despite signing on at Fort Alexander, he continued to be based out of Lac Seul, miles away from his mother, brothers, and sisters.[61] During the same era, Red River suffered through additional environmental failures. Grasshoppers returned, and there were failures in the Métis buffalo hunt to the west and in nearby fisheries.[62] To face the winter months, food was brought in from St. Paul, Minnesota, on sleighs but was expensive.

WHILE ELLEN AND HER FAMILY faced insecurity and tumult, the people and governance of Manitoba were awash in turmoil. Much of this upheaval was acted out in two places, Upper and Lower Fort Garry. Lower Fort Garry (downstream on the Red River and north of Upper Fort Garry) was not far from where Ellen and her family lived. Métis authority and activities were often based from these two locations. But the uproar was national in scope; it was about governance, by whom and under what conditions. The eastern provinces first became a Canadian Confederation in 1867, sparking interest in those lands west of Ontario, or what was called the Province of Canada at the time. Across the border, some Americans sought to extend Manifest Destiny to include prairie lands north of the forty-ninth parallel. In Manitoba, harsh economic and environmental problems helped coalesce a minority group of English speakers to call for the "annexation of Red River to Canada."[63] Turmoil in governance swept through the parishes hugging the Red and Assiniboine Rivers, hastening the HBC to sell Rupert's Lands to the young Canadian Confederacy on December 1, 1869, called by some the "Deed of Surrender." This was a strictly British transaction, between a British company and the Crown, with no consultation or affirmation from the residents, particularly the numerically dominant Métis.[64]

To the west, the Métis community of Portage La Prairie made an attempt at home rule, supplanting the fading HBC governance.[65] The arrival of a Canadian survey party at Fort Garry, in the heart of the Red

River, on August 20, 1869, was too much for the Métis to bear. Louis Riel led a group of Métis men who stopped the surveyors from their work. The Métis were anxious about their rights and homes along the Red River and elsewhere as many possessed the land through the right of occupancy rather than formal title. A smaller number of Métis had received titles to river lots from the HBC, but there was a question of if and how those rights would be recognized by the change in government. In fall 1869, support for Louis Riel grew, particularly among the French Métis, leading to the idea, and then actuality, of a provisional government of those living in Manitoba. After much discussion among the French and English Métis on December 9, a provisional government, or Red River Republic, was proclaimed by Riel. Facing the threat of being added to the Canadian federation without a voice, the provisional government listed fourteen rights as a condition of union. These included representation in parliament, a bilingual legislature, and recognition of certain land claims. These conditions were ignored.

Several men did not accept the provisional government and worked to undermine it. Riel's group arrested a few pro-Canadian men, called "Orangemen," for combatting local governance by the numerically dominant French Métis. Some of the pro-Canada men eventually escaped, some were freed, and a handful were recaptured. After a trial a few men were convicted but released, but one violent insurrectionary, Thomas Scott, was executed by firing squad. News of this incident incensed many in eastern Canada, redoubling calls and efforts to raise, equip, and send troops to quell the "rebellion" in Manitoba. After months of travel, Colonel Wolseley and his troops marched into Lower Fort Garry on a drizzly August 23, 1870. Riel fled across the border to the United States, but unofficial retribution began to rain down on the Métis. While Wolseley's soldiers were en route, the Canadian Federation formally admitted Manitoba into the union on July 15, 1870.

Ellen and her family were enmeshed in these events and indeed lived in the upheaval of Red River society. They lived between the stone Church of St. Andrew to the south, and Lower Fort Garry, the heart of HBC trade and governance, to the north. Ellen and her children walked along the river road to both sites, roughly four miles, until the spire of St. Andrew's Church was visible. From her house, the Stone Fort, or Lower Fort Garry, was about a half mile away, close enough where she could hear any gunshots and the bell. She would have witnessed the summer gathering of Anishinaabeg and Cree and government negotiators for Treaty 1 concluded at Lower Fort Garry in 1871—the first such treaty in the region. She lived near the river road, which was a main thoroughfare, and everyone passed that way: Métis, Louis Riel, HBC retirees, "loyalists" (those for joining Canada), soldiers, Anishinaabeg, Cree, and representatives of the Canadian Confederation. Ellen knew many of the participants, particularly in the provisional government, as they were essentially neighbors. The brother of next-door neighbor James Gunn, George, was in the Legislative Assembly of Assiniboia, as was Ellen's employer, Dr. Curtis James Bird.[66] Alfred Boyd, whose Hawthorne House dwarfed her own, was an English representative to the Convention of Forty, a prelude to the provisional government. Boyd was, in the words of Métis leader Louis Riel, "one of the most decided against us." Thus, Ellen lived literally in the middle of swirling and virulent viewpoints toward Métis government in Manitoba.[67]

For the English Métis, like the Linklaters, the Riel Resistance begged the question of their sympathies and allegiance. Some English Métis sided with their French Métis friends. Others were of a mixed opinion, one stating that the French Métis "were born and brought up among us, ate with us, slept with us, hunted with us, traded with us, and are our own flesh and blood. . . . Gentlemen, I for one cannot fight them. I will not imbrue my hands with their blood."[68] But where Ellen and family lived, in St. Andrews parish near the Stone Fort, "was a place of refuge . . . [for] . . . the troubled loyalists."[69] Or the home of those who might hide the main antagonist of Louis Riel, the provocateur and land speculator "Dr." John Schultz, who had escaped from the Stone Fort.[70]

Once the Riel Resistance was quelled, many English Métis suffered the loss of land, prestige, and self-governance, as did French Métis. Many French Métis fled west, once the hostility and power shift against them

View of Red River from St. Andrew's Church, 1858. The Linklaters lived nearby along the "River Road." Photograph by H. L. Himes. Courtesy of Beinecke Rare Book and Manuscript Library, Yale University.

was obvious. Bias against any Métis was rampant and bolstered by racial stereotypes of the day. One leading minister reported the "Scotch Half-breeds . . . were . . . middle-sized or under, steadier than the [French-Anishinaabe] Métis, somewhat slow in movement, stolid, fairly reliable, sociable, somewhat suspicious, intelligent."[71] Racial bias combined with antagonism toward any Métis self-governance made life hard, especially compared with the lives of the political elites, who would increasingly be made up of English Canadians from Lower Canada.

Ellen Linklater's married daughter Barbara Knott and her husband, Alexander Knott, lost their river lot despite Alexander's father being an HBC grantee of the land. Not helping the Métis was the delay in a Canadian ruling on what constituted "satisfactory occupancy" for a Métis family to be recognized as a legitimate owner.[72] River lot 48 left the Knott family, and they moved northward to Grand Marais along Lake Winnipeg. This took place despite both Barbara and Alexander (and their children) being awarded Métis scrip monies based on being Métis in Manitoba before it joined Canada. But the scrip monies came too late, in May 1, 1876, to save their farmland.[73] The Knotts lost their lands, as did up to 90 percent of Métis through one means or another.[74] But the owners of the adjoining river lot 47, Ellen's sister, Nancy Brown, and her husband, John, kept their place because of their financial success stemming in part from a longer tenure on the property prior to Manitoba joining Canada. The Browns holding their land was an exception to the rule, as was their relative prosperity from agriculture.

Despite having no legal title to a river lot, Ellen continued to live along the Red River. Another young family, the McAlsters, also lived between river lots 116 and 117.[75] Ellen was still struggling, evidenced by how many of her children were absent from the 1870 census despite their young age. Archibald, age fourteen, and John, fifteen, were elsewhere, beyond the reach of a census taker, likely already working seasonally for the HBC. Margaret, age twenty-two, was absent too but was already at Fort Alexander living with Pierre Swampy. William, the oldest, was visiting and was counted in the census. Barbara was already married to Alexander Knott, so only James and Charlie were at home. Two years later, James Stewart Linklater married Nancy Donald, and later that year they had a daughter, Ellen, named after her grandmother.

THE SAME YEAR, 1872, the Linklaters—William III and Eliza, Alice, and toddler John—canoed from Lac Seul to Fort Alexander. William renewed his contract there with the HBC on June 20, 1872, and eighteen days later the family was in Red River, and John James Linklater was baptized at St. Clement's Anglican Church. Only two years old, John could not remember the day. But his nearby extended family, "Kokum," or Grandma Ellen Linklater, the Browns, and perhaps an uncle or two attended the baptism. John was baptized by Reverend Henry Cochrane, a Métis pastor.[76] Before long the family turned around to head home, visited Margaret and Pierre Swampy at Fort Alexander, then began the arduous paddle upstream to Lac Seul.

None of these family observances uplifted Ellen for long. Less than a year later, she died a mysterious death. The newspaper accounts of her death are not kind:

> On Friday evening last a Mrs. Linklater of St. Andrew's was at a house in that parish, and proposed crossing the river, and on expressing a dislike to going alone, a young man present volunteered to accompany her and they departed together. The next day a shawl and bundle belonging to the woman were found beside a hole in the ice, and as she was missing it was supposed that she had been drowned and the river was dragged, for the body but without success. On Wednesday a person who was shooting in the woods opposite the premise of Mr. B.R. Ross, came upon the body of the unfortunate woman.[77]

Another newspaper account published a rumor that "she had been murdered" and, unmercifully, that the "deceased was addicted to drinking, and was under the influence of liquor when last seen."[78] The official inquest found she had perished from exposure.

It is likely that after Ellen's shocking death, her sister, Nancy Brown, took in young Charlie and perhaps Ellen's other children. Nancy provided support to the children, assisting them in applying for Métis scrip after her sister's death. Nancy and her husband also took in Barbara and Alexander Knott's daughter, Sarah, in 1881.[79] The arrangement was probably of mutual benefit as the Browns needed farmworkers and Sarah could stay in Red River and go to school. Sarah was John Linklater's first cousin. It is also likely that a young John Linklater spent a year or two at the Browns, as he went to an unnamed "big city" for schooling, but he became lonely and asked to go home.[80] Later, a newspaper man wrote about what John told him of this time:

> After infancy and early boyhood spent at a lonely Hudson Bay trading post, John was sent to his grandmother, who lived in a Canadian settlement that he might go to school. Apparently the life of the

village and the confining walls of the schools did not appeal to the young huntsman and, in the absence of more legitimate game, his grandmother's chickens fell before his bow and arrow.[81]

Perhaps while at the Browns, he would have met other members of the Richards, Linklater, Knott, and Swampy families traveling through Red River. And he might have learned more about his Richards family roots at Moose Factory, including that from this side he inherited some Welsh and English blood in addition to his Orkney heritage. The Richards family included two HBC captains who had plied the Atlantic, four generations of HBC employees, as well as one of the first acclaimed Indigenous visual artists, William Richards.[82] Richards's paintings are celebrated today but were likely unknown to John (Plates 1 and 2).

After Ellen's death and the sweeping political changes and land speculation in Red River in the early 1870s, her children moved away from a booming Winnipeg. Barbara and Alexander Knott moved north, as did her younger brother James and his newly wed wife, Ann Donald. James and Barbara and their families lived in proximity for a number of years, making the windswept Grand Marais, Manitoba, their home. Barbara and Alexander Knott were instrumental in establishing St. Jude's Anglican Church in Grand Marais, continuing the Linklater fidelity to the Anglican faith.[83] Younger brothers John and Archibald moved northwest, likely with temporary HBC jobs, though these are rarely recorded. After they left Red River, their jobs took them through Lake Manitoba and along the English, now called Churchill, River. Before long John settled in or near Prince Albert, Saskatchewan. John married a Métis woman from the area, Mary Brass, and lived there until her premature death.[84] As a widower he moved to North Dakota among other Métis, remarried a Métis widow, and became a farmer. He identified himself on a U.S. census as "Cree" as there was no category for Métis. Archibald started year-round employment with the HBC in the English River District, whose district center was at Île-à-la Crosse. He steadily moved up through the ranks from laborer to interpreter and was finally postmaster at Souris River in northern Saskatchewan. After thirteen years of service, he left HBC employment in 1890, or, more likely, his contract was not renewed in a reorganization or austerity move.[85]

Margaret Linklater married Pierre Swampy and settled in the Fort Alexander area. Pierre and his older brother, George, also worked for the HBC, at Lake of the Woods and the Rainy River District. George worked as an HBC fisherman at Lake of the Woods in the 1860s, catching whitefish for the post.[86] Only two years later Pierre was hired as a canoe man.[87] Pierre and Margaret had a child, Helene, in Rat Portage in 1882, named after Margaret's mother. Unlike her siblings Margaret converted to Catholicism.[88] Eventually the family returned to Fort Alexander, and she was accepted as a member of the tribe, identifying as Anishinaabe rather than Métis or Cree. Government rules stipulated she was now an Indian. She lived a remarkably long life.[89] Margaret and Pierre's sojourn at Rat River and the Rainy River District may have effectively introduced her brother, William III, and Eliza to the area. The close relationship between the Anishinaabeg families from Fort Alexander with those of Lake of the Woods also may have played a factor in their move and stay there. The William Linklater III and Swampy families also lived nearby in Rat River during the early 1880s. Like John and Archibald when they moved northwest, the siblings often stuck together in pairs when they could. William and Eliza saw Pierre and Margaret repeatedly at Fort Alexander and later at Lake of the Woods.

John Linklater's youngest uncles, Archibald and Charlie, traveled far and led dramatic lives. After being laid off by the HBC, like John's father, "Archie" went farther north and west to Yukon Territory. There he eventually married a Gwich'in woman and started a family. Archie was quite a bit older than his wife, and not long ago, his grandson became a chief of the Gwich'in tribe.[90] Archie led a noteworthy life in the outdoors, in one instance taking a fifty-four-dog team to Dawson City for the Royal Mounties. He also took a dog team over the Rocky Mountains to investigate the oil boom at Fort Norman. In another frantic sled dog trip, he tried to get his daughter to the nearest doctor 225 miles away, but " the girl's life could not be saved."[91] Archie was also known as a fiddler, and he brought Red River jigs to the Gwich'in, where the fiddle music is played today.[92] But once Archie went to Yukon Territory, he left the extended orbit of his siblings, never to reconnect.

"Uncle Charlie" was only nine years older than his nephew John. Charlie's young life was tough. His father died when he was three years old, and his mother when he was twelve. He was born at Osnaburgh House, not Moose Factory, unlike all but one sibling. He remained in Red River after his mother's death, and in 1880 he married Margaret Donald, sister to his brother James's wife, Ann.[93] In 1885 "he volunteered in the 91st Regiment . . . and saw all the active fighting of the [Second Métis] Rebellion." Charlie fought for the Queen and against the French Métis and their Blackfeet allies. He was awarded a medal for his service that remains in the family.

After a return from the 1885 Rebellion, he and his family moved to Rat Portage, and while there he must have seen his older brother William, and his family, including John.[94] Charlie, too, took to the fur trade as a trapper, though not as an HBC employee. One of his long, 320-mile dog team trips with his ten-year-old daughter was glamorized in a Minnesota newspaper, as was a hunting trip when he shot a moose, thought it was dead, and was kicked by it, requiring a six-month recovery.[95] Charlie identified as Cree and told stories of the Cree trickster, Wesakchak, appearing in a book of Indian legends.[96] Charlie's life was tragic; two of his sons were killed in World War I. John was connected enough to his uncle and family that he knew three of his cousins had enlisted. Only later did he learn two had died in Europe.[97]

By the time John Linklater had come of age in the late 1880s, his uncles and aunts were scattered across western Canada, most living north of Winnipeg. John traveled from Rat Portage to Fort Alexander on occasion, likely staying with his auntie and uncle, Margaret and Pierre Swampy.[98] It was a commonly traveled canoe route of 149 miles. Most of his uncles and aunts had turned to the woods and trapping or trading, but Uncle John became a farmer. All but Margaret and Archie applied for and received Métis scrip. Through his HBC postings, William, the oldest, literally went his own direction south and east to Rat Portage, to Lake of the Woods, and eventually to Pine Portage in what is now the Quetico Provincial Park. John and Alice learned about the far-flung members of the extended Linklater family through the smaller get-togethers with Aunt Margaret and Uncle Charlie and their families.[99]

John and his older sister, Alice, remained very fond of one another, despite being apart much of their adult lives. A letter written to John by his young granddaughter says it best: "Your sister [Alice] wants to see you very badly. They were coming here [Embarrass, Minnesota] but they haven't any car."[100] Just a year different in age, they had been together at Lac Seul, Rat Portage, Lake of the Woods, and Wabigoon. Leaving Wabigoon and her family, Alice married Daniel Morriseau and lived along the Ontario–Minnesota border. Only ten years later Daniel died. Alice remarried and lived into her nineties but saw many premature deaths in her life.[101] She helped her parents raise younger brothers and sisters, all of whom would die young except for John. She took care of her eight-year-old sister Clara after her mother died and her father could not. Another brother of Alice and John, Charles Edward, age five in 1881, must have died shortly after the census information was taken.[102] And perhaps worse for Alice, many of her children died as infants.[103]

Throughout their lives, Alice and John had to "negotiate" the categories of what it meant to be Indian or Métis, as recognized by the Canadian and American governments. Alice applied for and received Métis scrip from the Canadian government in 1894, affirming her Métis status. She chose to receive monies (rather than scrip for land) and received $240 as a Métis born in "Keewatin," or Northwest Ontario. Key points in her application mulled over by the Canadians were that she had not received treaty payments at Lac Seul like her mother, who "was married to a non-treaty man [William Linklater, thus] their children had no right to receive treaty [payments]."[104] In other words, in the eyes and under the rules of the Canadian government, she was not an "Indian"; instead she was Métis.

Four years later, her Métis husband Daniel died. She initially stayed on Lake of the Woods at a commercial fishery with her father-in-law and her younger sister, Clara.[105] Sometime after 1901, she moved across what some Métis called the "medicine line," or border.[106] The first record of Alice living among Bois Forte Band members was 1908; however, she likely was there years prior to that time.[107] In the first census where she appears, she was already listed as "Mrs. Frank Wakemup." Frank Wakemup, or May no kwince, was considerably younger than Alice. By 1909 and 1910, the Indian agent noted that although she was a "Canadian Indian," he "asked the Dept authority to pay this woman" as a Bois Forte Band member. As such, she was eligible to apply for an allotment. After years of delay, Alice Wakemup was granted an eighty-acre allotment in remote St. Louis County off the Little Fork River on August 25, 1920.[108] In the eyes of the American government, Alice was an "Indian," or more specifically a member of the Bois Forte Band, and as a landowner, a U.S. citizen.

Her brother, John, was typically called an Indian by U.S. census takers. He never applied for Indian status or was a member of a specific band, nor was he a citizen in the United States or Minnesota. Rather, in the official "Alien Registration" in 1918 during World War I, the recorder listed him, under miscellaneous remarks: "Halfbreed but not ward of the U.S. nor Canada."[109] John was born only three weeks after the July 15, 1870, cutoff date to apply for Métis scrip in Canada. And his July 15, 1889, immigration to the United States foreclosed a late application as a Métis even when the cutoff date was rolled back. Technically speaking, John was neither Indian nor Métis in Canada and not even a U.S. citizen. He was, officially, an alien in the United States, neither White nor Indian. And while the 1924 Indian Citizenship Act finally recognized Indian citizenship in the United States, it would not apply to John, as he was not born in the United States (the act presumed birth on an Indian reservation to be a citizen). While John and Alice were only a year apart, shared a childhood at remote HBC posts together, and as adults lived relatively close to one another, their histories as Canadians and potentially Americans were conceptually worlds apart. Remarkably, almost none of John's White friends knew of his ambiguous status nor suspected it. Nor seemingly were they aware of his sister. For his White friends, his family history was generic and romanticized.

But John's relatives repeatedly faced hardship and the structural inequities of being Métis. Ellen Linklater suffered from the adversity of prematurely losing her husband, being pregnant out of wedlock, and the discriminatory hierarchy of the HBC. Societal forces and biases bore down on her. Reliance on family was one buffer to adversity. Steadfastness to family was deep-seated among the Linklaters. Even when William Linklater I returned to Orkney, he took with him his wife and youngest daughters, unlike so many other HBC retirees. But difficulties repeatedly forced family members to move, to leave home for a new one, days or weeks away by canoe.

The Linklaters' story was geographically sweeping as families tried to settle, became uprooted, and started anew in the prairie lands of Red River or the boreal forest of Lac Seul or Pine Portage. Clinging to the Anglican faith in the form it took within Métis culture brought some comfort to generations of Linklaters. The Linklaters were not unique: their family history echoes that of other geographically scattered Métis. And yet, few non-Métis understood or appreciated those stories, which were hardly known (or told) in the United States in particular. Few could guess at John's and his sister Alice's past and heritage or knew of the imperiously devised difference between the two. Few knew much about John's mother's and father's life and death. And yet, their lives were as heroic as any others and in the case of Kokum Ellen Linklater, heroic and uncommonly tragic. Out of family hardship and fidelity, John and Tchi-Ki-Wis Linklater forged a partnership that furthered their resilience and fashioned truly extraordinary lives.

CHAPTER 2

The Anishinaabeg Family
and Artistry of Tchi-Ki-Wis

TCHI-KI-WIS, OR HELEN ROBINSON, met John Linklater when they were both teenagers. He was not more than nineteen years old, and she was sixteen. In 1889 they immigrated to the United States.[1] But moving may have been simply canoeing from a border lake to the southwestern reaches of Basswood Lake, such as to Jackfish Bay. Tchi-Ki-Wis's family, along with other Anishinaabeg, had long roots in the Basswood Lake region. While it never became a reservation or reserve in either country, it was a long-standing Anishinaabeg home. Tchi-Ki-Wis's mother and father, Laposh and Mandaquabeek, John and Susan Robinson, lived on the American side of Basswood Lake as early as 1885. The border was effectively invisible in Susan's youth, but with time it had growing consequences because of the two countries' differing governing regimes.

Tchi-Ki-Wis and John lived in a time of great change. The quiet forests and waters of canoe country, their homeland, were suddenly inundated with surveyors, engineers, Indian agents, construction men, miners, railroad workers, and eventually settlers. One of the sweeping changes in their midst was the building and use of the "Dawson Trail," or "Dawson Route." The Canadian government wanted a transportation system from Lake Superior to the prairies for two pressing reasons. First, the Canadian government sought a way to get a military contingent to Red River to counter the threat of Métis governance in Manitoba, or in plainer terms, quash the Riel Rebellion. Second, farmers in eastern Ontario and the

Tchi-Ki-Wis with raven, Birch Island, Isle Royale, circa 1928. Photograph from Warner Wirta. Courtesy of Iron Range Research Center.

Maritime Provinces were clamoring to have access to the fertile farmlands of the prairies. One problem of getting Canadians to Red River was the geography of the Canadian Shield with its checkerboard of lakes, river, swamps, and granite. The country defied the easy movement of troops. A second problem to a more practicable solution of taking railroads through Minnesota to Red River, was American greed, owing to the cultural belief in Manifest Destiny, which drove the United States to want to acquire the prairie lands north of the forty-ninth parallel. Accordingly, many Americans opposed Canadian military forces in the region. To remedy these problems, the Dawson Trail was hacked through the forests and strung along waterways for 618 miles from Thunder Bay to Manitoba. The actual "trail" slashed through what is now Quetico Provincial Park, entering the northeast end of the park and exiting roughly at Lac La Croix, on the southwest. From there it followed the border waters until Lake of the Woods, where it returned to exclusively Canadian soil and waterways.

Construction of the Dawson Trail began in 1868, and only ten years later the route was effectively abandoned. But in those ten years, and especially in 1870, men flooded into the area. More than eight hundred workers and voyageurs were toiling along the route, and more than 150 large boats were stationed on various lakes.[2] Fourteen hundred military men (with four cannons in tow) paddled, rowed, and portaged across the route in 1870, sometimes helping to improve the road along the way. Led by Simon J. Dawson, men built coffer dams to raise water levels to improve navigation, cut wood for the small steam engines, and built way stations along the route.[3] One way station, at Pine Portage on the southwest end of Pickerel Lake in today's Quetico, would after abandonment by the Canadian government become an HBC post and a place where treaty payments were made to the Sturgeon Lake Band, or Kawawaigamok Anishinaabeg.[4] The Linklaters knew this place well. Despite all this effort, the trail remained a work in progress. A traveler recounted: "One Englishman said he would sooner be hanged in England than die a natural death on the Dawson Route."[5] In 1873, two hundred men were still working on the route. It was used primarily by Canadian military forces in 1870 (both

going west and then returning eastward). In 1871 men crossed it to counter
the threat of a Fenian raid. In 1872 and 1873, the first police recruits for
the North-West Mounted Police made their way along the route.[6] When
effectively abandoned in 1878, roadhouses, gardens, small steamers, and
property were left along the trail, a boon to area Anishinaabeg short on
tools, iron, stoves, and nails.[7]

A job on the Dawson Route brought John Robinson into the country.
At the height of the construction in 1870, forty-seven men were hired at
Sault Ste. Marie, likely including John Robinson, Tchi-Ki-Wis's father.[8] He
was not originally from Lac La Croix. Instead, Robinson was a common
name at Garden River (just east of Sault Ste. Marie) and at Batchawana
Bay on the eastern shore of Lake Superior. Unfortunately, we do not know
what job Robinson did, but before long he met Susan somewhere along

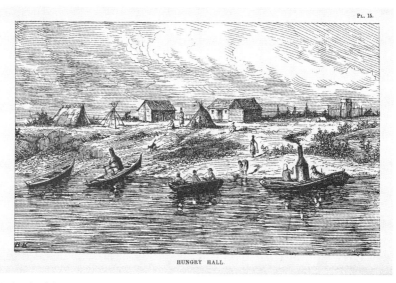

A sketch of the Dawson Trail where the Rainy River meets Lake of the Woods, then called
Hungry Hall, circa 1872. Note the small steam vessels, which were stationed on the larger
lakes along the Dawson Trail and used to pull travelers' boats. Courtesy of University of
British Columbia Library, Rare Books and Special Collections.

the Dawson Trail. He was a powerfully built man, half Anishinaabe and half French, and spoke French fluently.[9] His surname was first rendered "Laposh," "LaPoash," and then "LaPoste" on the Lac La Croix treaty paylists and was a rare French name and "Roman Catholic" in the early records. He likely knew Pine Portage between Sturgeon and Pickerel Lakes, as a "Robson" is recorded there in 1890.[10] If so, he certainly would have interacted with William Linklater, John's father. In the 1920 Census, "Robinson John" was listed as a "trapper." After Tchi-Ki-Wis's and John Linklater's deaths in 1934 and 1933, Robinson died alone suffering from dementia in Duluth, Minnesota.

Tchi-Ki-Wis and her father, Laposh/John Robinson, who wears a top hat and plays the mandolin, Birch Island, 1929. Frank M. Warren photograph. Courtesy of University of Minnesota Duluth, Archives and Special Collections.

All the while the Dawson Trail was being constructed and during its first years of use, a mining boom was ongoing at Silver Islet outside Thunder Bay. The amount of silver mined there made a fortune for a few. The discovery of gold in 1871 at Jackfish Lake, not far off the Dawson Trail (and just northeast of the present borders of the Quetico), kept mining and prospecting in a frenzy.[11] Jackfish Lake was also beyond the boundary line of the 1850 Superior Robinson Treaty because it was west of the height of land separating the Lake Superior and Hudson Bay watersheds. In other words, it was Anishinaabeg land. Chief Blackstone, also called Magatewasin, objected to the mine and made the miners leave and return to Fort William. That an Anishinaabe leader did so was an immediate national scandal and caused a great deal of consternation among Euro-Canadians not used to such a forthright act. The mine manager, oozing White superiority, assumed that Blackstone had not acted alone but was instead "tampered with" by Simon Dawson (of the trail fame) to remove the miners.[12] The eviction of miners was an act of courage as it came on the heels of Blackstone having watched and reluctantly agreed to the movement of hundreds of men, soldiers, and a few women and families across his homeland on the Dawson Trail.[13] Nor did Blackstone's reputation among non-Indigenous people improve, as he was a believer in Anishinaabeg religion and actively put off missionaries in his midst. At one point Blackstone debated an Anglican missionary. In turn, some Whites started an incendiary rumor that Blackstone had participated in the U.S. Dakota War of 1862.[14] This rumor, repeated by Anglican churchmen, is preposterous as the Anishinaabeg and Dakota were traditional enemies at this time and Blackstone lived far from central Minnesota. But it was true that Blackstone's sphere of influence extended beyond Lac La Croix, and he could often be found in the larger region defending Anishinaabeg rights.

Tchi-Ki-Wis grew up during the time when Blackstone was a widely respected chief ogimaa. She was likely related to Blackstone. She was a cousin (most likely first cousin) to Sophie and Charlotte Connors, who were Blackstone's granddaughters. Blackstone had more than one wife—three, in fact—as was common at the time for men who were good pro-

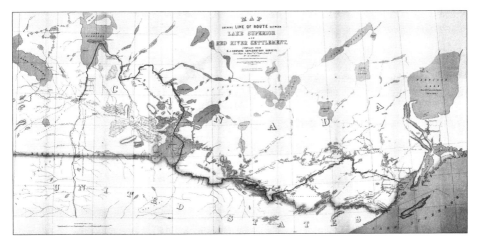

The route between Lake Superior and Red River Settlement, compiled from Simon J. Dawson's exploratory surveys, 1870. Courtesy of University of Manitoba Archives and Special Collections.

viders and often Anishinaabeg leaders. Tchi-Ki-Wis may have been a granddaughter or grand-niece to Blackstone but from a different maternal line than the Connors. Still, his presence marked her youth. Blackstone held strong beliefs, expressed by an Indian agent: "As a general rule they do not seem to wish to be Christianized."[15] A traveler through the country, Rev. George M. Grant described Blackstone, who was "said to be their most eloquent chief, and accordingly set down as a great rascal by those who cannot conceive of Indians as having rights, or tribal or patriotic feelings."[16] Blackstone's eviction of miners at Jackfish Lake caused an uproar and led to treaty negotiations so mining and exploration could resume in the area, and the Dawson Trail would be "secure, and plans for the Canadian Pacific Railway could confidently proceed."[17]

Chief Blackstone was one of a handful of Anishinaabeg leaders who negotiated Treaty 3 with Canadian government representatives, one of whom was Simon Dawson. The 55,000-square-mile treaty area ran eastward from the Northwest Angle of Lake of Woods along the border until it met the height of land (and the west border of the Robinson Superior Treaty area) and then northward as far as Lac Seul and the English River. One Anishinaabeg request that was ignored by the commissioners was "that the river should be left as it was formed from the beginning—that nothing be broken." The Anishinaabeg were worried about the effects of damming and altering the river that might impact fishing and wild rice gathering. Treaty 3 led to the creation of reserves within the area, including one at Lac La Croix and a second, "Wawa Bay," sometimes called "Sturgeon Lake" (the Sturgeon Lake in the center of Quetico Provincial Park). Two years later, Treaty 3 was amended by adding a "Halfbreed Adhesion," which is the first formal Canadian government document to recognize the Métis people as having Aboriginal rights. One of the people included in the document was a "John Linklater" married to "Tchi-Ki-Wis."[18] Possibly a distant relative, the older John Linklater's spouse, somehow had the same name as the Tchi-Ki-Wis, or Helen Robinson from Lac La Croix. The older Tchi-Ki-Wis was perhaps the namesake for Helen Robinson, or Tchi-Ki-Wis.[19] The younger Linklaters may have deeply admired the older woman.

A photograph by Wright Bros. of Rat Portage, Ontario, shows the conclusion of negotiations for Treaty 3 at the Northwest Angle in 1873. Copyright Manitoba Museum, Winnipeg, Manitoba.

The treaty permitted Whites to log, mine, and settle in the area. It also reserved "Indian" hunting and fishing throughout the area. To encourage farming among the Anishinaabeg, and thus more assimilation, it provided tools such as hoes, plough, scythe, auger, and one box of carpenter tools and enough wheat, barley, potatoes, and oats to seed the land. Payment was five dollars a year for each Indian, but each year it seemed one of the Indian agent's main goals was to remove Indians from the treaty paylist. When Tchi-Ki-Wis was a young child, the first year of payments there were 106 people paid at Lac La Croix. In 1881, the agent removed 23 Indians from the Lac La Croix paylist; 7 had died, and the rest were deemed "not belonging to the band."[20] This left only 87 Lac La Croix Anishinaabeg who received treaty payments in 1882. In the same year, "There were nine Robinson [Treaty] and twelve American Indians struck off the pay-sheets last year" among the Kawa (full name: Kawawaigamok Bay), or Sturgeon Lake Band.[21]

We tend to overestimate the borders, the separation, between Anishinaabeg bands. In reality, the Lac La Croix and the Sturgeon Lake people were deeply interrelated. For example, Blackstone's sister had married Chief Kaybaigon, the leader of the Sturgeon Lake Band, or Kawawaigamok Anishinaabeg. A cousin of Tchi-Ki-Wis, Julia Charlotte Connors, was born at Kawa Bay, part of Kawnipi Lake, east of the Dawson Trail.[22] In turn, Sturgeon Lake, or Kawa Bay, people were related to other bands in the area: Seine River, Lac des Mille Lacs, and Grand Portage and Bois Forte. Thus, it is not surprising that a visiting Indian agent recorded the daughter of the chief of Kawa Bay was married to a Grand Portage man. Wasagabowe, who was "formally a councilor" at Kawa Bay, now lived at Grand Portage.[23] And the two sisters of Chief Kaybaigon were married to American Indians.[24] Marriages were most often to a spouse from another place/band, which created strong ties between Indian communities (and in this case across the border). Lac La Croix, like many Indian people in the Midwest, encouraged intermarriage with outsiders, creating networks with other places, bands, and some non-Indigenous families. Both John Robinson/Laposh and John Linklater were examples of this and were welcomed into the greater orbit of Lac La Croix people at Basswood Lake.[25]

Lac La Croix winter lodge, 1932. The U.S. Forest Service derisively labeled this structure "Birch Bark Igloo." Note the stove pipe. Photograph by J. W. Trygg, U.S. Forest Service Records, National Archives.

At Chief Blackstone's death he was succeeded by his son, John Blackstone, also a traditionalist, like the majority of this band.[26] Indian agents often noted they were "pagan," particularly in Susan and John Robinson's young adulthood at Lac La Croix. With a reserve population between 85 and 110, Lac La Croix was larger than Kawa Bay but still a relatively small reserve. In 1890, the Indian agent remarked Lac La Croix "is more isolated than any others and the most difficult to reach." Only four years earlier the agent assumed that the Lac La Croix men would transport the treaty cattle from Fort Francis to the reserve, a difficult task at any time of year. Access to Lac La Croix changed with the coming of the Dawson Trail, and later, the railroad to the north, but it was still only accessible by canoe. Treaty payments and gatherings were often held at Savanne, distant from Lac La Croix, along what is now the Trans-Canada Highway (Highway 17). Savanne in 1878 "consist[ed] of a river going one way and the railway track going the other way, three log houses and a barn or two."[27] Later Savanne, barely a hamlet today, became an HBC post and a regional district for the Canadian Department of Indian Affairs.[28] Along with the railroad and

Birch-bark teepees on Basswood Lake near Washington Island, 1903. Chief John Black-stone is in the foreground. Photograph by William Trygg. Courtesy of Superior National Forest.

indeed settlement came the "whiskey peddlers." Two men camped on the American side of Lac La Croix in 1883, 1886, and 1888, when a peddler from Tower, Minnesota, came to Lac La Croix.[29]

Tchi-Ki-Wis was born roughly when Treaty 3 was signed and Blackstone was at the height of his powers. While Susan and John Robinson lived only occasionally at Lac La Croix village, they remained on the treaty rolls. When they lived on Basswood Lake, they would sometimes skip one year's payment and the next year travel to Lac La Croix to pick up two years' payments. As John was primarily a trapper, they moved seasonally, including when he might find a rare cash-paying job. The year the Robinsons officially settled in the United States, the family continued to move routinely for subsistence. The neighboring band at Kawa Bay also moved seasonally throughout their homeland. The agent wrote:

> I visited this band on the 31st of May, and distributed their garden
> seeds. I found only three families on the reserve. Arrived here again
> on the 12th of July, and found no one on the reserve. The whole Band
> were camped down the lake six miles, making canoes. They returned
> when I sent for them. I called a council and talked to them pretty
> strongly for neglecting their duties on the reserve [no structures,
> little agriculture].[30]

While the agent was decreeing staying on the reserve, as agriculturists in
one place, the band was continuing their traditional lifeways, dependent
on canoes. They continued to live on fish (especially the much sought
after whitefish), caribou and moose, wild rice, and berries.[31] The band's
traditional lifeways, dispersed through their homeland, were impacted by
the reserve system, the effects of increasing centralization of people in one
small reserve, and individuals moving elsewhere for jobs.

　　Susan Robinson's life history is obscure. She appears in few records.
Her birth date differs in three censuses in which she is listed, being born
sometime between 1854 and 1860.[32] According to a White friend of the
family, Susan was a "full blood."[33] More important than her age and blood
quantum was the gathering of relations she lived among, likely many of
whom were of the same clan and extended family, clans being a primary
organization of traditional Anishinaabeg society. Known clans at Lac La
Croix were and are muskrat, moose, bear, catfish, lynx, kingfisher, caribou,
and eagle.[34] Anishinaabe elder Milt Powell believed his mother, Sophie
Connors Powell, and Clara and Margaret Linklater were second cousins.[35]
Working up the family line with what has been documented leads to the
likelihood that Susan Robinson was a sister to one of Blackstone's three
wives. With this uncertainty, it is impossible to know if Sophie Connors
and Susan Robinson were of the same clan. Susan's Anishinaabemowin
name, Mandaquabeek, is also difficult to translate. It does not appear on
treaty paylists, as typically only men were named. But since Susan was
related to Blackstone's sister, Shawbegeezigoh, who was married to the
Kawa Bay Chief Kaybaigon, Susan was related by marriage (and likely by
blood) to the Kawa Bay people as well.[36]

Margaret (Maggie) *(seated)* and Clara Linklater, studio portrait, Ely, Minnesota, circa 1910. Photograph from Warner Wirta. Courtesy of National Park Service, Isle Royale National Park.

The Basswood Lake Anishinaabeg hung together—the Robinsons, Hoffmans/Cooks, Linklaters, Kingfishers, Fishers, LaBots, Caribous, Ottertails, Gesicks, Chosas—until the flu pandemic of 1918, when Indian agents cruelly dispersed the "Canadian Indians" from Basswood during World War I. The full Jackfish Bay community never recovered.[37] Many of them reassembled, briefly, at Winton, Minnesota.[38] Some went to Nett Lake, some to Lac La Croix, and a few, such as the Linklaters, Robinsons, Defaulds, and Chosas, returned to Basswood. Jackfish Bay neighbor Grandma Hoffman, thought by some to be Tchi-Ki-Wis's sister, was part of the Basswood Lake Anishinaabeg.[39] Like the Linklaters' home, Grandma Hoffman's place was tucked below a rocky hill facing south on Jackfish Bay, on a point of a small bay. Her Anishinaabemowin name was Ma-Me No-a-go-shish, according to a state census taker.[40] It is not clear that she ever received Lac La Croix treaty annuities like her "sister" Tchi-Ki-Wis (but never as a daughter of Laposh and Mandaquabeek). She was married twice; first to Vincent Defauld in 1882. He died in 1910. She then married a German immigrant, Joe Hoffman, a laborer and clerk for Swallow and Hopkins Lumber Company.[41] Grandma Hoffman's daughter, named Mary, married a railroad engineer, Joseph Cook Sr., and they raised a large family primarily in Winton, but they also visited Jackfish Bay regularly.[42] The Hoffmans outlived the Linklaters by only a few years; Joe died at Jackfish Bay of pneumonia the day before Christmas in 1936. Grandma Hoffman and her daughter Mary Cook died in October 1938, when they drowned in Fall Lake in a boating accident.[43] Grandma Hoffman and Tchi-Ki-Wis lived much of their adult lives a long stone's throw apart on Jackfish Bay. With their husbands away at work for days or even weeks at a time, they were sometimes the only two there. With their deaths, the village on Jackfish Bay was abandoned, though trappers continued to use the buildings for some time. The Linklaters and Hoffmans resided there for more than thirty years but never owned the land.[44]

Another family, the Caribous, shared the Robinson name or were relatives of Tchi-Ki-Wis and Grandma Hoffman. The Caribous, Robinsons, and Linklaters all lived on Basswood Lake for several years.[45] Paul Caribou

Tchi-Ki-Wis with two grandchildren in front of a home, early 1920s. One grandchild is
bundled in a beaded dikinaagan. Courtesy of Quetico Provincial Park.

sometimes guided with Jack Linklater.[46] Paul married Topsey Ottertail,
further linking Lac La Croix families together. Their son Walter was born
on Jackfish Bay in 1914. In an interview, elderly Walter Caribou struggled to define the connection of his grandmother, Ga-Ga-Gey, or Mrs.
Crow, with Susan Robinson, being either that of a cousin or half-sister. He
remembered Susan Robinson and his grandmother Gag-Ga-Gey together
at the Lac La Croix Reserve. He was told they regularly stayed together in
a house on a hill overlooking the village.[47] Like much of her life, Susan's
death is unrecorded, occurring between 1920 and 1926.[48] But the Caribou
family—and thus by extension the Robinson family—also had Grand Portage roots. Addikonse, or Little Caribou, had been an important Grand
Portage ogimaa and was one of the Grand Portage leaders that signed
the 1844 Isle Royale Compact ceding the lands to the U.S. government.[49]
Little Caribou knew Isle Royale. Walter Caribou was a direct descendant
of Addikonse; Tchi-Ki-Wis was more distantly related.[50]

The family of John Ottertail in front of a summer lodge at Lac La Croix, 1921. Mrs. Ottertail was likely related to Tchi-Ki-Wis, as they had a mutual relative, Ga-Ga-Gey. All were
from Lac La Croix First Nation. U.S. Forest Service photograph. Courtesy of the Forest
History Society, Durham, North Carolina.

The Linklaters' interest in, and indeed fondness for, Isle Royale elevates the question of their roots there.[51] Were Tchi-Ki-Wis's grandmother and her family before her deeply familiar with Minong? Was this connection to Isle Royale one of the missing links of historic Anishinaabeg use and presence on Isle Royale? Tchi-Ki-Wis's experience as a child paddling to the island from the mainland suggests there were deeper family roots to Minong than we are able to confirm. The missing link is specific early records of an Anishinaabeg presence on Minong. We know there were earlier Anishinaabeg on Minong, but their identities are uncertain. Tchi-Ki-Wis's ancestors were likely some of the people who used Minong, knew Minong, and made the difficult paddle there, but their names have gone unrecorded.[52] This question can be even further focused. Did Tchi-Ki-Wis's family have connections to Birch Island/Indian Point in McCargoe Cove? Were the Linklaters attracted to the Birch Island fishery because Tchi-Ki-Wis had camped nearby as a child? Or perhaps John liked it, stemming from when he had previously worked for Captain Francis.[53] McCargoe Cove was the primary historical entry point for Anishinaabeg paddling to Isle Royale from islands outside Thunder Bay, one of the safest crossings. Tchi-Ki-Wis's family roots at Minong on the east and at Lac La Croix on the west are also evidence of the strong relationships among Anishinaabeg bands along the border. We often think of tribes being distinct, separated by geography (and now by state or country). But the relationship of the people who went to Minong is not distinct and includes those from Lac La Croix, Bois Forte, Seine River, Fort William, and Grand Portage. An interrelationship of families and clans blended these bands even while they were distinct by name and lived on geographically distinct reserves and reservations.

TCHI-KI-WIS'S CREATIONS

They took time in making what they needed like blankets, clothing, moccasins, mitts and all the other things they made from hides. A lot of things that they made were out of animal hides. Some of the things were made from bones from animals, birds, fish and sinew from animals. Pots and plates were made of clay, spoons from wood. People also worked on things until they were completed, they never left anything unfinished. Every little thing they had to use was handmade.

—ELDER WALTER CARIBOU[54]

Tchi-Ki-Wis was a multimedium artisan. The range of what she made is stunning. As her White friend Ellen Hanson said, "She could do anything."[55] She made a wide variety of objects for home use and use by her family, including clothing and moccasins, mittens, gear (such as dog harnesses, tumplines), canoes, bead work, birch-bark work (mukuks, or storage baskets, wild rice winnowing trays), quill work, cedar-bark mats, tanning/leather work (including booties for dogs to wear on crusty or icy snow), bags, tobacco pouches, rabbit skin blankets, snowshoes, and more. She also made many objects to sell to White tourists, including miniature canoes, birch-bark baskets, leather bags and pouches, cedar-bark mats, and snowshoes. The list of what she made for her family and friends is longer than those objects she made for sale. The two lists are just for those objects for which we have documentation. Fortunately, a number of the things she made survive today. From looking at historic photographs, we can supplement the list of known types of objects and appreciate the skill and care she brought to her craftsmanship. Her daughter, Clara, was known as a remarkable seamstress and must have learned some of her skills and aesthetic from her mother.[56]

Tchi-Ki-Wis made several winter parkas, an unusual kind of outerwear for the area at that time. Many were made of a wool blanket as the outer fabric, trimmed with coyote or wolf fur ruffs. They were pullover parkas extending to midthigh with a full ruff on the hood to keep the face from freezing in cold weather when driving dog teams. Besides cutting and sewing the fabric, Tchi-Ki-Wis tanned the coyote and wolf furs and stitched them on. The parkas were made large, so a thick inner layer could be worn underneath. The sleeves were large enough that they slipped over

Tchi-Ki-Wis and John Linklater hold two model birch-bark canoes. They are with John Robinson *(back right)* and Frank Nelson on Isle Royale, circa 1930. The canoes were among the many items Tchi-Ki-Wis made for sale to tourists on the island. Donald Wolbrink photograph. Courtesy of National Park Service, Isle Royale National Park.

mitts. She made several parkas for Minnesota Game and Fish wardens, including Bill Hanson. They were practically a winter uniform for the wardens based out of Winton. None of the parkas survive today, but they appear in photographs worn by various wardens. Ellen Hanson remembered a notable dog team trip where she wore a parka Jack had loaned her. It had a drawstring on the hood and one inside, likely at the waist. Jack's parka was made of a different outer fabric and had large V-shaped pockets in front. The other parkas do not appear to have had those types of pockets. Most commonly when photographed with other wardens, Jack is not wearing one, often having loaned his to a colleague. Tchi-Ki-Wis also made a heavy leather mitten, like what we call a "chopper" today. Jack and fellow wardens wore these with a liner or work glove inside while on dog runs in cold weather.

"I think Jack was the one who introduced the parka to this area. . . . It was the first I ever heard of such a thing. Wish I had one now." Ellen Hill Hanson would be one to know. She was born in Winton in 1905 and lived there most of her adult life.[57] Ellen knew Tchi-Ki-Wis well. On Isle Royale, she lived with Tchi-Ki-Wis on the three-acre Birch Island during summer 1927, and despite a language barrier they became friends. While Jack brought knowledge of parkas with him, it was Tchi-Ki-Wis who made them. No historic photographs of earlier parka use have yet been located that dispute Ellen's avowal that Jack and Tchi-Ki-Wis "introduced" parkas to the Ely-Winton area. The type of parka that Tchi-Ki-Wis made does have antecedents among the James Bay Cree, where a couple of generations of Linklaters lived and intermarried. While parkas are typically associated with Inuit farther north, a practical and similar parka was worn by Jack's Cree forebears. Where Jack learned of it is unknown, but it was worn by Cree on traplines along the James Bay lowlands and up the Albany River, perhaps as far as Osnaburgh House.[58] Some Cree parkas had the outline of animals with eyes and mouths painted on the inside hide. It was believed that "the garment possessed the powers of speed, endurance, or cunning of the living animal, and was able to convey them to the wearer." Jack shared a parallel belief that when he ate moose or deer meat, the animal "brings me what he has—youth and strength and quickness,"[59] When Jack lived in the Jackfish Bay–Winton area, he imported not only knowledge he learned from his curiosity and experience but also layers of knowledge that his parents, grandparents, uncles, and aunties had taught him.

The Linklater canoe is the largest surviving object of Indigenous presence on Isle Royale. It is also one of only two surviving canoes representing the means of transportation to Isle Royale for millennia.[60] It was likely made by both Linklaters, Tchi-Ki-Wis doing all or most of the bark work, spruce root sewing, and collecting of the materials for the pitch (bear fat, spruce gum, and charcoal), and John doing the work to hold the bark in place and driving the stakes in the ground to hold the sides of the bark up until the ribs, planks, and gunnels were put in place. It was made in

Bill Hanson and John Linklater on a winter trip, circa 1926. Hanson is wearing a parka made by Tchi-Ki-Wis. Courtesy of Quetico Provincial Park.

Minnesota and then brought to Isle Royale.[61] A canoe of similar size and construction likely conveyed a young Tchi-Ki-Wis and her grandmother to Isle Royale decades earlier. Even if we did not know the makers of the canoe in the collection, its distinctive shape is a telltale sign of who made it and where it was made. It is a "long-nose Ojibwe" canoe made by border lakes Anishinaabeg, such as those from Lac La Croix.[62] The canoe is relatively short by modern standards, only fifteen feet six inches long. It does not have a carrying yoke or seats; paddlers would kneel instead.

The canoe is unusual for another reason. It was made as a birch-bark canoe, but canvas was added over the birch bark and then tacked in place by gunnels running its length. Canoes are generally made with birch bark or wood and canvas but not both. With the extra layer of canvas, it could get heavy, as the canvas would trap moisture between it and the bark. The canoe was undoubtedly built on a smooth canoe bed made of sand. Stakes would be driven into the sand to give the canoe a preliminary shape. Bark would be placed inside the stakes and held down with rocks. The frame would then be built within the canoe bark. The bark would typically be stitched together with split spruce root. In a short movie clip preserved at Isle Royale, John is shown mending the canoe with a birch-bark torch, melting pitch to make it watertight or perhaps even to seal torn canvas. Unfortunately, the grainy footage does not make clear the problem he is fixing. The use of a birch-bark torch to heat pitch to repair a canoe is a traditional technique used by Native Americans and then fur traders. The canoe is a fusion of mostly Aboriginal technology with European materials—canvas and tacks to hold the canvas in place.

Tchi-Ki-Wis's canoe was used by John and Frank and Alice Warren on Isle Royale to conduct their moose studies. When paddling solo, John built a brush blind in the bow as he stealthily paddled toward the moose. He also used this canoe to guide Dr. Frank Oastler during his report on whether Isle Royale was of national park caliber. After the Linklater era, it was used casually by several people but eventually was given to the park. In tough shape today, it needs restoration to ensure it lives on as evidence of the Linklaters' and Anishinaabeg life on Minong.

Frank Warren with a duckling in foreground and John Linklater in a canoe at Isle Royale, circa 1924. Note the shape of the canoe and the wrinkles in its shell from birch bark pressing against the canvas exterior. Tchi-Ki-Wis and John Linklater made this canoe. Frank M. Warren photograph. Courtesy of University of Minnesota Duluth, Archives and Special Collections.

Also finding their way into the park's museum collection is a pair of paddles Tchi-Ki-Wis made. These paddles may have been made while she was on the island, as Ellen Hanson recalled being with her when a paddle broke. Tchi-Ki-Wis went ashore, found a small cedar, cut it down with an axe, and shaped the paddle into form with a knife.[63] The paddles were made of a single piece of wood, unlike the fancy composite paddles of today. The paddles do not show much wear, so they must have been carved in the last few years of the Linklaters' tenure on Isle Royale, 1929 or 1930. Their shape, like the canoe, tells a story. The relatively thick throat of the paddle and only the smallest of handles at the top are common among field-carved paddles. Tchi-Ki-Wis knew these paddles were unlikely to be used on long trips, such as a lake crossing, where weight is a paramount factor, and thus left them purposefully thick so they lasted longer.

According to artist Carl Gawboy, a Bois Forte band member, when paddling, the upper hand grip was on the paddle shaft, not at the top.[64] A "no handle" top was most common among the border lakes Anishinaabeg.[65] The blade of the paddle is narrower than what today's canoeists would be familiar with. The shape of the end of the paddle blade is unusual, being slightly pointed in the center. Two paddle experts thought that a paddle with a sharper end to it, like the Linklaters', is quieter when it enters the water.[66] And it would handle more wear and tear, as it could be trimmed off once the center end was frayed from use against rocks or sand. Few similarly shaped paddles are found in museum collections, but those that do exist are from the border lakes Anishinaabeg. When carving these paddles, Tchi-Ki-Wis made them the way she was taught and modeled them after a common shape she had seen at Lac La Croix or on Basswood Lake.[67] The paddles, like the shape of the canoe, tell the story of who she was and where she was from.

One constant for Tchi-Ki-Wis, when either in canoe country or on Isle Royale, was the tanning of moose hide and its use for a myriad of purposes. Even when on Isle Royale, where hunting moose was prohibited, John "would hunt for hides for his wife to use."[68] With a female moose hide being one-eighth inch thick and a mature bull moose hide being one-quarter inch thick, tanning was heavy and laborious work. Various steps were required, often repeated and taking several days, to flesh the hide (scrap off remaining fat), remove the hair (often requiring soaking it in water), make the hide more supple, tan it in brains (or fatty substitute), and dry it. A large kettle at Birch Island appears in several photographs and was likely instrumental in the tanning process.[69] A final step was carefully smoking the hide to ensure it would remain supple if it got wet. Once the hide was fully tanned, Tchi-Ki-Wis used it to make moccasins for her family and friends, webbing for snowshoes, mittens, or "choppers," (if appropriately hunted and treated, perhaps drum heads), and bags. Tchi-Ki-Wis likely learned how to make all these objects by watching and listening to her mother and older women; learning by quiet observation was a highly valued Anishinaabeg trait.

Canoe paddles made by Tchi-Ki-Wis from a single piece of wood, circa 1929. Warren Collection. Courtesy of National Park Service, Isle Royale National Park (ISRO 1088).

Tchi-Ki-Wis also tanned moose hide for dog harnesses. She made the lines and traces (for both a single file of dogs and for a tandem hitch for two dogs abreast) and the collar out of moose hide. The collars she made were of a horse collar style that came to North America with Europeans likely even before William Linklater I arrived at Fort Albany. They were patterned after the work collars used by draft horses to pull wagons and plow fields. The Hudson's Bay Company men and trappers used these heavier types of collars and harnesses for years. They were sometimes available for trade at HBC posts. The horse collar style was used in Manitoba as recently as the 1970s. Frugal or remotely located mushers made these horse collar style harnesses at their camps. No photographs showing Linklater's dogs include harnesses outfitted in an "Aboriginal" style used by Cree or Anishinaabeg—a strap-type harness, more akin to what is used today for skijoring. The horse-type collar was made of moose leather wrapped over an oval-shaped ring made of bent willow. Moose hair was often stuffed between the inner wooden ring and exterior leather to provide padding for the dogs as they pulled heavily laden toboggans.[70]

Tchi-Ki-Wis was a prolific maker of moose-hide moccasins. Most of those she made were utilitarian, often unadorned with beads. She and her father, John Robinson, wore these moccasins often. They had a round toe, a plain leather vamp, and at ankle height a drawstring in front that could be tightened. Those in photographs were often worn with this "cuff" turned up and tied by a leather throng to provide further protection when in the woods. While Tchi-Ki-Wis and her father are seen dressed in European-style clothing, they did not trade their moccasins for boots often. It is likely they preferred the moose-hide moccasins because of their comfort, and their cost was only Tchi-Ki-Wis's time, labor, and skill. Oxhide shoes, made in a moccasin style, had been available at HBC stores for a while, but most Anishinaabeg at the time preferred the homemade moccasins.[71] They were part of "Indian identity" and persisted in use long after other "Western" clothing had been adopted by Anishinaabeg.[72] Tchi-Ki-Wis made moccasins for her daughters, father, and friends. She made dozens of moccasins of all sizes. After Ellen Hanson gave birth to her daughter Ardis, Tchi-Ki-Wis went to see the baby and measured her tiny feet. Not long after she went back with beaded moccasins for Ardis to wear. Once Ardis had outgrown them, the Hansons used them as Christmas trimming.[73]

In contrast to Tchi-Ki-Wis and John Robinson, John Linklater is usually pictured wearing boots. Many Native men who worked in lumbering, particularly on slippery logs in mill ponds or around hoists or engines, swapped their moccasins for boots. John wore a pair of moccasins, fancied up, in a staged photograph with his friend Chilson Aldrich, or Studge, as he liked to be called. The two men are fooling around with a camera, John sitting on a big rock with moccasins and fancy, heavy socks prominently displayed. Both are jauntily smoking curved pipes. The photograph is grainy, but John is wearing a center seam/vamp moccasin in which the vamp is beaded. There is also beadwork on the folded-down cuff on the sides and behind, but only part of it can be seen. This is an older, traditional, and common method of making Anishinaabeg-style moccasins.[74] The floral vamp is prominent, with a rose design, also a favorite

John Linklater and Chilson "Studge" Aldrich, log cabin architect, ham it up for the camera, mid-1920s. Note the elegant design on Linklater's moccasins. Wirta Family photograph. Courtesy of Iron Range Research Center.

of Anishinaabeg beadwork. The beadwork stands out on the front of the otherwise unadorned moccasin. There may be a drawstring hidden behind the beaded vamp, holding the moccasins in place. The graceful beadwork strongly suggests these had more special than practical use. The photograph is obviously posed, with John purposefully displaying the upper portion of his socks, which had both a checkered and a slashing pattern near the upper end. Why John wanted his footwear so prominently displayed, other than to show obvious pride in them, is beyond our interpretive reach.

One pair of Anishinaabe moccasins, likely made by Tchi-Ki-Wis, survives in the Isle Royale museum collection (Plate 3).[75] The vamp and cuffs are beaded in floral patterns and trimmed with red wool. The vamp is made of a dark wool, a customary choice. The rose and tulip designs and the red trim were also a common choice among Anishinaabeg women beaders at this time. Some of the floral design elements on the vamp are repeated on the cuffs. These moccasins were made for Anishinaabeg regalia (or customers with high dollars) as the cuffs were meant to be seen, not folded up like the utilitarian moose-hide moccasins Tchi-Ki-Wis and John Robinson regularly wore. The bright seed beads used to make the floral designs also illustrate an Anishinaabeg love of bright colors and vivid contrast between beads and dark background in their fancy and symbolic attire.[76]

Tchi-Ki-Wis and her daughter Clara were expert beaders, like so many Anishinaabeg women at the time. And both were accomplished seamstresses; Tchi-Ki-Wis hand-stitched John's woolen shirts. John preferred wearing wool, as did most woodsmen of his day. Tchi-Ki-Wis also made most of the cotton house dresses she wore. Clothing did not have to be made at home, as textiles, particularly cotton textiles, were available through mail-order companies, such as Montgomery Ward. Ready-made clothing, particularly pants, were also available for purchase. Charity boxes of used clothing from well-off urbanites were sent to reservations. And boarding schools, which Clara briefly attended, taught sewing skills to Indian girls. Indeed, in some circles the wearing of Western clothing

John Linklater wears a wool shirt made by Tchi-Ki-Wis while guiding the Warrens on Isle Royale, circa 1926. Frank M. Warren photograph. Courtesy of University of Minnesota Duluth, Archives and Special Collections.

signified the degree of the Indian wearer's assimilation. This belief (and hope in assimilation) was bolstered by an older practice where Protestant denominations gave new clothes to those who converted to their faith. The opposite was also believed to be true, that "blanket Indians" (those in traditional clothing, which was a blanket wrap in some tribes) were less civilized and less assimilated.[77]

Clara in particular was interested in making clothes that reflected both contemporary fashion and her proud Indian past. She put these disparate interests together in the 1920s flapper-style clothing she made paired with beautiful Anishinaabeg regalia.[78] Fortunately, these outfits were captured in paired photographs taken at Cyko Art Studio in Ely, owned and operated by O. Hokkanen. Hokkanen, in turn, printed these images on postcards for sale. A similar set of paired photographs of Josephine and Annie Sloan from White Earth Reservation, at approximately the same time, was taken by a different photography studio.[79] It is not known how or if

Clara and Charlotte Connors agreed to this arrangement or if they sought it out. But these photographs do capture much irony as well as startling contrast. Paired together, they make a stunning visual statement about the two different worlds that the women thrived in.

Charlotte and Clara are dressed in shorn beaver fur coats, which were the craze among young people in the early 1920s. Some called this "Fur Pimp Coat Craze," but most young people could buy only the cheaper raccoon fur coat. In a turnabout of fortune, Clara likely made these two beaver fur coats from pelts trapped or acquired by her father. The coats might have been a prop for the photography studio, worn by clients, as they were expensive for anyone. There is a sense of pride in wearing them for the photograph that would not have been triggered by wearing a borrowed coat. These were made at the height of their fashion; Babe Ruth, for example, wore a raccoon fur coat in 1924. They are both wearing loose-fitting and fashionable below-the-knee dresses. Even the two hats are trendy. They appear to be a design blend of a French beret and a Scottish tam-o'-shanter. Both hats, as well as the upper part of their dresses, have embroidery, also deemed fashionable at the time. Charlotte's hat and perhaps Clara's have embroidery elements that come from Anishinaabeg design. Charlotte and Clara wear a bobbed hairstyle fashionable in the day, perhaps just styled for the photograph. Even with the most contemporary of interests, Clara is purposefully mixing her Anishinaabeg heritage with Anglo-American style.

While it is not pictured in this remarkable photograph, a stunning beaded purse in the Isle Royale museum's Warren Collection would have fit right in (Plate 4). A beaded purse was a stylish accessory at the time, but this one is of an obvious Anishinaabeg floral design. The beaded purse and a pair of moccasins survive, and thus we can see the color scheme on them, which cannot be seen in the black-and-white photographs of other objects, such as bandolier bags and velveteen women's dresses. The use of color in the purse and moccasins is relatively conservative, and if Tchi-Ki-Wis made them on Isle Royale, she would have had limited access to beads, only those she brought with her.[80] She used blue, white, light

Charlotte Connors *(left)* and Clara Linklater in contemporary clothes. Cyko Gallery
postcard, Ely, Minnesota, circa 1920.
Photograph from Warner Wirta. Courtesy
of Iron Range Research Center.

Charlotte Connors *(left)* and Clara Linklater in Anishinaabeg regalia. Cyko Gallery
postcard, Ely, Minnesota, circa 1920.
Photograph from Warner Wirta. Courtesy
of Iron Range Research Center.

and dark green, orange, and pink "seed beads" in both objects. Even with
limited colors, both objects are beaded on a black background with the
strong color contrast common in Anishinaabeg beadwork. Both objects
use red trim as edging, the purse with red beads on the bottom and the
moccasins with red fabric trim.

The photograph of Charlotte Connors and Clara Linklater in regalia
is stunning, even in black and white. Both are dressed in beaded black
velveteen dresses, leggings, and moccasins. Charlotte is also wearing two
gashkibidaagan, or bandolier bags, more commonly worn by men with
other regalia. The velveteen dresses were not as commonly worn with the

bandolier bags.[81] Clara may have known that her father would decline to wear these bandolier bags; hence she made them to go with dresses she made for her future models. The same floral designs favored in most men's regalia in the early twentieth century were also used in the few beaded velveteen dresses worn by women, such as in this photograph. The effort to make these two bandolier bags, two beaded velveteen dresses, two pairs of beaded leggings, and two pairs of moccasins, not to mention the contemporary outfits, was astounding. It took "Clara all winter to make that [robe]."[82]

The exact origins of bandolier bags are only conjectured. Anishinaabeg bandolier bags were considered some of the finest made, evidenced by their high status as an early trade object with the Dakota. Their high value is reflected in the trading terms: one bag for a pony.[83] It is thought that the intricate beadwork on bandolier bags starting in the late nineteenth century grew out of earlier porcupine quill–designed bags. There were two primary methods of making bandolier bags, both evident in the photograph. The older method was to do loom beadwork resulting in geometric designs. Both bandolier bags worn by Charlotte Connors are a combination of loom geometric design and the freer, spot-stitched floral design favored at the time these bags were made. Loom beadwork was more common among Tchi-Ki-Wis's generation than her daughter Clara's.[84] Spot stitch was more recent, an applique technique, in which the bead worker typically secured the beads to the surface every two or three beads.[85] Both front panels—the largest bead block of the bag—were made on a loom and finished in an unusual way. Clara, likely with Tchi-Ki-Wis's assistance, finished it with small rectangular beaded tabs at the bottom, before the loom-woven tassels were tied off.[86]

A bag made much later, on Basswood Lake by Paul Piska, and a couple from Bois Forte have this same design.[87] It must have been one of a few preferred options used in their home area to finish off loom design. One of the *gashkibidaagan* straps is loom woven, the other is spot stitched on a black fabric, likely velveteen. The *gashkibidaagan* that is spot stitched on the strap has an otter-track design to form its edge, a very popular

Anishinaabeg bandolier bag design. One element that does not change from one bag to the other is the size of the front panel and straps and the length of the bag. The leggings, though partially covered in Charlotte's case, use favored spot-stitched designs, such as the bunchberry and a stylized rose on Clara's. Perhaps the most dominant spot-stitched design of the two outfits is on Clara's velveteen dress. The floral designs are quite large and go from her shoulder to below her waist with one break at her waist. White or pink dominate and lend the strongest of contrast with the black fabric. The density of the mirror image beadwork on the garments Clara is wearing is also atypical for much beadwork done in Minnesota at the time.[88] All together the regalia with their exquisite beadwork are a fusion of traditional and innovative elements, and of typical and atypical design and scale. Most important, they are worn proudly.

The regalia and flapper-era photographs of Clara and Charlotte, with the same "models" in the same position, are meant to be paired so as to contrast with one another. Both sets of clothing are show pieces, demonstrating the maker's mastery of design and execution. This pairing, intentional or not, is revealing as it confirms the two very different sides of the Linklaters' world. The flapper-style clothing speaks of Clara's interest in contemporary fashion and a movement away from the utilitarian artwork of her mother. Still, Clara does not abandon traditional designs and colors; for example, she uses the elongated arrowhead design in the purse, a not uncommon Anishinaabeg design at the time. With Tchi-Ki-Wis's assistance and know-how, Clara made this White and Anishinaabe ceremonial clothing by hand. Clara seems to be making a statement that she was of both worlds—or that she found herself in two different realms and decided she belonged to both. The photographs suggest she is comfortable in both realms and in combining them, with the unstated but overt support of her cousin Charlotte.

MANY OF THE WOVEN-LOOM TECHNIQUES in Clara's beadwork are anticipated in her mother's cedar-bark mat weaving. Instead of being fashioned from strings of beads woven on a loom, the mat is made of cedar-bark strips woven together, the strips being three-quarters to one and one-quarter inch wide and six to eight feet long. Both crafts require meticulous attention to details as well as substantial forethought in design to create and maintain a desirable geometric pattern. In the case of cedar mats, the maker must keep track of weaving in and out of seventy or so strips of cedar bark (weft) with the strips hanging down (warp) vertically from the frame. Just as Clara learned sewing techniques from her mother, Tchi-Ki-Wis likely learned cedar-bark mat making from her mother, Mandaqua-beek, and other Lac La Croix women. It was a traditional Anishinaabeg craft, learned by watching, imitating, and reflecting on past efforts.

Surprisingly, ten of Tchi-Ki-Wis's cedar-bark mats survive today, the largest collection of any Anishinaabe craftsperson/artist (Plates 5–14).[89] This remarkable collection is even more poignant because the art and craft of making cedar-bark mats has largely been lost, with few being made after 1925.[90] As Anishinaabeg moved into log or frame structures and moved less often, they had less need for mats originally used in bark lodges as flooring and door flaps, or as mats to dry fruits and berries on in the sun.[91] Instead, hooked rugs became popular. In at least one instance, a cedar mat was even used in Midewiwin ceremonies.[92] If walked on, the mats would be swept clean or wiped off, and their life expectancy was fifteen to twenty years.[93] For a short period of time local fairs in northern Minnesota, for example, in Cook County and at the "Red Lake Fair," awarded prizes for the best cedar mats. At the 1917 Cook County Fair, Mrs. Jim Morrison of Chippewa City won first prize, as did Mrs. Frost in 1921. And in 1912 "Indian work in the form of baskets and cedar bark mats" made in Cook County were exhibited at the Minnesota State Fair.[94] These efforts to recognize the artistry of cedar-bark mat making did not continue, and the craft and art of making them languished.[95]

Today there are revitalization efforts to relearn mat making in Anishinaabeg communities. The cedar mats are called *gii-zhi-ika-náa-kaan* in Anishinaabemowin.[96] In English they were locally called "Ojibwe linoleum," "rugs," and "carpets." Anishinaabeg also made mats of bulrush and sweetgrass. One of Tchi-Ki-Wis's bulrush mats also survives. But in the border country, with the availability of white cedar growing in low spots and along lake shorelines, most of the mats were made with cedar. In fact, the greater canoe country was a core area of mat making. This area included Isle Royale, where Indians attempted to sell a cedar mat to a copper miner in 1847.[97] Cedar mats have been collected from Grand Marais, Seine River, Nett Lake, Vermilion Lake, and Grand Portage. Another surviving mat, made by Charlotte Connors (Tchi-Ki-Wis's niece), was made on Saganaga Lake and is in the National Museum of the American Indian in Washington, D.C.[98]

The timing for making of cedar mats is prescribed by when the cedar bark best "slips," typically in June or early July. The bark can be harvested at later dates, but it comes off the tree easiest when the sap is actively flowing, in early summer. Because of this timing and the optimal time to use the bark, when it is fresh and most pliable, Tchi-Ki-Wis would have made these mats with cedar bark collected on Isle Royale. And nearby, indeed visible to the east from their fishery, were plentiful cedar trees lining Brady Cove. If she and John followed traditional gender roles in the making of cedar-bark mats, John would have done much of the rough harvesting of the cedar.[99] After the proper length of the strip plus some extra on either end is measured, the bottom and top of the section to be removed are marked and chopped, allowing sections of the bark to "slip" or be pulled free. Care is particularly taken with the face of the inner bark that will become the front of the mat, as it dries into a rich brown color if undyed. A knife or scissors is used to trim the roughly cut strips into more regular dimensions, and the rough outer bark is removed. The strips of the inner part are then coiled for carrying back to where the mat will be made. If only part of the bark is harvested, the tree may survive, but harvesting could also involve cutting the tree down and using all the available bark.

Once back at Birch Island, Tchi-Ki-Wis would take charge. The roughly cut strips were immediately worked to a more uniform width, three-quarters inch or slightly larger or smaller. Working around knot holes and twisting of the grain make this difficult. While Tchi-Ki-Wis prepared the strips to be used as the warp and weft of the mat, John or Tchi-Ki-Wis's father, John Robinson, would erect a rectangular outdoor frame to be used to weave the mat. The frame was often assembled in a shady spot to keep the strips from drying out when they were woven in place. Once the cedar strips were cleaned and the proper size, Tchi-Ki-Wis began the process of dying the cedar strips to create her geometric patterns. Ellen Hanson witnessed some of Tchi-Ki-Wis's effort while on Birch Island.

> There were bundles of ribbon-like strips hanging from several trees. She said (to Frankie [her grandson]) that they were cedar strips that she had cut and put up for drying. Some of the stripping would be colored in shades of green, blue and red, with dyes Tchi-Ki-Wis made from roots, plants, and bark. . . . I enjoyed watching the rug [mat] making process and even learned the intricate way to finish the edges.[100]

Tchi-Ki-Wis used all natural dyes in her mats. She preferred "natural colors—deep red and a deep green. [Those were] her colors. Those carpets she made were just gorgeous."[101] Ellen Hanson was right: four of the ten mats (and possibly one more) have green, and three of the ten (and possibly one more) have red dyed cedar stripes. The age and fading of the colored bark make it difficult to discern the original colors of the mat, particularly the blues. Tchi-Ki-Wis also used plant dyes for a dark brown/black color. Ellen Hanson did not witness Tchi-Ki-Wis collecting plants for dyes on Isle Royale, but she knew of times when Tchi-Ki-Wis "went into the woods to find roots to make the dye."[102] These roots were boiled in a large kettle to produce the colors she sought. Boiling the tips of root of bloodroot (often mixed with ash) created a deep red or mahogany color. Hazel is an important ingredient in creating dark browns and blacks. According to anthropologist Frances Densmore, "The Chippewa in Minnesota do not color green with native dyes."[103] But Tchi-Ki-Wis preferred green in her craft. She likely used tansy, available on Birch Island,

Mary Boshey, an Anishinaabe woman, weaves a cedar-bark mat on Burntside Lake, date unknown. Courtesy of Ely–Winton Historical Society.

and yarrow to produce the vibrant green. Tchi-Ki-Wis also made a cedar bag, dyed with green strips, that survives in the Warren Collection. It was rare for Anishinaabeg women to use a mordant to help set the color, but the colors persisted through the expected lifetime of the mats.[104]

To begin the weaving, the cedar strip warp was lashed to cord loosely wrapped around the upper horizontal crossbeam of the frame. The warp, variable in number (from 50 to more than 138), hung from the cord nearly to the ground. Another term for this type of weaving is "suspended-warp weaving" as the warp hangs free.[105] Cord attached the warp to the upper crossbeam and was draped down near the vertical posts, with extra left over for eventual use on the bottom edge. In Minnesota, often the cord used in edging was fabric repurposed from burlap sacks, or even twine made from basswood tree fiber. With no basswood trees and little burlap, Tchi-Ki-Wis had to improvise, using in several instances older cotton twine from the Birch Island net house. The twine came with the fishery and was meant for tying floats on gillnets and similar purposes. All the weaving was done by hand; no tools were used. The weaving was akin to the finger-weave technique that Tchi-Ki-Wis and other Anishinaabeg women used to make sashes. The design chosen for each mat determined the weaving technique; for example, weaving the weft in a one-over (the waft) and one-under technique was called "plain plaiting" or "checker weave." Or if Tchi-Ki-Wis chose a diagonal or twilled pattern in her mat, she would insert the weft in a two-over (two waft strips) and two-under technique. To create complex geometric patterns, such as a chevron design, the weaving technique was built on the formula of two over and three under. However, if the location of the chevron pattern moved where it appeared in the mat, the basic formula had to wait until the pattern was called for; in other words, each weft strip was woven differently from the one above it. Once the desired size of the mat was reached, the edges were bound to secure them.[106] The cedar-bark "end" was wrapped partially around the twine and a filler fiber and then tucked in under itself.

All but one of Tchi-Ki-Wis's ten surviving mats are large, about three to four feet by six to seven feet in dimension. The largest is more than five feet by eight feet three and half inches. They were large enough that at her Jackfish Bay home Tchi-Ki-Wis used "a lovely woven cedar mat hung from the roof rafter concealing a corner of the room."[107] In theory, it took John and Tchi-Ki-Wis thirty-five hours to create one mat (for the entire effort, including procuring all the cedar needed, getting the strips ready, finding roots for dyes, and weaving the mat).[108] The size and complexity of the weaving could, of course, increase or decrease the time. Once the materials were ready, the actual weaving appears to have been done in one productive day. But even in one day, Tchi-Ki-Wis might have had to move the frame to stay out of the sun to keep the cedar strips pliable while weaving.

A tremendous amount of skill is required to create a pleasing mat. Besides keeping the pattern in mind, when adding each waft strip, the weaver must take care to keep the weaving square and symmetrical. This is done by producing the same amount of tension in the weaving from one end to another. If the strips are tighter on one end than the other, the shape of the mat and the pattern are distorted. Another skill is working with cedar strips of varying widths. Effort is taken to make them as close to the same width as is possible, but inevitably the cedar grain will not allow it. So Tchi-Ki-Wis had to be mindful of using varying widths (a narrower strip after a wider one) to ensure the patterns stayed symmetrical. Maintaining symmetry in the weaving was also important because of the "framing" of a design that was common in her work. Tchi-Ki-Wis often framed a mat with plainer pattern around the edges, then completed a more complicated design in the center. If the framing is not symmetrical, the mat is less pleasing to the eye. Keeping the binding on the edges the same in size and method is also important to give the mats an attractive look. Like other Anishinaabeg women, Tchi-Ki-Wis sought a tight weave with little space between the warp and the weft. If the mats were going on a wall of a cabin or cottage where they were effectively an art piece, consistency in the tightness of the weave would make the mat less prone to sag in the middle when hung.

Tchi-Ki-Wis wove these mats for tourists or non-Anishinaabeg clients. Hence, the designs she chose must be seen from the perspective of what she thought would be appreciated by Isle Royale summer cottagers. Given whom these mats were going to, she would likely not have used designs that had a revered meaning in an Anishinaabeg sense. But she did seem to have favorite designs. She often created a "plaid check" design with different colored strips, much like in a shirt. Another common design was a chevron woven using only natural-colored strips. One mat with a sequence of chevrons gives the illusion of hearts, rather than the hard corners of a classic chevron design. She also produced a diamond design using two contrasting colors, sometimes filling in the center with a dark color or creating a checkerboard effect in the center. A mat with a similar diamond design was made by her cousin Charlotte Connors Deschampe.[109] Like many other mat makers, Tchi-Ki-Wis used a zig-zag pattern to great effect. Two of Tchi-Ki-Wis's surviving mats are comparatively unique in their design. The first is a maze-like design outlined in green that might be called a "Little Chippewa Village" design.[110] It is unlike any others, as it is made of small squares and short blocks with only vertical and horizontal lines (versus the diagonal design of chevrons). Its effect is unusual and has few antecedents in Anishinaabeg design. The second is also made with green cedar strips, which are used to create large Xs in the center and slanted rectangles as a frame around the mat. Some believe the Xs in beadwork are a thunderbird, an important Anishinaabeg spirit being. If so, this would mean Tchi-Ki-Wis was using a highly reverential pattern in a mat meant for someone who likely would not understand or fully appreciate its meaning.

THE SURVIVAL of so many cedar mats created by Tchi-Ki-Wis is a fortuitous coincidence. Ten surviving mats by the same maker are rare. Indeed, her surviving output appears to be the largest collection of Anishinaabeg mats made by one person anywhere, including the Smithsonian National Museum of the American Indian. There are relatively large and important collections of cedar mats made by Indigenous peoples of the Pacific Northwest Coast.[111] But there is only a sprinkling of Anishinaabeg mats in museums. Many, if not all, of Tchi-Ki-Wis's surviving mats were made in only four years, the years she spent extended periods of time on Isle Royale, 1927–30.[112] They were made on Birch Island, in between her helping at the fishery and taking care of guests and family.

So many of Tchi-Ki-Wis's mats survive because of the friendship between the Warren and Linklater families and the Warren family's appreciation of the Indigenous crafts coupled with their advocacy for the fledgling Isle Royale National Park.[113] For example, the Warrens chose to purchase a canoe made by Tchi-Ki-Wis instead of the wood-and-canvas canoes that were becoming popular at the time.[114] The Warrens purchased mats from Tchi-Ki-Wis and John, brought a few home to Minneapolis, and hung others on the wall of their Isle Royale residence. Other island families followed suit, including the next-door Morse family, who had a mat made by Tchi-Ki-Wis "hung over the fireplace just above the branches

Minong Lodge, Tobin Harbor, Isle Royale, circa 1926. This view is from the upper deck of the steamship *America*. Frank M. Warren photograph. Courtesy of University of Minnesota Duluth, Archives and Special Collections.

of balsam and yew."[115] Other families bought her mats sold on consignment at the Rock Harbor Lodge. At one point five island families (Warren, Morse, Cochran-Savage, Alfred Merritt, and the owners of Crystal Cove) all owned cedar mats made by Tchi-Ki-Wis. John's friend Reuben Hill, a maintenance worker and eventual master boat builder, purchased a small mat from Tchi-Ki-Wis as a honeymoon present. He bought it for $1.50. Rock Harbor Lodge sold mats for $6.00 and $8.00 dollars. Bertha Farmer, who ran the lodge, took a 10 percent commission.[116]

The death of Jennie Warren, Frank Warren's mother, in August 1940 set in motion efforts to have the baskets and curios she collected in the Southwest and California donated to the then imagined Isle Royale museum. Jennie Warren's enthusiasm for collecting Indian souvenirs was passed along, to a lesser degree, to Frank and Alice Warren. As friends of the Linklaters, it was natural that they were interested in and either purchased or were given these striking mats made by Tchi-Ki-Wis. Frank and Alice Warren had no children, so there were no direct heirs for these objects, but they wanted to ensure they were well cared for. Further, they were strong advocates of Isle Royale National Park. The Warrens believed the objects, and particularly those of Tchi-Ki-Wis, were a natural fit for the park's collection. The park, in turn, was discretely conflicted about accepting the objects. As one superintendent stated in a memorandum to his superior as late as 1967, "We have not catalogued the Warren Indian Collection as it is not considered suitable for use at Isle Royale."[117] The National Park Service accepted the collection, in great part, because of the Warrens' influence in helping establish the park.[118]

Only recently has Isle Royale fully embraced the story of historic Indigenous peoples as part of its interpretation work. For years, the park was comfortable with the distinction made that prehistoric (Native) copper mining was an important island theme, but historic use by people like the Linklaters and the Bushman and Caribou families of Grand Portage was not. Isle Royale initially resolved this dilemma by accepting the Warren Collection and, when staffing permitted, transferring much of the basketry to southwestern parks and Yosemite. Many other objects were transferred to the Science Museum of Minnesota on a long-term loan, including one of Tchi-Ki-Wis's mats. Other mats that hung on the walls of Isle Royale cottages eventually made their way into the park collection as the owners of the cottages died. This is not unlike how other keepsakes from the island, and from shipwrecks, found their way into the park museum collection. Essentially, Tchi-Ki-Wis's mats were frozen in time on the walls of vacant buildings or moved to corners of park buildings employed as temporary curatorial facilities. For years, the mats were stored at park headquarters on Mott Island, largely forgotten. The survival of these many mats is serendipitous as they originally were seen more as superfluous than an asset. Mats that were taken off the island often suffered worse fates, such as the mat given to Frank and Alice Warren's niece that was proudly displayed but then damaged so severely by movers that it was discarded.[119] That mats were left on the island during the winter (whether in makeshift storage areas of the National Park Service or on cabin walls) helped preserve this remarkable collection.[120]

Tchi-Ki-Wis's material creations are important for another reason, as such art has become a symbol of Indian survival. They are testimony that she and others preferred their artistic and utilitarian traditions and by doing them refused to be fully absorbed into mainstream America. She affirmed her Anishinaabeg culture in her crafting of the mats and in their purchase and display on cabin walls. For white cottagers on Isle Royale, the mats were esteemed because they combined beauty with a sense of a different world, a different aesthetic that was stimulating to those who bought them.[121]

But Tchi-Ki-Wis was also more than a gifted and extremely versatile craftsperson. She was, according to her grandson Warner Wirta, a "medicine person."[122] She knew a great deal about using plants to dye mats and, like many of her contemporaries, had extensive knowledge of herbal remedies. Her penchant for traditional Anishinaabe knowledge of plants fit with her participation in Midewiwin ceremonies. And, according to Wirta, she was a "master," or a highly trained Mide. The "Breathing Life" ceremony is a traditional complex and essential ceremony for many Anishinaabeg.[123] Anishinaabe author Basil Johnston describes the Midewiwin as "a society of medicine men and women that was formed to preserve and advance the knowledge of plants and healing and to establish the relationship between health and upright living, known as walking in balance."[124] Because of efforts by Whites to suppress it, the ceremony was often conducted discreetly, even underground, for many years. Tchi-Ki-Wis's discretion matched a larger tribal survival method of being cautious about letting outsiders know about important information and customs. Thus, we know little about what level of degrees she received in Midewiwin and about how much she practiced as a Mide. It is possible that the plants Tchi-Ki-Wis collected on Isle Royale were used in Midewiwin ceremonies on Basswood Lake or nearby because they were seen by some to be particularly potent.[125] Tchi-Ki-Wis was a traditionalist who protected herself and culture by quietly conducting many profound aspects of her life in private, escaping the notice of others who might refer to her or these practices derogatorily.

But Tchi-Ki-Wis was highly "visible" as a prolific and skilled crafts-person. She could, as Ellen Hanson said, "do anything." Birch-bark moose calls were etched with neatly spaced and wonderfully executed design (Plate 15). When leading tourists hikes on Isle Royale, John and Tchi-Ki-Wis created an interest in moose calls:

> If you are on the trail and ask John to give you a sample of moose calling he will cut a strip of bark from a birch—first going back in the deep timber so that the peeling of the tree may not mar the loveliness of the trail for visitors who pass—roll it into a megaphone and he is ready. But if you want a moose horn of your own to carry away from Isle Royale as a souvenir he will leave the task of making it to his wife and when it is finished the horn will be a thing of faultless symmetry and beauty, sewn along the seams with spruce root, bound at the edges with a willow withes and ornamented with designs laid on with native Chippewa dyes.[126]

Miniature canoes were made for sale, but few shortcuts were taken in their making. Birch-bark containers called mukuks were made yearly for storing food, particularly wild rice. Birch-bark souvenirs were made and sold for much needed cash. Moose hide was tanned and cut and fashioned into dog harnesses. She and John made canoes, which were essential for Anishinaabeg life, much like horses were for the Plains tribes.[127] To make so many different objects, Tchi-Ki-Wis had learned diverse skills, designs, and methods. None of her mats have the same design; they are all differ-ent, requiring multiple weaving patterns. To keep the geometric design regular, Tchi-Ki-Wis must have had a mathematical knack. She must have enjoyed trying out new designs to challenge herself. She paid a great deal of attention to proportion in beading, canoe making, and mat making. She had her own aesthetic, using classic designs and employing eight or more colors of beads in an object to effect both brightly contrasting colors and subtle shifts, from light to darker green, for example.

From a lifetime of making objects large and small—and harvesting many of the materials to make them—Tchi-Ki-Wis had strong hands. The breadth of what she made required her to do fine work with porcupine quills as well as to fashion large objects such as canoes or mats. She knew the right time to slip the inner bark of white cedar in between making copious amounts of strawberry jam. While Tchi-Ki-Wis made hundreds of objects in her lifetime, most were used up or were given away. She was productive working alone; few people saw her make mats or canoes. If she or John or a friend needed it, Tchi-Ki-Wis would make it. Her artistry integrated beauty with utility, and she expanded that artistry to make goods for sale to sustain her family. In the end, Tchi-Ki-Wis used ingenuity in her craft in a desire to live well and purposefully.

CHAPTER 3

Finding Their Way

THE LINKLATERS' EARLY YEARS

MEMORY IS QUIRKY. Thirty years after the fact, John Linklater recalled one particular day, June 15, 1889, in an officious U.S. document. It is when he went to Tower, Minnesota, and when he stated he immigrated to the United States. But he had already been trapping, trading, and paddling along the border. Why remember this day and place? It is likely he did not arrive alone; Tchi-Ki-Wis was with him.[1] On this day, John was not quite twenty, and Tchi-Ki-Wis was younger, her exact age unknown. There were not any immigration officials to report to as there are today, only a new rough-and-tumble mining town. Why not make a start in Ely or Winton, which were closer to Basswood Lake? John remembered the exact day and place mostly likely because the couple became *nabem gaye wiw*—husband and wife—in St. Mary's Episcopal Church in Tower. There was no such religious affiliation in Ely, and the Linklater family were Anglicans, of which Episcopalians were a part. John's father, William, was nearby (at Lac La Croix or Pine Portage), and perhaps he attended the event.[2] And if John's mother was still alive, she, too, may have attended the church wedding. A marriage William and Eliza might attend would be memorable and honor the family steadfastness to the Anglican faith and John's baptism.[3]

We do not know exactly how John and Tchi-Ki-Wis met. John likely came to the area with his father; in his teenage years perhaps John even worked as a temporary employee of the HBC, as was common. William had worked in the HBC Lac La Pluie (Rainy Lake) District before, and he was reemployed there in 1886.[4] His HBC posting at Pine Portage beginning in 1889 placed him in the area. Any time after this, William and John might have stopped or traded at Lac La Croix or Basswood Lake and possibly met Tchi-Ki-Wis there. Maybe something caught John's eye that kept him in the Basswood area, such as the unusual short canoes, a few decorated with red and blue paint, unlike those found at any other place he had been.[5]

Another event in 1889, six weeks later, may have encouraged the newly wed Linklaters to stay at Basswood Lake and not return to Lac La Croix. Efforts of the Indian agent Albert McCraken resulted in the deposing of the hereditary ogimaa, Bakandagisik, or John Blackstone. Bakandagisik had only succeeded his father, the renowned Blackstone, for four years. But the agent made various charges against Bakandagisik, including giving away or selling his "chief's coat" and medal to American Indians. McCraken raised the stakes by then accusing Bakandagisik of being a "bad example," "thief," and "untruthful." Perhaps what was worse from McCraken's perspective was that Bakandagisik was frequently "absent," or living on the American side of the border. McCraken refused to give Bakandagisik his (and his immediate family) treaty payment.[6] This implicit threat pressured the Lac La Croix men from reelecting Bakandagisik as their principal ogimaa. After Bakandagisik was deposed, he frequented Basswood Lake, away from Lac La Croix village. But he was not alone; family members and perhaps other clan members also lived on Basswood. This may have influenced the Linklaters to remain there, as Tchi-Ki-Wis was likely a Blackstone relative and perhaps a fellow clan member. Tchi-Ki-Wis was closely related to Mrs. Ed Connor, or Margaret Blackstone, who, in turn, was Bakandagisik's sister.[7] Thus, if they shared a paternal grandfather, they were fellow Caribou clan members (clan membership running along paternal lines).[8] Perhaps Bakandagisik was just continuing to live on traditional lands on Basswood, or maybe he was trying to distance himself from McCraken or even the indignation of being deposed. This heavy-handed action by the Indian agent may have made Basswood Lake even more appealing to the Linklaters, as Tchi-Ki-Wis could reside there in the company of family and clan members.

An Anishinaabeg family travels in a birch-bark canoe on the Basswood River near Wheel-barrow Portage, 1915. Courtesy of Superior National Forest.

By 1893 the Linklaters were living on Basswood Lake, perhaps in Jack-fish Bay.[9] They initially moved around the region, following traditional lifeways. One year the Robinsons and Linklaters collected their treaty payments at Savanne, northeast of Quetico. One of the Linklater daughters may have been born on Baptism Creek (in the northeastern corner of Quetico) one winter when John was trapping.[10] Baptism Creek was only a long day's journey from William at the HBC post at Pine Portage. Again, while John trapped during another winter, they lived on Poplar Lake off the Gunflint Trail in Minnesota. By 1895, the Linklaters, Robinsons, and at least five other Lac La Croix families were at home on Basswood Lake.[11] Through this seasonal movement, John's geographical knowledge grew, both of the boundary waters area and northward, linking to his childhood home territory of Lac Seul. John's older sister, Alice, after the death of her first husband, Daniel Morrisseau, in 1898, moved eastward along the boundary waters from "Hungry Hall" on the southeast corner of Lake of the Woods to Nett Lake, much closer to her brother and perhaps even her father, William.

The Linklaters were drawn to Basswood Lake, and Jackfish Bay in particular, for its abundant resources: woodland caribou, moose, fire-managed berry patches, and dense wild rice beds nearby. The wild rice on Basswood Lake was bountiful enough that Anishinaabeg left markers to one another, pointing the way to a bed of "exceptional quality . . . (with) . . . a stake three or four feet high driven into the sand near the edge of the water. Attached to the stake in a horizontal position was a bunch of wild rice, the heads pointed in one direction."[12] The plentiful wild rice beds also meant abundant waterfowl to hunt. A partial shotgun barrel found at their place confirms their waterfowl hunting.[13] The two streams entering Jackfish Bay ("jackfish" being a slang term for northern pike) meant nearby spawning grounds of fish, or reliable concentrations of pike, and in deeper water whitefish and walleye. Among the Basswood Lake Anishinaabeg, whitefish was the favorite fish, and if "obtainable, many thousand are caught every fall, and kept for winter use."[14]

Through time the Linklater place grew from traditional bark lodges to small cabins, repurposed from abandoned lumber camp buildings, windows, and wood. John and Tchi-Ki-Wis were there at least as early as 1897 and likely earlier, prior to the construction and then abandonment of the Swallow and Hopkins logging camp.[15] Years later their place was disdainfully described as "three shacks and a teepee."[16] Their main house was made of cedar.[17] They may have added a sweat lodge and wooden shelters for their sled dogs.[18] Tchi-Ki-Wis had a productive garden.[19] Her parents lived nearby. Grandma Hoffman and the German immigrant Joe Hoffman lived only a few hundred feet away. Hoffman clerked at a succession of logging camps in the vicinity. Early on, others may have also lived nearby, especially when dozens of Swallow and Hopkins lumberjacks were cutting pine close by. A Swallow and Hopkins logging railroad spur terminated in a small bay in view from the Hoffmans' place. The rail line linked up with other rails going as far north as Horse Lake to transport logs to the Winton sawmills on Fall Lake. The rail line was eventually known as

Linklater grandchildren play in a birch-bark canoe with bows and arrows (which are blunt tip for killing birds), early 1920s. This rare photograph includes a partial view of the Linklater home at Jackfish Bay. Courtesy of the Warner Wirta Family.

the Cloquet Line, and after it was abandoned and the rails pulled up, it became a walking path to and from Jackfish Bay. When the lumberjacks were not around, Jackfish Bay had the further advantage of being away from the hubbub of a bustling sawmill town. Indeed, it was also mostly away from Indian agents, the stifling borders of Lac La Croix reserve, busy roads, and the whims of most White residents and tourists.

John and Tchi-Ki-Wis lived a subsistence lifestyle augmented with a few paying jobs. It is likely that John first worked as a commercial fisherman on Basswood Lake to earn very welcome cash. His sister and brother-in-law were already fishing on Lake of the Woods. Commercial fishing on Basswood began as early as 1892, and three years later the Lake Superior Fish Company announced plans to build a narrow-gauge railway to transport their fish from Fall Lake to Basswood Lake. Commercial fishing on the border lakes and shipping the catch to Winton continued until 1921, when it was banned.[20] The Linklaters also fished for their own subsistence.

Recently, gillnet lead sinkers were found at the Linklater place, suggesting that fish were also caught to feed themselves and their sled dogs.[21] In their early years, they only occasionally visited town. Other Anishinaabeg coming to town were permitted to sleep in a barn if they had to overnight in Winton or Fall Lake.

John initially made a living from what he had learned when coming of age: trapping and preparing and selling furs. He worked alongside his dad at HBC posts, and at Lac Seul, and likely trapped with his mother's family, particularly his uncle; he knew trapping and could fall back on it when needed. Occasionally, their trapping success was documented in newspapers for animals for which there was a bounty. In 1906 they received forty dollars in wolf bounty for six animals.[22] In 1907, "The auditor's records show that two women, Mrs. John Burnside and Mrs. John

Leo Chosa at a dock on Basswood Lake, 1916. Chosa ran a commercial fishing business on Basswood. Note the large fish boxes and metal frame on which an upturned canoe could be hauled. U.S. Forest Service photograph. Courtesy of the Forest History Society, Durham, North Carolina.

Linklater each killed a wolf last year and collected a bounty. One of the women is said to have shot a wolf as it was slinking through the dooryard of the homestead on which she and her husband reside."[23] In all, the Linklaters are recorded collecting wolf bounties in 1906, 1907, 1908, 1909, and 1916–17. The last record makes clear he had a trapping permit for three timber wolves, two brush wolves (coyotes), and two red foxes.[24] After his father was let go by the HBC, John worked briefly with William as an independent fur dealer along the border.[25] John reportedly worked with trader Ed Connors prior to his death in 1910. Dorothy Powell recounted "Linkletter" bartering with Indians after they received treaty payments: "Linkletter would accompany them on the return trip and when they camped he would set out his wares and barter with the Indians. By the end of the trip Linkletter would have most of the Indians' money and the Indians would have depleted his packsacks of his trade goods. All would return home happy."[26] Linklater stressed that his and others' trading must be fair and honest.[27] For John, trading was second nature, having grown up at HBC posts and accompanying his father. Trading, like trapping and commercial fishing, was part of a hardscrabble, adaptive strategy to provide for his family and himself.

John and Tchi-Ki-Wis were devoted to one another.[28] John regularly paddled from Hoist Bay on the southeast arm of Basswood, where he worked, to their home. Later, he walked the sixteen miles from Jackfish Bay to Winton and then returned the next morning, bringing medicine back for Tchi-Ki-Wis.[29] Tchi-Ki-Wis was attentive to John, making sure he was comfortable and well fed and clothed. She sewed many of his beautiful and sturdy wool shirts. The couple assumed traditional Anishinaabeg roles and were extremely productive individuals. While John trapped most animals, Tchi-Ki-Wis skinned them. She was renowned for her moose-hide moccasins, which she sometimes lined with rabbit fur booties for warmth in the winter.[30] Tchi-Ki-Wis taught her daughter Clara how to snare and then weave strips of rabbit fur into blankets; similar blankets were made by John's Cree ancestors to the north. Tchi-Ki-Wis and John regularly picked berries and sold them to the many resorts springing up on Basswood Lake.[31] Guests to their home remember dinners of moose meat, whitefish, wild rice, potatoes, and strawberry jam. Moose meat was shared among the families on Jackfish Bay. Meat not immediately consumed was dried or jerked over a fire. Later, when the Linklaters lived in Winton, their diet adapted to purchased foods: basics in bulk, flour, sugar, salt, baking soda, beans, butter, coffee, tea, raisins, powdered milk, meat (sometimes slab bacon), cabbages, prunes, dried apples, rice. On one trip, they purchased five dozen cookies.[32] John had a reputation as a good cook, and he cooked a lot of pancakes, meat, beets, and dishes flavored with salt pork.[33] Their "in town" diet appears to have been little different from their non-Indian neighbors', except that they ate few canned goods.

They spoke to each other in Anishinaabemowin rather than English. Their grandson, Frankie, growing up with them, was not as fluent and sometimes struggled to understand what they were saying.[34] But when a young adult, Frankie showed a great deal of deference to his grand-

Quetico Provincial Park rangers transport a bull moose in a canoe on Basswood Lake, circa 1915. The moose has been field "dressed," or cut up into manageable sizes. Courtesy of Superior National Forest.

mother and grandfather, evidence of traditional Anishinaabeg customs.[35] When the Linklaters ran a commercial fishery at Isle Royale, Tchi-Ki-Wis would sometimes assist on the lake, working their pound and gillnets on the open water, which was a traditional role among Anishinaabeg. But it was unusual at Isle Royale at that time among the predominantly Scandinavian immigrant fishermen, who often had male hired hands.[36]

Tchi-Ki-Wis and John had two daughters, Margaret (Maggie) and Clara. Margaret was likely born in 1892, and Clara in 1894.[37] They grew up primarily at Jackfish Bay, but the family still traveled to trap, fish, and harvest food when they were young. Clara attended boarding school at Vermilion Lake and

Clara *(left)* and Margaret Linklater model bandolier bags, likely in front of the Linklaters' Jackfish Bay home at Basswood Lake, circa 1905. Photograph from Warner Wirta. Courtesy of Iron Range Research Center.

eventually married Samuel Victor Wirta. They had five children together before she tragically died, only two years after her mother. Wirta remarried a Finnish American woman, which had the unfortunate consequence of downplaying and effectively cutting the children off from their Native heritage. Like her mother, Clara was a remarkable seamstress, and many of her contemporaries remembered her as soft-spoken and beautiful.

Margaret died young. The circumstances of her death are enigmatic and unrecorded, as are most details of her short life. We do know that on August 26, 1911, Margaret gave birth to a son, Frank H. Nelson. John and Tchi-Ki-Wis raised Frank, or Frankie as he was called after Margaret's death. They sometimes introduced him as their son rather than grandson.

In Frankie's Social Security enlistment, he named his father as (Arthur) Elmer Nelson, hence his last name.[38] Maggie's death was suspicious, according to family and a brother of Frankie's first wife, perhaps the result of domestic abuse or neglect. It is not known what Maggie died from or where. There is no newspaper or official record of what happened, and no charges were brought forward. At this time convicting a White person as complicit in the death of an Indian woman, particularly in a remote location, was unthought of.[39] Sometime close to Frankie's birth and Maggie's death, Frankie's father moved to Canada and married a non-Indigenous woman. Years later, the Nelsons moved back to the United States to Bemidji, Minnesota, and then Arthur, as a widower, moved to the West Coast, keeping a distance from Winton and Basswood Lake.[40] Margaret was perhaps interred in a grave house not far from the Linklater place on Jackfish Bay.[41] The shock of Margaret's death, and the circumstances of it, must have been a fierce blow to her parents. They never talked of it to their friends. But Tchi-Ki-Wis regularly cared for the spirits of those in nearby grave houses (likely her mother and daughter). Their memories and spirits and the pain of their deaths reinforced her resolve to stay nearby. Worry about the new trickle of recreationists in the area, some who disturbed and even looted grave houses, may have further caused Tchi-Ki-Wis and John to remain in Jackfish Bay as much as possible.[42]

NAMES HAVE POWER and even the blessing of a *manidoo* in Anishinaabeg culture. They were a "source of sustenance throughout one's lifetime."[43] Accordingly, in the Linklaters' day, Anishinaabeg names were not casually given or received. An individual might have multiple names, some from childhood, from parents, or from a naming ceremony. Only John's closest friends, Bill and Ellen Hanson, knew his Indian name, "Chi Wais-askonse," translated as Great Muskrat.[44] The muskrat is an important Anishinaabeg and Cree creature who in *aadizookaan,* or sacred legend, brought the first soil back from the bottom of the great flood. First, the beaver and the otter tried to retrieve mud from the bottom but failed. In a version told by John's Uncle Charlie Linklater, muskrat, in a heroic attempt, reached bottom, grasped a lump of clay in his paws, but drowned before surfacing. Out of this mud, Nanabushu (or among Cree, Wesakchak) re-created Earth.[45] Likely following the Linklaters' lead and out of respect for them, the Hansons did not publicly use John's Anishinaabeg name. John surely received this name at Lac Seul through a naming ceremony requested by his mother or grandmother. A spiritual leader, through fasting, dreams, and prayers, named the child and assumed some responsibilities for him. A feast concluded the ceremony. John's name bespeaks his traditional background, unknown to all but a few of his White friends and coworkers.

We do not know Tchi-Ki-Wis's Anishinaabeg birth name. Tchi-Ki-Wis's cousin remembered that she had an Anishinaabeg name other than Tchi-Ki-Wis but could not or would not recall it.[46] Friends believed John had given her the name Tchi-Ki-Wis, or a personal name, but if so, it was not likely given to her through a naming ceremony. It is more probable her parents gave her this name. But the name Tchi-Ki-Wis was significant to the Linklaters because it was her name affirmed in their marriage.[47] The exacting meaning of "Tchi-Ki-Wis" is unclear; grandson Warner Wirta understood it meant "spirit woman." Frank Warren explained further: "In the Chippewa Indian lore, Tchee-kee-wis was woman of supernatural powers but a pleasant and benign character."[48] Others have said it meant "Lady of the Woods" or "Grand Lady."[49] Most of these explanations come later from interested friends and family who had limited knowledge of Anishinaabemowin and culture.

Tchi-Ki-Wis is a fairly rare Anishinaabeg personal name. It is puzzling and does not easily translate into English. It appears to be missing a first syllable, not uncommon in English imitations of Ojibwe words.[50] In only one instance, a 1911 Canadian census, does a fuller rendition of her name appear: "Ma che q wis." More often the full name is transcribed into English as "Majikikwewis," but also Maji-qua-wis, meaning first-born daughter (using *qua* or *quay* to denote female). It is an old name, dating back to "proto-Algonquian" language. First-born daughters (and sons) had an important distinction and honor in Anishinaabeg society. In legend there was also a group of "wayward and impulsive sisters" with the name of Majikiwewis; these sisters "are tricksters and most of their tricks backfire."[51] Tchi-Ki-Wis might be interpreted to mean "eldest daughter," or "foolish maiden," though the latter does not seem to fit Tchi-Ki-Wis's character.[52] A similar sounding name, Madjikiwis, was used for a male and early Bois Forte ogimaa. He was said to have witnessed the first White man on Lake Superior.[53]

The most curious happenstance of her name is that only fifteen or so years before she met John, another Tchi-Ki-Wis was recorded as the wife of a "John Linklater," who was one of the Métis men and families recognized in the "Halfbreed Adhesion" to Treaty 3, a treaty between the Anishinaabeg and the Canadian government. This is a seminal event in Métis history as it is the first instance of the Canadian government for-

Tchi-Ki-Wis with a washboard in front of a canvas tent, likely on Isle Royale, circa late 1920s. Courtesy of Christina Woods.

mally recognizing the Métis in a treaty. The John Linklater who signed the adhesion was much older than the younger John, and with his Tchi-Ki-Wis already had six children.[54] If John gave Tchi-Ki-Wis her name, he may have wanted to honor and remember the older namesake with the reuse of her name.[55] Even with our cloudy understanding of its meaning, the act of naming someone after another was an act of respect in both Anishinaabeg and Métis culture.

Naming customs were changing at the time the Linklaters had children. Their daughter Clara was given the name of "Sha-no-bik," or Swallow woman, which was more broadly known. Some traditional Anishinaabeg customs and beliefs were resilient, sometimes being spoken or enacted in sequestered places, while others were changing in the course of contact with lumberjacks, schoolteachers, ministers, nearby Finnish American neighbors, and expanding technologies such as railroads and mines.

The Basswood Lake region, in light of what quickly happened after 1890, had the fault of its virtues: large stands of old-growth white and red pine. At that time, it was the epicenter of one of the largest swaths of white pine left in Minnesota.[56] Cutting and hauling the pines consumed the region, and companies set up sawmills on Fall Lake in the newly bustling town of Winton. The company operating closest to Jackfish Bay was Swallow and Hopkins. In its heyday, there were more than fifty Swallow and Hopkins camps with an average of one hundred men and sixteen draft horses per camp.[57] Swallow and Hopkins and the St. Croix Lumber Company had logging railroads throughout their "cut" area. Once they were done in an area, the rails were pulled up and used to access the next location. Rail lines were also installed on portages to transport logs from one lake closer to Fall Lake and the mills. Swallow and Hopkins operated in the region from 1898 until 1922, when the operation was sold to the Cloquet Lumber Company, part of Weyerhaeuser's growing lumber empire.[58] John Linklater began working for Swallow and Hopkins circa 1901.[59] Only a few Indians worked for lumber companies, but John and Vincent Defauld, both of mixed heritage, did.[60]

Swallow and Hopkins Lumber Company operation at Winton with Fall Lake in the background, early 1900s. Courtesy of Ely–Winton Historical Society.

Swallow and Hopkins log hoist operation, 1902. Logs were hoisted from Basswood Lake onto small railroad cars, which carried them to Fall Lake, where they were then floated to the Winton mill. Courtesy of Ely–Winton Historical Society.

The volume of trees cut was staggering. "So extensive were the rafts of logs that older Ojibway in the area recall the heavy deposits of pine bark chips that settled in shallow bays of Basswood Lake. This bark inhibited the growth of wild rice, seriously reducing the harvest for over a decade. The effect was temporary, however."[61] Logging was a dangerous business, and quite a few men were killed or maimed by the work. Reminiscing years later, the general superintendent of Swallow and Hopkins wrote:

Two of the Basswood [Lake] Indians, namely Vincent Default and John Linklater, were a perfect pair to work together hoisting the logs out of Basswood into the railroad cars. We first used a jammer with cable and crotch chains (two chains attached to the end of the cable) with a hook at the end of each chain. The hook of each chain was fastened to each end of a log and then hoisted by the jammer to be loaded on a car. This system hoisted only one log at a time and there-fore required two good fast workers to get the logs loaded on the cars quickly. Linklater and Default (pronounced Defoe) were fast and nimble on their feet, as well as being good workers. . . . We had two steam locomotives, one to haul a train load of logs across the portage, while the other engine switched cars which were being loaded by Linklater and Default. Al Oakes was the locomotive engineer for the log haul, he was an interesting character, always friendly and helpful. He would never pass up anyone going across the portage, and would often pick up a whole family of Indians, the squaw and papoose and youngsters riding on the bunks of the "Russell" cars.[62]

The Four Mile Portage became a rail line, and the lifting operation on Hoist Bay meant Basswood Lake pine could be transported to Fall Lake and the waiting sawmills. As new innovations changed the operation, Linklater and Defauld (who died in 1910) went on to other jobs. Linklater likely worked as part of a small locomotive crew on a logging railroad west of Basswood Lake. He also probably worked on the railroad spur into Jackfish Bay, which swung into the south end of the bay, arriving at the water not far from his place. The branch line to Jackfish Bay was built in 1912 and operated until 1920. Logs from Jackfish Bay were then loaded by a hoist onto this spur line.[63] In the 1920 census, John reported his occupation as "fireman" on the (logging) railroad.[64] Doing different jobs, Linklater worked twenty years for Swallow and Hopkins in the Basswood Lake region. This long work history and the connections he made on the job paved the way for the Linklaters to use the company's abandoned buildings.

Linklater's labor for Swallow and Hopkins was not full-time work. He appears to have worked during the summer months when logs were moved. There is no record of him sawing down pine in the winter, though he might have done so. Instead, during this same era he relied on another of his suite of skills and knowledge: dog mushing. Dog teams were somewhat of a rarity in Ely early on, especially ones owned by non-Indians. One of the first jobs Linklater used his dog team for was to deliver "fast

Rangers from the U.S. Forest Service use a rail car to transport canoes and gear along Four Mile Portage between Fall and Basswood Lakes, circa 1921. Courtesy of Barbara Wenstrom Shank.

express," or news, from the senior officials of one iron mine to those of another.[65] "As a trainer of dogs for the harness," he was "one of the finest."[66] One canoe party recorded seeing Linklater and "two small papooses holding puppies" circa 1915.[67] Linklater knew dogs and tripping as they were part of his family heritage. A stray comment by his grandfather in 1862 makes this evident: "I am happy to say that Mrs. Linklater and her family is in good health. One—one of my little boys lost his little finger to the bite of a dog."[68] The Linklaters at Moose Factory, Fort Albany, Osnaburgh, Lac Seul, and Red River used and were around sled dogs. Often the drivers/ trippers were relatively young; William II once delivered mail by dogsled along the coast from Moose Factory to Fort Albany and back. They were a critical part of the HBC communication network.

Having grown up around dogs at posts and villages, Linklater heard many stories about them, some even shading toward the exotic. He might have heard about hungry sled dogs that learned how to fish for pike on their own: "As they [jackfish, or pike] crowd along in these shallows, often with their back fins out of the water, they are observed by the dogs, who quietly wade out, often to a distance of many yards, and seize them with such a grip that in spite of their struggles, they are carried in triumph to the shore, and there speedily devoured."[69] Owning, training, and feeding sled dogs were a family tradition, and Linklater had his own string of dogs until his death.[70] Whenever possible, the Linklaters fed their dogs fish soup and extra meat if they had it. Linklater was better known as the primary dog "pilot" and caregiver for the string of sled dogs the Game and Fish Department had, based at Winton. While Leo Chosa originally brought Canadian dogs for the Game and Fish operation, only a year later he left, so Linklater assumed the main role in running and caring for the dogs. One game warden observed:

> He had wonderful control over dog teams and could perhaps get more out of them than anyone I knew. He was not cruel to them; on the contrary, he was most considerate of the dogs. He was never known to get his own supper until his dogs had been fed and boughs placed

on the snow for them to bed down for the night. One cold night four of us stopped at Charley Cling's cabin out of Winton. I use the word "cold" in its proper sense, as the thermometer registered 52 below. Jack and his partner were going north from there; my partner and I were returning to Winton with the dog team. My partner and I were hitching the dogs to the toboggan when they went into a free-for-all-fight. When six huskies enter into a fight, it is not just for fun but for the survival of the fittest. Jack came to the rescue, rushing out of the cabin in his stocking feet with a piece of kindling wood. He soon had them quiet. Again came his brief words, "They are all right—you can hitch them up now."[71]

When the new Game and Fish station was built, it included log dog kennels and "five compartments each with separate wire enclosed runways—taking care of twenty to thirty-five sled dogs."[72] The howling of the team at Winton before they were fed (corn meal mush and storm-damaged herring from Grand Marais) at 6:00 p.m. was a community event. John sometimes hitched up three of the tamer dogs, with "Moonie" as the lead, so that Winton kids could go for a ride on the frozen Fall Lake.[73] Tchi-Ki-Wis and John made dog harnesses, and he repaired them.[74] The dogs were used to haul supplies out to game warden trappers, resupply Forest Service cabins, transport wardens close to a stake-out, and for miscellaneous tasks such as hauling gear for the U.S. border surveyors. One man wrote about when he saw Linklater running a team across frozen Horse Lake:

> In the early morning light, the dogs trotting along in good form, clouds of steam rising from their mouths in the still air. Their barking and all and Jack calling out to each dog by name . . . made a picture for eye and ear. . . . It was perhaps worth the whole trip just to see our team of nine dogs traveling along in its various moods, from mornings' gayer irresponsibilities to the dignity of evenings' more weary trot, with Bill or Jack's cheery encouragement of "atta boy, Whitey," "Wolf, whatta doin', get up there" or "trot along, Twoshine."[75]

John Linklater with a five-dog team on patrol in the Superior National Forest, mid-1920s. Note the horse-type collars on the dogs. Tchi-Ki-Wis made and repaired these types of dog harnesses. Courtesy of Iron Range Research Center.

"Whitey" was a lead dog for the Game and Fish team, and either Linklater or Hanson talked a Minneapolis outdoor writer into caring for him when he was retired from ten years of "service in the harness." Whitey was a character, and his exploits were captured in a newspaper article. Even in retirement he was headstrong and a

> battle scarred old brute . . . hides a heart as gentle as a child's. . . . I can't picture Whitey as perfect . . . and he has his faults. His morals in the matter of property rights to food are most elastic. Recently he helped himself to $2.65 worth of bacon from the Crane Lake Trading Post and departed hastily, bidding them charge it to me—which they did.[76]

Linklater's own lead dog, Nanook, was remembered for being both a "pet" and strong. That Linklater named him Nanook after the main Inuit character in the 1922 docudrama *Nanook of the North* substantiated his pride in Indigenous people, the Arctic, and Hudson Bay.

John Linklater in a parka with his leader dog, Nanook, circa 1925. Grandson Warner Wirta was told Nanook was part German shepherd and part wolf. Courtesy of Ely–Winton Historical Society.

The dog teams were also a centerpiece of a public relations stunt to cross the forest from Winton to Grand Marais during two different winters. Linklater, Hanson, and other wardens with the dog teams hauling gear led VIPs, such as the mayor of Minneapolis, on a trip for eight days and 157 miles.[77] Linklater impressed the VIPs then and others on different occasions, as he often ran in front of the dogs to break trail, a technique he probably learned from his HBC forebears. His stamina for breaking trail impressed everyone. As one of his contemporaries remarked later, "No one around here who knew much about dogs then. . . . Linklater's regular warden mushing duties took him from Winton along the border to the Cook County line at Ottertrack Lake, then southward to Koma, Parent Lake, Isabella, and Gabbro Lakes and out. It was a twelve-day trip, with an average of fifteen miles a day with stops and duties along the way. Linklater was paired with another warden for the trip, each taking turns breaking trail."[78] Linklater's expertise with dogs and his White neighbors' lack of knowledge about his early years led Ely resident Lee Brownell to presume the Game and Fish Department "bought him down [from Canada] because he was a skilled dog driver."[79]

Linklater was also well known for guiding canoe parties, which were beginning to recreate in the borderlands, even while working for Swallow

John Linklater hauls a dory and small outboard motor out of the water on a boat slide, Rock Harbor, Isle Royale, 1925. Frank M. Warren photograph. Courtesy of University of Minnesota Duluth, Archives and Special Collections.

and Hopkins. Indeed, one party called him "Mr. Swallow's Scotch-Indian guide."[80] An outdoor newspaper columnist described meeting Linklater on the trail: "John Linklater, middle-aged, finely set-up, pleasant of speech, in every way the master woodsman and guide he had been pictured to me."[81] Another called him the "dean of the guiding profession."[82] Needing paying work, Linklater guided anyone, including fishermen and hunters, a couple on honeymoon, surveyors, and mining engineers. A number of those he guided became friends for years. Around 1897, Linklater guided Frank M. Warren, a mining engineer from Minneapolis. They became lifelong friends. Later, when Warren and his newlywed wife, Alice Rockwell Warren, vacationed at Isle Royale, they brought Linklater along as a handyman and guide.

In 1914 Linklater guided Chilson (Studge) Aldrich and WCCO radio personality Darragh Aldrich, who later became close friends of the Linklaters. Darragh wrote an article about a summer trip they took with John. It began in a storm on Jackfish Bay:

Along about ten minutes to 9 o'clock, we looked out over the lake through the rain, and lo! we saw a canoe fighting against a heavy head wind.

"Company!" says "Tommy." "No," says I, getting the glass and training it on said canoe. "Jack" says I. And in a little while he lifted his birch [bark canoe] and small pack up on the rocks and came up to the tent.

"Why Jack!" I said, "I didn't suppose you'd think for a minute that we would start out today!"

"I told you I'd be here 9 o'clock; bad rain, head wind; little late," says Jack. ("Some Indian," I say).

Known for his punctuality and keeping his word, Linklater defied stereo-typical notions about Indians that circulated among the White residents of canoe country. After waiting out the storm, the party restarted:

We packed up, made the first portage falls and went on down the Basswood River, coming to other rapids. "Tommy" and I would walk over the portage, while Jack "shot" the rapids with first his canoe, then ours, having divided the load.

To clean a large trout, Linklater removed birch bark from a tree to use as a fileting plate, but soon thereafter the fishing became poor:

He paddled me around that lake for miles, and I tried all the baits and ways of fishing that I knew and all the different depths from shallow to 175 feet deep, and did not get three fish. After three days of this, he said, "We try Indian way." The next morning he asked for hooks, black thread, etc. and sat down on the shore and made some baits that "Tommy" immediately named "Fish Babies" she said they resembled the papoose in its "dick-e-na-gan" or board on which they are carried on the squaw's back. This bait was a willow stick about five inches long, split part way with a large hook inserted and the

John Linklater (with axe) and a fellow camper hang a coffeepot over a fire. Linklater made a tripod to support the stick on which the pot is hung. Frank M. Warren photograph. Courtesy of University of Minnesota Duluth, Archives and Special Collections.

stick wrapped tight again; then the slab side of a small bass; taken the day before in another lake, wrapped around the stick with the hook protruding, and this well wrapped with black thread, giving a mottled effect with the white meat; then a small wooden peg fastened by a black thread to the wire leader, thus holding the bait in a nearly horizontal position.

The fish hit "one after another, as fast as I could play them out," recalled Darragh.[83] Guides like Linklater were expected to know "tricks" so campers could improve fishing success, camp in comfort, find good campsites, and so on. Guides also had to deal with unexpected, and sometimes fortuitous, circumstances, as one Anishinaabe guide did when he made an impromptu fish smoker with rocks, bark, and sand to dry the many fish caught on one trip. The result: "when taken out [the fish] were found to be delicious."[84]

Indian guides were common in the early days of recreation in the boundary waters and Quetico. A number lived on Burntside Lake and were engaged to guide there. On one trip, a young couple from Philadelphia on their 1897 honeymoon remembered their guides:

> These Indians have the most remarkable powers of observation, and they see and hear things that are simply not revealed to the poor White man. Suddenly they stop paddling in the canoe; Cutahbonis, our "bow oar," looks off in the distance and whispers, "Shesheep"; that means wild duck. They pull the canoe along a little further, the ducks still being invisible to all the clear-visioned strangers and the Indian remarks, perhaps, "Cowin nishinshin shesheep," which being interpreted is "the ducks are no good."

Or not the right kind of duck (mallards), which they were hoping to hunt for food.[85] But guides, and Indian guides in particular, added tremendous knowledge to those observational skills. The same guide offhandedly remarked after the days' weather and seeing northern lights in the evening that cold weather was coming, and it indeed did come on that trip.

Linklater guided in Minnesota, Ontario, and Isle Royale in his later years. One of his most compelling skills was his ability to reach a non-Indigenous audience, old or young. After his death, his ability to inspire Boy Scouts and canoe campers was noted by many. In one account, the Boy Scouts were visiting Linklater and his dog team and "got Buckshot going," or talking:

> Jack was not an eloquent speaker, but at the same time had a gentleman's command of the English language. His tale progressed, with an occasional "oh" or "ah" on the part of some wide-eyed youngster, until it neared conclusion. Instead of merely ending the adventure, the story was skillfully brought to a climax which contained the lesson that in conquest of the wilderness, or in ordinary life for that matter, the thing that counts is to play the game according to the

Plate 1. William Richards, *Man and His Wife Returning with a Load of Partridges from Their Tent,* watercolor, circa 1805–11. The artist was John Linklater's great-uncle. Courtesy of Hudson's Bay Company Archives, Winnipeg.

Plate 2. William Richards, *A South East View of Albany Factory: A Winter View,* watercolor, circa 1805–11. John Linklater's paternal grandfather was likely born at Albany Factory around 1822. Courtesy of Hudson's Bay Company Archives, Winnipeg.

Plate 3. Beaded wool felt moccasins likely made by Tchi-Ki-Wis. Warren Collection. Courtesy of National Park Service, Isle Royale National Park (ISRO 1029).

Plate 4. A purse with a beaded Anishinaabeg floral design by Tchi-Ki-Wis. Warren Collection. Courtesy of National Park Service, Isle Royale National Park (ISRO 1027).

Plate 5. This is the largest mat that survives (8 feet, 3½ inches by 63 inches), with more than 140 warp cedar strips, which hung vertically when it was woven. In excellent condition, it features a complicated design with medicine eyes in a checkerboard background with alternating vertical strips. This is likely one of two mats Frank and Alice Warren took home to Minneapolis, then donated to the park years later. Warren Collection. Courtesy of National Park Service, Isle Royale National Park (ISRO 1133). Photograph by Travis Novitsky.

Plate 6. A simple over-and-under weave pattern. The dark color, now quite faded, may have been blue or black. This mat was recently given to the Grand Portage Band by the Olmsted (Minnesota) Historical Society and was likely owned by the Wallace and Thelma Merritt family of Tobin Harbor, Isle Royale. Photograph by Travis Novitsky.

Plate 7. Detail of edging of a mat made by Tchi-Ki-Wis. Note the irregularity of the cedar strip widths. She compensated for a wide strip with a smaller one; one strip has a small knot in it. This was a plaid-check design, with extreme fading of the red color. Tchi-Ki-Wis's mastery of the craft is evident in the particularly tight weave of this mat, which measures 6 feet, 5 inches by 4 feet, 1 inch. Warren Collection. Courtesy of National Park Service, Isle Royale National Park (ISRO 1136). Photograph by Travis Novitsky.

Plate 8. A detail of one of the original mats given to Isle Royale National Park by the Warren family in 1941. In deeply contrasting colors, it is perhaps the most unusual design, called by some "Little Chippewa Village." Tchi-Ki-Wis chose to carry the design throughout the mat and to the edges. Warren Collection. Courtesy of National Park Service, Isle Royale National Park (ISRO 1134). Photograph by Travis Novitsky.

Plate 9. On this smaller mat, Tchi-Ki-Wis made the cedar strips (both weft and warp) narrower than in a larger mat. This mat once hung above the mantel at Crystal Cove, Amygdaloid Island, one of the larger and more elaborate summer places on Isle Royale. Warren Collection. Courtesy of National Park Service, Isle Royale National Park (ISRO 1078). Photograph by Travis Novitsky.

Plate 10. Long and narrow compared to the other surviving mats, the cedar strips in this mat have been varnished or waxed, giving it a shiny appearance. Its history is unclear. Tchi-Ki-Wis integrated multiple design elements together, including diamonds, chevrons, and plaid made by weaving one over, then one under. Warren Collection. Courtesy of National Park Service, Isle Royale National Park (ISRO unnumbered). Photograph by Travis Novitsky.

Plate 11. This large mat (8 feet by 4 feet, 8 inches) features three colors and a plaid design with medicine-eye pattern. Tchi-Ki-Wis rounded the corners of her mats, unusual among cedar mat makers. The upper left corner is square; she likely started her weft weaving here, moving left to right. Warren Collection. Courtesy of National Park Service, Isle Royale National Park (ISRO 1135). Photograph by Travis Novitsky.

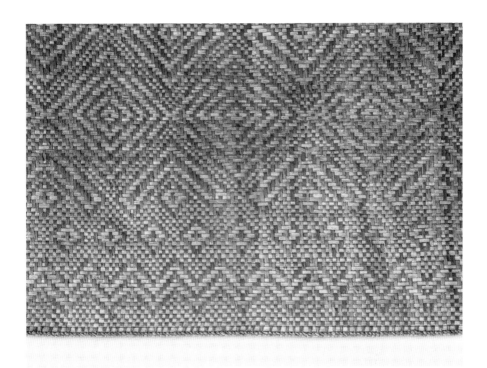

Plate 12. Natural and a faded green cedar form an otter-trail border around a medicine eye/diamond center. Isle Royale boat builder Reuben Hill bought this mat from Tchi-Ki-Wis for $1.50 as a wedding present for his wife, and they hung it at their home in Larsmont, Minnesota. It is the second smallest of the surviving mats (61 by 35½ inches). Warren Collection. Courtesy of National Park Service, Isle Royale National Park (ISRO 4232). Photograph by Travis Novitsky.

Plate 13. The cedar mats are fragile. A woven mat typically lasted fifteen years, and over time the edges became the most vulnerable to tear. On this mat, Tchi-Ki-Wis repurposed fishing line as the core to the edging, which is exposed here at the bottom. Warren Collection. Courtesy of National Park Service, Isle Royale National Park (ISRO 1138). Photograph by Travis Novitsky.

Plate 14. An alternating design with plaid ends, two panels of diamonds, and facing chevrons. The mat uses natural-colored cedar strips to create essentially two colors and textures, one vertical and the other horizontal. This mat was recovered by Isle Royale park staff from the former Savage–Cochran family boathouse in Tobin Harbor. Warren Collection. Courtesy of National Park Service, Isle Royale National Park (ISRO 1138). Photograph by Travis Novitsky.

Plate 15. A moose call made by Tchi-Ki-Wis from birch bark. Warren Collection. Courtesy of National Park Service, Isle Royale National Park (ISRO 1051).

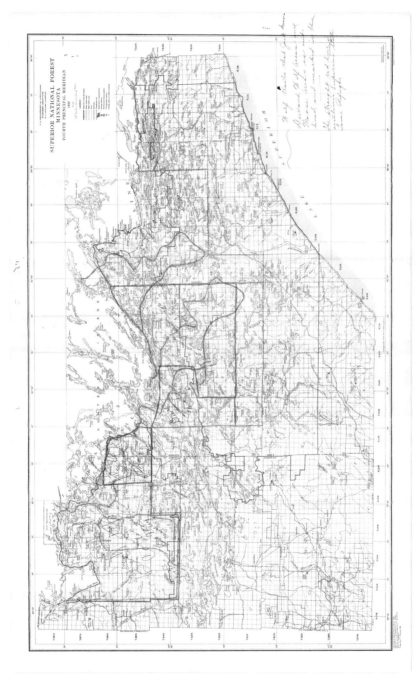

Plate 16. Wolf trails and areas of moose and deer in the boundary waters, mapped by John Linklater for Sigurd Olson, circa 1927. Sigurd F. Olson Papers. Courtesy of the Minnesota Historical Society.

Two boys admire John Linklater as he carves a paddle at Rock Harbor, Isle Royale, 1924. Frank M. Warren photograph. Courtesy of University of Minnesota Duluth, Archives and Special Collections.

rules of fairness, giving every ounce of energy towards reaching the goal. "The wilderness had made hard rules, but they're for our own good. If we follow them, we survive and succeed. If we break them, we may succeed for a time, but failure is eventually certain and we may perish. The same applies to everyday life." Thus, without moralizing, he brought home to the group of impressionable boys one of the most valuable lessons they could ever learn.[86]

Linklater had a presence about him, as "a swarthy appearing woodsman of the old school," according to the same obituary writer, but he also could bring that presence, experience, and authenticity alive in people he met.

John Linklater, with pack, inching around a rock face while guiding a boundary waters
canoe trip in 1917 with Frank and Alice Warren. Frank M. Warren photograph. Courtesy
of University of Minnesota Duluth, Archives and Special Collections.

Linklater's penchant for guiding and seeing and understanding wildlife morphed into another realm as he got older: he became adept with both a still camera and a movie camera. When he was out with his friend Frank Warren, who was deeply concerned about the welfare of moose on Isle Royale, they took hundreds of photographs and much movie footage of the moose. One of their common techniques was for Jack and a partner, sometimes Alice Warren, in the bow of a canoe to chase the moose to shore while Frank took photographs or filmed them. They were trying to gauge the relative health and to some degree the behavior of the moose. The irony of Linklater becoming a cameraman prompted one newspaper-man to write a piece of about how Linklater had progressed from the use of bow and arrow in his youth, to hunting with a gun, to finally hunting with a camera later in his life.

One consequence of Linklater's reputation as a guide was that more well-off and well-connected people sought him out. Linklater guided mayors, businessmen, engineers, filmmakers, architects, scientists, and biologists—including the head of the Department of Conservation at the time. Noted conservationist Ernest Oberholtzer tried to arrange a U.S. Senate committee member tour to Isle Royale and to begin the whirl-wind tour at Linklater's cabin in McCargoe Cove.[87] Linklater befriended powerful people, such as Frank and Alice Warren. Alice Rockwell Warren became the first woman regent of the University of Minnesota.[88] With the Warrens and others, Linklater found a way to maintain his dignity, sometimes in the face of patronizing behavior. He was tested but stayed quiet. It was his habit to be reticent in their company, which was also an act of self-preservation. In more than a dozen trips with the Warrens on Isle Royale, he was helpful, ingenious in solving problems, and outwardly comfortable in the midst of family but usually kept his distance. In the many photographs of the family on outings, Linklater is there, eyes usually averted from the camera and with a little bit of extra space between him-self and his patrons. Avoiding eye contact was considered a sign of respect in Anishinaabeg culture at the time. If they are standing, he is squatting, or if they are sitting at a camp table, he is usually sitting a little bit farther away. On the other hand, Linklater was comfortable enough to give Alice Warren an Anishinaabemowin name, Sheesheeb, or duck.[89]

The Warrens and Linklater were quite close, and Frank in particular "considered Jack the best friend he ever had."[90] Frank looked out for Linklater and his family's welfare, including convincing him to buy a life insurance policy. Linklater was searching for his own economic opportunities, such as commercial fishing on Isle Royale and guiding from his camp. In 1929 he worked with an advertising writer for the Northern Pacific Railway Company to promote his guiding trips across the island.[91] The idea was later seized by Mrs. Farmer at Rock Harbor Lodge on Isle Royale, so that she could increase the guiding opportunities she could offer and encourage Tchi-Ki-Wis to produce more handicrafts for sale at the lodge. In one letter to John, Mrs. Farmer was enthusiastic about the business opportunity growing out of the national park designation of Isle Royale:

Alice Warren and John Linklater with stacked canoe gear, including multiple Duluth packs, at the start of a canoe trip into the boundary waters in 1917. Frank M. Warren photograph. Courtesy of University of Minnesota Duluth, Archives and Special Collections.

I am already getting reservations, and many of them are asking about your camp and what about the trips advertised in last year's folder. I do not think, John, that you can afford to stay away from the Island with all this development going ahead up there, and feel that you will get something really good from the government if you are on the job up there and taking care of tourists according to our plan. I am going to press with my folder the latter part of this month and surely want to feature you and your part of in our excursions. . . . We need you and you need what the Island can give you this year, I am sure.[92]

We do not have Linklater's reply to Mrs. Farmer, but Frank Warren, being aware of this enticement, was not happy and wrote John a confidential and stern letter.

Mrs. Farmer is in town today [Minneapolis] and is very anxious to make arrangements with you to guide people across Isle Royale this summer. Last summer, she says, it was not a success because we took you off the job in August. . . . So far as I am concerned, we brought you to Isle Royale and we like your company too well to give you up so that she can make a few extra dollars by being able to have parties go across the island to your camp. We are willing to be generous but this is going too far. I would not talk this way to you if you and I both did not know that there is many times as much money working for us as it is possible to get out of that arrangement with Mrs. Farmer.[93]

Warren was not used to being second fiddle to anyone, let alone Mrs. Farmer. He used his trump card: not money but their long association (and concern—there is a paragraph in the same letter about Linklater's life insurance policy) to wrangle Linklater into returning to be Warren's guide and handyman. Less attractive to Linklater, perhaps, was that in most years when he went to the island to work for the Warrens, he went alone. Tchi-Ki-Wis stayed at Jackfish Bay.[94]

The Warren family had known the Linklaters a long time. In summer 1891, George Warren, Frank's father, had taken his ailing wife and his teenage son to canoe country. They were guided by Vincent "Defoe" (Defauld), who was married to Tchi-Ki-Wis's "sister."[95] Frank Warren wrote that on July 5, 1897, he met John Linklater in Ely, likely for a trip where Linklater was the guide.[96] According to the guest book at the Warren place on Isle Royale, Linklater was on the island as their handyman for at least twelve different years. As their friends, the Warrens were helpful to the Linklaters beyond employment. When lumber baron Edward Backus threatened to build a dam at the outlet of Basswood Lake (and other dams) and impound its waters, Frank Warren was extremely active in helping Ernest Oberholtzer and the Quetico–Superior Council defend the canoe country.[97] After Jack's death, Frank Warren was solicitous about Tchi-Ki-Wis's well-being and later begrudgingly gave monies to grandson Frank Nelson during his tough times in the Depression.[98] At the same time, Frank Warren's concern was of a superior to a subordinate, of a well-off White elite to an Indian.

Linklater's growing reputation as a remarkable individual and guide led to powerful or well-connected folks wanting to introduce him to a much wider audience. Their intentions were likely honorable, but the effect was to essentially put him repeatedly on display. Thus, the state Game and Fish Department set him up to take their dog team, by train, to the Twin Cities to greet and welcome the Arctic explorer Donald Baxter MacMillan, when he visited.[99] This was the second trip for Linklater to the Twin Cities with the dogs; they traveled there in 1924 for the Minnesota State Fair.[100] While in the Twin Cities with friends, such as the Aldriches or Warrens, Linklater was taken to a bank, the Zoological Museum's wildlife display, and a house party to mix with guests. Similarly, in a publicity stunt, Linklater led a canoe trip with four women that was filmed by a California director, supposedly to make a film to show at the 1933 Chicago World Fair that would demonstrate that canoe trips in the wilds were safe and entertaining for women.

A privately funded, publicity seeking, archaeological expedition, the McDonald–Massee Expedition, arrived at Isle Royale on two palatial yachts in August 1928.[101] The objectives were to dispel or confirm a number of archaeological theories, such as the existence of a supposed "Norse Fort" or lost city, and that Aboriginal peoples could not have been the prehistoric miners because they lacked the "industrial organization, the social system nor numbers necessary to do this work."[102] The group opportunistically engaged Linklater to guide them in exploring the prehistoric mines near McCargoe Cove and inland. He showed the expedition leaders some of his finds, including stone points, white flint and black chert points, a stone axe, or celt, and part of a stone pipe found near Siskiwit Lake.[103] Linklater's efforts and consultations led to a place of honor on Commander McDonald's yacht, a hundred dollar bill as payment, and a top hat.[104] The publicity machine of the expedition was not so kind. He appeared in one newspaper article as "Lindlater [sic], the Indian who had run his trap lines and fished the north shore near the old mines was brought to the *Naroca* (yacht) in a sea sled at a speed that left him gasping."[105] Thus, Linklater as a guide had to overlook the whims and amusements of wealthy and influential men who might be warm to him in person but also publicly condescending, making him out to be a stereotypical Indian, unacquainted with motors and the modern world.[106] Still, they relied on Linklater and were privately impressed. One of the few trained archaeologists along, George Fox, later corresponded with Linklater and tried to lure him to a "Camp Manitou" in Georgian Bay, Lake Huron, to "instruct the boys in the proper handling of a canoe and to show them the tricks of woodcraft." Linklater declined and sent Fox a photograph of "Indian paintings," or pictographs, to ease the sting of "no."[107] Linklater proved to be a skilled diplomat in addition to being in demand.

While recreationists were growing more impressed with John and Tchi-Ki-Wis, events engulfing them foreclosed other opportunities. The creation of both the Superior National Forest (though much smaller then than today) and the Quetico Forest Reserve, both in 1909, circumscribed the opportunities and movements of the Linklaters and other Native peoples in the area. The 1910 winter eviction and forced relocation of the remaining members of the Sturgeon Bay, or Kawa Bay, First Nation in the

John Linklater guides on Isle Royale, circa 1927. Frank M. Warren photograph. Courtesy of University of Minnesota Duluth, Archives and Special Collections.

Quetico had impacts beyond those who trudged through the snows to Lac La Croix. The Kawa Bay and Lac La Croix people had been communally using the lands and lakes to hunt and gather plants and medicines.[108] Suddenly they were not welcome. A year after this forced removal, the Linklaters' daughter Margaret died. Both the removal of their Anishinaabeg kin and Margaret's death in 1911 deepened their bond to their home on Jackfish Bay.

For Indigenous peoples, the rise of conservation interests and particularly the presence of game wardens led to a period of "criminalization of the[ir] seasonal round."[109] Ancient Anishinaabeg traditions were circumscribed by new rules. In 1921, the Canadian Department of Indian Affairs published a circular aimed at their agents to "dissuade, and if possible, prevent them from leaving their reserves."[110] The administrative closing of the Sturgeon Lake, or Wawa Bay, Reserve in 1916 impacted their connections to the Quetico country. The Linklaters and others were watching warily while remaining on the American side of Basswood Lake. The removal of many of the Anishinaabeg from Basswood during World War I left the Linklaters and the Hoffmans alone on Jackfish Bay.[111] They were overlooked in the move, unlike many others, because Hoffman was a German immigrant and Linklater was not a recognized Canadian Indian subject to the Indian agents' decrees. Both had jobs with Swallow and Hopkins Lumber Company. The end of the logging boom around them in the early 1920s foreclosed job prospects for Linklater.[112] The lumberjacks living in their midst and in Winton moved on. The end of logging momentarily returned Jackfish Bay to the Linklaters, Hoffmans, and Robinsons. They could live on in the cast-off Swallow and Hopkins buildings and use the old logging spur, the Cloquet Line, to get to town. With the mills dismantled, railroad tracks pulled up, and the labor force gone, Winton became a shadow of its former self.

CHAPTER 4

"Talk to John"

Guide, Teacher, Warden

It BEGAN WITH THE VISITORS strapping on pistols in Grand Marais, Minnesota, dressed in clean wool knickers, thick knee-high socks, bulky coats, and cabbie hats with the earflaps pulled down. Later, when this group of twenty-three sportsmen mixed with the northern game wardens, they snowshoed to an old logging camp on Cascade River. The next day they joined other wardens and sled dogs and followed the packed trail to Brule Lake. In conversations along the way, the wardens learned that some of the men from the Twin Cities fancied themselves as woods wise, as experts. Still, the wardens played host and endured these conversations from those "who knew it all and learned nothing from others and little from their own experience." This was a trip where the wardens were to explain their jobs, conditions in the game refuge, and their strenuous efforts to hold off outlaw trappers.

On the snow-packed trail to Brule Lake, the taciturn fishery biologist spotted lynx tracks. Many of the party stopped, looked, and then started talking and thinking lynx. Tents were pitched on the ice, and an old logging shack was cobbled together as a dining hall. That night stories were told by the veteran wardens, even by Linklater, and the businessmen and mayors listened intently. In the darkness around a large fire, eyewitness accounts were told of isolated trappers who were ambushed and injured by lynx. Pistols were relocated and made handy. When the party broke up, the newcomers decided to go out in groups, and those without pistols

A gathering of VIPs before a winter trip across the boundary waters, 1924. John Linklater is among the group; other wardens wear parkas made by Tchi-Ki-Wis Linklater. Courtesy of Ely–Winton Historical Society.

asked the cook for knives. They adjourned; the city men slept in the canvas tents with stoves and on mounds of balsam boughs, the wardens in an unheated shack.

The next day, the party took inspection trips with the four dog teams, each piloted by a warden from Winton. Linklater organized and took care of the dogs—he was the dog wrangler and pilot. Assembling for dinner, the party told of their experiences as the light faded. Before long, a fair distance across Brule Lake, some of the men saw the red eyes of a lynx glowing, others heard a lynx scream. The city men reached for their pistols and shot at the lynx, driving it away. Anxious (at least many of the thirty-eight men), they went to bed.

The men took more dogsled trips down the length of Brule Lake the following day and over a portage or two to check browse conditions for deer and moose or for signs of illegal trapping. Talk was of last night's near lynx attack and better preparations. In camp, the men gathered around a dead sled dog said to have had its throat slashed by a lynx. Pistols were fondled. Dinner came slowly, then twilight. The sled dogs rose from their beds and started howling madly. Linklater stood up and started speaking animatedly in Anishinaabemowin, a warden or two translating that he was asking the wild beasts to stay away and that he was their brother. Not long after, a large lynx reappeared in twilight but closer, moving jerkily along the ice. Shots rang out again, and the lynx disappeared. The city men went to bed with pistols and knives, thinking they must have killed it, but they weren't quite sure.

The next morning, the wardens felt guilty about their prank and showed the men the poster-board lynx. Linklater had made it out of materials he had found at the logging camp and had mounted it on two runners so it could be pulled along the ice by a rope. The red-eyed lynx of the night before was a Linklater creation made of a tin can with two holes, red transparent paper from a filmmaker, and a flashlight. Linklater made the faux lynx tracks by hand. The unfortunate sled dog (and favorite of the mushers) had to be put down on the

A poster-board "lynx" made as a prank by John Linklater while on Brule Lake, 1926. Photograph courtesy of Robert Maki.

trip from Winton to Brule Lake. That the commissioner of Game and Fish showed him to the city men gave further license for his wardens with their prank. Some of the city men didn't believe it and thought there really was a lynx out there, still out there, and others went home laughing about it for weeks.[1]

MORE OFTEN than being a lighthearted job, being a game warden was dangerous and demanded long hours. In one stretch in May and June 1931, Linklater worked thirty-two days straight.[2] As fellow warden Bill Hanson's wife, Ellen, stated, "not good for family life." Still, she supported his and Linklater's efforts. The first year on the job, the state required new wardens like Hanson and Linklater to furnish their own equipment, packs, tents, and canoe.[3] Linklater's first work for the State of Minnesota was conducted from a birch-bark canoe that he and Tchi-Ki-Wis made. A year later, the state reversed course and agreed to equip wardens. Early game wardens and their commissioner were political appointees and as such could lose their job with a change in state administration, such as in 1928 when Commissioner James Gould was replaced.[4] During Linklater's time, one game warden was shot but survived, another died in a motorcycle accident on the Gunflint Trail, and a third was shot and killed. Bill Hanson, Linklater's friend and boss, was on the two-month manhunt to arrest the killer.[5] Linklater was shot at more than a few times, but all wardens assumed they might become targets. To elude Linklater, another man punched a hole in his canoe. Linklater could be fearless, once snatching a rifle aimed at him by a much larger man.[6] Making this job even less desirable was unreliable pay; wardens were funded from the State of Minnesota's sale of illegal or permitted furs and fines. If the fur sales revenue was not enough, wardens might be unexpectedly laid off, as happened in fall 1924 and throughout much of Linklater's career.[7]

The Superior National Forest was created out of the conservation interests of progressive Republicans. Teddy Roosevelt established the forest in 1909, and across the border the Quetico Provincial Forest Reserve was created the same year. Coincidentally, the State of Minnesota banned beaver trapping in 1909, in response to their very low numbers statewide and indeed nationwide.[8] The beaver trapping ban lasted through 1939, six years after Linklater's death,[9] although permits to trap "nuisance beavers" were first issued in 1919, as their population grew and expanded. The establishment of the Superior Game Refuge, staffed by state rather than federal employees, led to state citizens having a heightened interest in the area. The game refuge and national forest were roughly contiguous, and the refuge was the largest in the state by far. State wardens often worked together with Forest Service rangers. A handful of state game wardens patrolled the refuge and completed tasks such as licensing and monitoring hunting and fishing, fire control, predator control, stocking fish, and clearing and posting the boundaries of the refuge. Wardens were to stop game law violations by apprehending "outlaws." Not long after, both would appear in court, with the warden presenting the evidence against the accused. Wardens also regularly checked freight for shipments of illegal game and occasionally participated in stings by impersonating illegal fur buyers. Wardens had to be in good shape and able to go miles on snowshoes or foot or by canoe. The wardens also built a string of cabins to use in nasty weather or as a base for operations, such as the cabin on Insula Lake (on state land) that Bill Hanson and Linklater built. It stood until the Pagami Creek Fire burned it to the ground in 2011.

Left to right: John Linklater, Merwin Peterson, and wardens Jim Hoffman and Bill Hanson, late 1920s. Hoffman and Hanson are wearing parkas made by Tchi-Ki-Wis Linklater. Courtesy of the M. W. Peterson family.

One of the lesser-known programs advocated in the 1920s was the planting of wild rice to combat declining rice beds. The cause of the decline was debated in *Fins, Feathers, and Furs*, the Department of Conservation's magazine. One sportsman maintained that the lack of muskrats to seed the beds hastened their decline, but warden Leo Chosa replied that the draining of marshes, logging, and pollution was the cause. The Game and Fish Department, in turn, advocated that citizens plant rice, and in 1925 identified 112 people as doing so. The more than one hundred sportsmen planted rice as a food source for waterfowl and not for the well-being of Anishinaabeg, who relied on wild rice for food.[10] Linklater planted wild rice in the boundary waters, but one friend thought he did it more "for his people" than for feeding ducks.[11] The concern over wild rice and the planting program mirror a larger sense among conservationists of the day that aggressive human intervention was the remedy to newly identified environmental problems.

"Predator Control" was the sad epitome of this belief in aggressive human response to a supposed problem, in this case, the alleged blood thirst of predators as well as their impact on game and furbearers. Animals deemed to be problems included coyotes, lynx, foxes, crows, and especially "the menace" wolves. Even rabbits were deemed to be serious adversaries at the time as a "hindrance" to reforestation.[12] The state commissioner, James Gould, and Forest Service officials endorsed predator control, and not long after Linklater started warden work, a federal predator control specialist, J. Stokley Ligon from New Mexico, was brought in to trap and poison wolves.[13] While a few biologists asked questions about the value of predator control and poisoning, it was employed in the Superior Game Refuge the winter of 1924–25. Linklater, as the most knowledgeable warden about the refuge geography, dog mushing, and indeed wolves, became Ligon's guide. Their first trip was in a motor-driven canoe, and after freeze-up they traveled by dog team. Other trappers working under the permit system were also trapping and poisoning wolves. Linklater spent one week with Ligon near Oyster Lake in the fall and two more weeks with him in January along Lac La Croix. A few days later, after Ligon left in midwinter, Linklater ran the trap/poison line and "secured two big wolves."[14] One of these wolves was noteworthy for its size, but earlier Linklater had trapped a "timber wolf on Crooked Lake . . . that weighed 150 pounds and whose skin stretched to 8 feet, 4 inches."[15] Only a few years later, in 1928, the state policy on predatory animals changed, except that for wolves.[16] By the winter of 1931–32, Linklater was picking up poison bait meant for wolves and destroying it.[17] He told Sigurd Olson that wolves had learned to be wary of returning to old kills to eat, as they associated them with danger stemming from either trappers or poison.[18]

Unfortunately, we do not know what Linklater thought of poisoning animals, nor did anyone ask him about it. The positive and prominent position of the wolf, *ma'iingan* in Anishinaabemowin, in Anishinaabeg belief must have caused Linklater some consternation. And yet we know that he trapped wolves for their bounty, also setting up a clash between the immediate needs of the day with traditional beliefs about *ma'iingan*. Perhaps, Linklater, like other Anishinaabeg, reconciled their trapping of wolves and other animals with their deep beliefs through their respect of and proper conduct toward the animal spirit. In this view, how an animal was treated—respectfully, when alive or when killed—was imperative. The Anishinaabemowin word root *nitaage*, with the twin meaning both to kill game and to mourn a death, demonstrates that killing animals and respect and sorrow were intrinsically linked.[19]

In Linklater's day, the real action, or really temptation, was illegal trapping of beaver. In the 1920s and 1930s, beaver pelts were comparatively worth a lot of money in a cash-starved area. Illegal beaver hides in Minnesota were selling for $22.00 in 1923, while the average price for a beaver pelt in Canada, where it was legal to trap beavers, was $20.22 in 1924–25, and $26.73 in 1927–28. A large prime pelt might bring up to $45.00 (more than $680 in 2021).[20] It was illegal to trap beaver in the game refuge without a permit from a warden. Thus, a cat-and-mouse game of illegal trapping by outlaws and the wardens' attempts to catch them began. In several cases, the outlaws were citizens in good standing. And when caught, a number on the Iron Range and North Shore were acquitted by juries made up of sympathetic peers.[21] One warden on the North Shore had a problem that other wardens did not; without a road to travel on, he took the steamer up the shore, and the ship's pilothouse horn whistled before each landing, warning off any men hoping to ship illegal furs.[22]

Linklater was renowned for his persistence. One account made this clear:

> For he, unlike the others, could travel at night without a sound. . . .
> The poachers worked days and slept at nights. Linklater travelled by darkness, and by day concealed himself beside the traps to watch for their owners.
> He could turn sleep on or off.

In Ely, two fur trappers display three months' catch from the Superior National Forest in 1922, valued at about three thousand dollars. The furs were taken under a trapping permit issued by the state Game and Fish Department. U.S. Forest Service photograph by William L. Barker Jr. Courtesy of the Forest History Society, Durham, North Carolina.

He was hunting one of the "toughest" poachers of the north woods. He had been traveling for nights, searching for a trail. On Mud Lake, near Winton, he found a beaver colony around which he read, in the muds and grasses, the presence of a poacher. Investigating closer, he found the traps.

Rain was pelting down behind a northeast wind. In the wet, the half-breed lay down behind a log to await the poacher.

For two days the rain stung down. And for two days, Jack lay behind the log, moving only when he had to. It was still raining when the "tough customer" came down to his traps.

He pulled his traps from the water (a beaver, upon being trapped, dives and drowns), and sat down ashore to skin the catch. Interested in the job, he was. Finally, he looked up, Jack stood behind him. Wringing wet, he was a bedraggled sight.

But his voice was nonchalant—almost detached. "I guess," he said, "you'd better come with me." The "tough customer" went.[23]

This was a vintage Linklater bust: finding the location of the illegal activity, secreting himself, watching the poacher for some time, and surprising the men by being in their midst before they knew anyone was around. Or as one old-time poacher put it years later, he and his son

were hiking down a trail one early spring with packsacks full of illegal furs, talking about their trip, when all of a sudden they had a three-way conversation going. Without a sound, Linklater had moved in and was walking between them. They paid their fines.[24]

Linklater enjoyed locating and surprising outlaws, or as he once reportedly said, he "would much rather hunt outlaws than deer, it was more challenging."[25]

Hanson and Linklater showed a lot of discretion in their work during the Depression, as many folks were hungry. One Ely resident remembered, "we lived off the country more or less: deer, rabbits, partridge [grouse].

We'd meet Linklater in the woods and he would let us go by, never searched us. Until some of the guys couldn't keep their mouths shut. Then they were caught."[26] Local historian Tauno Maki stated, "people needed to outlaw for meat on the table. They needed to trap for money for their families."[27] A letter written to Maki makes this point:

A rare formal portrait of John Linklater wearing his game warden badge, circa 1924. Photograph from Warner Wirta. Courtesy of Iron Range Research Center.

> Your description of Linklater is right on the button. Several of us Section Thirties, "Jerk" Doran, Ray Carpenter and myself in the winter time would go to the "point" to play cards at George Carpenters. We got there one time when "Link" was there. And after some visiting and card playing by us "Link" turned to Ray Carpenter and told Ray the time of day, the date and that it was off Queen's Bay that Ray had shot a deer. Out of season of course. Ray admitted "Link" was right and "Link" explained that he knew the size of the Pete Carpenter's family and figured they had a need for meat and so he watched Ray gut the buck, drag it to the canoe and watched him head for home.[28]

Hanson and Linklater wouldn't go after "penny-ante stuff," but when they did, Linklater caught the outlaw, and Hanson was complimented by judges for the well-documented cases he brought to the court.[29] Many community members understood the rule: brag about poaching, leave meat to spoil, take more than you and your family might eat, and you became a Linklater target. Concern that Linklater was around was an effective deterrent. The rule had a further subsection; if Linklater or Hansen caught you roasting venison or a partridge out of season, or with more than your limit of fish, but it was intended for consumption by your needy family, if you confessed, they would often let you go. Without a confession you became a target for prosecution the next time. Linklater and Hanson both might amble up to someone in a store or on the sidewalk and tell them the day, place, and time they shot a deer out of season or fished with too many lines. The effect of this deterrence technique was that many locals assumed that when they were in the woods, Linklater was watching. Or as one stated, "When Linklater was after someone, he was caught."[30] Some locals knew Linklater's territory and avoided it, or alternately went to the territory of wardens who "were slow in summer and more so, if possible in winter. Neither [warden] could catch a porcupine."[31]

One task Linklater assumed that few others did was being a mentor to new wardens. Indeed, new wardens, if they knew of Linklater, wanted to get started with him. Besides teaching the new wardens woodcraft, "he helped them see how important the job was." He was "a very dedicated conservationist. I don't think anybody loved nature more than Jack did." Further, "he instilled confidence in the new men."[32] He was proud of being a game warden with a badge, though some of the other wardens teased him about this.[33] Sometimes the new wardens or those new to the area did things that Linklater could only marvel at and for which he had to "cover" their ignorance:

> One time we were driving in sub-zero weather from Tower to Winton when we overtook a woman and a small boy afoot, the woman carrying a large pack. We stopped for them. She was an Indian acquaintance of Jack's going from Lake Vermilion to Burntside Lake. Stepping out of the car I helped her with the pack and proceeded to lash it to the fender, as we had considerable luggage in the car. She made a remark in the Chippewa tongue and Jack burst out to me, "Bring the baby in—do you want it to freeze to death out there?" Jack said a few words to her in Chippewa then translated it. He had assured her that I meant no harm to the child but that I was a bachelor and did not know any better. Actually, I had not realized that the pack contained a papoose.[34]

When Hanson and Linklater were on a leave of absence in spring 1927, temptation got the better of Hanson's replacement, Jim Hoffman. Hoffman and two trapper-wardens "skimmed off" a number of beaver pelts from the state's possession and sold them for their own profit. "The Beaver Scandal" was bad publicity for the Game and Fish Department. Hoffman eluded capture for three months and even faked his own suicide in California. For Hanson, this was a bitter pill, as Hoffman was a trusted subordinate.[35] More broadly, the scandal meant the end of the trapper-warden system in Minnesota. However, ending the system created another challenge, a drop in revenue to pay for the salaried wardens. Still, Commissioner Gould quickly rehired Hanson and Linklater.[36]

HANSON, LINKLATER, and other men created a community of game wardens at Winton. The Game and Fish Station was named by Linklater Wa-wa-tay Post for the northern lights. It had rooms with double bunks, always "a crackling fire going in the fireplace," and a radio. Each bunk had Hudson's Bay blankets, and if the men got cold, eiderdown sleeping bags. The wardens cooked and ate together.[37] Both Hanson and Linklater made fish-head stew, Hanson cooking it as a Finnish dish, and Linklater as an Anishinaabeg food. Intentionally or not, the six to eight wardens working there created a group comradery that ameliorated the long hours, separations from home, and the dangerous work. Linklater's job, on the trail and at the Game and Fish Station, changed how much time he spent with Tchi-Ki-Wis at Jackfish Bay. The job meant they were apart more, sometimes for weeks. On occasion, Tchi-Ki-Wis came to town, but more often John visited, traveling to and from Jackfish Bay or whenever a warden task or patrol took him that way.[38]

Leo Chosa first hired Linklater to be a game warden in 1923. But within a year, Chosa had left, and Bill Hanson became the supervisory warden at Winton. Chosa was an innovator and willing to take chances. He had commercially fished on Basswood Lake for years. He brought in the first sled dogs to serve the wardens. He had an automobile that ran on the four-mile railroad line.[39] He understood publicity trips, once taking female school-

John Linklater and architect Chilson (Studge) Aldrich in front of the Game and Fish Station, or Wa-way-tay Post, under construction. Aldrich helped design the building, and Linklater, Bill Hanson, and others constructed it in the mid-1920s. Photograph courtesy of the Wirta family.

teachers out on a winter trip, and he was instrumental in making the first winter trek across the boundary waters go well. Like Linklater, Chosa was of mixed descent (Anishinaabeg and French) and was originally from the Keweenaw Bay Indian Community of Michigan.

Chosa was also a fighter for his and other Indians' rights. When the Ontario government threatened to move the Kawawaigamok (Kawa Bay) people in midwinter 1910, he wrote blistering letters to the Canadian government condemning their cruelty. Chosa also did not always accept the rules of the day, especially if they were somebody else's rules. Game wardens had cited him for fishing violations in 1916, illegal possession of a moose in 1917, and illegally trapping beaver in Cook County, Minnesota, in 1922.[40] The Game and Fish Department then thought the best way to apprehend illegal trappers was to hire an outlaw trapper themselves. They hired Chosa.[41] Chafing at the rules, he resigned or was fired (depending on who you talk to). By 1925 Chosa was again caught, after bragging that the wardens could never catch him. Linklater tracked him down, and Hanson brought him to trial.[42] Chosa likely never blamed Linklater or Hanson, as he, after all, had arrested his brother for game violations only a year before.[43]

In 1917 there was a newspaper squabble between the arresting warden and Chosa. After insulting Chosa by calling him out as a "squaw man," Warden Wood went on to accuse Chosa and two others of multiple game violations and even being responsible for the disappearance of caribou. Chosa replied that he was within treaty rights to possess a moose (for his family to eat). After a trial he was convicted; however, the treaty rights issue was not addressed. Wardens, and indeed the state, did not recognize off-reservation hunting rights at the time and actively pursued Indians in their traditional hunts.[44] In Cook County one arrest was even made for hunting on the reservation. For his part, Chosa was stretching his rights, as today we would understand that a Keweenaw Bay man did not have treaty rights in northeastern Minnesota. On the other hand, his family members likely did.

Bill Hanson and John Linklater were an effective team, likened by one man to being "Mounties of the Superior National Forest."[45] Hanson, a second-generation Finnish American, treated Linklater as an equal. Linklater occasionally dined at Ellen and Bill's home while they strategized on locating and bringing in game and fish violators. They would have a beer together (despite Prohibition it was easy to get a beer in Ely), but Linklater was careful to limit his consumption. Hanson was the boss, but they were also friends, and in December 1926 they bought a commercial fishery on Isle Royale together. Ellen said they purchased half of the Francis fishery on the strength of Linklater's word.[46] Their friendship crossed racial lines, as did relationships among several Finnish Americans and Anishinaabeg in the area. Hanson took a number of risks having Linklater on his warden force. Hanson might even have helped Linklater fabricate parts of his application about his family history. It is unclear what Hanson

John Linklater *(left)* on snowshoes with Leonard Des Rosier at Cache Bay on Saganaga Lake, 1926. Linklater would often break trail (compact snow) to make for easier pulling for the dogs. Courtesy of Quetico Provincial Park.

might have known about Linklater's origins, but the two seemed to accept that it was best to keep Linklater's background vague. And at least from Linklater's perspective, if others had his story of his origin wrong, such as his mother being full-blood "Sioux" from North Dakota, so be it.[47] For some, especially those who did not know Linklater, the accepted prejudice toward Indians was enough to disqualify him from being a warden in the 1920s. In reality, Linklater was the very antithesis of prejudicial stereotypes: neat, on time and reliable to a fault, rarely drank, and worked days on end if need be.

Through time Hanson and Linklater's working relationship evolved: Hanson did more paperwork, supervised the wardens, and dealt with his superiors downstate. Linklater mentored new wardens and was often paired with inexperienced ones, tracking outlaws and running the mushing operations. While Linklater was more likely to find and catch a game violator, Hanson was on the arrest and usually was the warden in court. But Linklater was accepted by all—judges, juries, and the accused—as being expert at identifying the person who skinned the pelts by the particular knife marks on the hide and how it looked and had been dried.[48] They developed a remarkable degree of trust. Despite their age difference

(Hanson was younger than Linklater), on occasion they were sometimes mistaken as brothers.[49] And Ellen Hanson became a warm friend and admirer of Tchi-Ki-Wis.

One of the most striking gaps in stories about Linklater as a game warden is that none of them considered what it must have been like for him as an Indian arresting, mostly, White men. Being an Indian game warden, or, in Anishinaabemowin, *gizhaadigewinini,* wasn't easy. One tragic event had a major effect on wardens: when a pioneer warden was killed by "outlaw Indians from White Earth Indian Reservation. The murderers were not punished."[50] In response to this incident and more pointedly court decisions enlarging the role of the State of Minnesota in Indian affairs, game wardens became, in effect, instruments of power used to curtail off-reservation hunting and fishing (the notion being that these actions would ensure more game for sportsmen).[51]

Even traditional hunting and fishing practices on the reservations were to be further curtailed, and it was the game warden's job to make this happen.[52] From the Anishinaabeg perspective, game wardens had significant powers and could tragically exceed those powers, such as when two wardens killed a Wisconsin Anishinaabeg leader for refusing to go along with them after being cited for hunting out of season.[53] More often than not, there was an adversarial relationship between wardens and Indians. Wardens knew little of Indian treaty rights off and on the reservation or about traditional practices, increasing the likelihood of friction and conflict.

Despite this ambiguity and hardship, the State of Minnesota hired a few Indian game wardens. The first appears to be "Star Bad Boy" of Mahnomen, of whom the *Minneapolis Tribune* reported, "the only Indian we had as a game warden is a Republican." Jim Gesick, from Lutsen, was another game warden. More common were Anishinaabeg who were successful trappers, such as James Morrison Sr. and Jr., of Chippewa City outside Grand Marais, whose knowledge made them attractive as trappers–game wardens.[54] These men were predecessors to Linklater, although Linklater's ten-year work tenure (up until his death) was atypical in its timespan. He was an Indian game warden working among mostly Euro-Americans.

Due to the dangers of the work and the reality of being an outcast in the community being patrolled, turnover was high among game wardens. This was especially the case in Ely after 1910, when a game warden had shot and killed a man illegally netting fish; charged with murder, he was acquitted in a trial in Virginia, Minnesota. After the shooting, a mob grew in protest (of both of the murder and of the threat to their subsistence needs) and had to be dispersed.[55] On another occasion, Bill Hanson's father found a note on his woodpile that read "Bill Hanson is a yellow bellied Finlander and Linklater smells men's tracks."[56] This insult unintentionally captures one of the assets Linklater brought to the job—his reputation of being able to track anyone, anywhere. This "hunting instinct," as Hanson called it, was built on stereotypes of Indians reinforced in this case by Linklater's record. It did not decrease the danger of the job, as Linklater, like other wardens, was shot at. But this tracking ability, linked with an arsenal of skills, knowledge, persistence, and reputation, made him a remarkable, some say legendary, game warden.

How did he become such an effective and unquestioned game warden? Linklater had a calm, quieting presence that commanded confidence.[57] He was well liked and had a reputation for fairness that countered any doubts about his citations and arrests. He and Hanson were discreet; there are no records showing they gave away the identity of sources for tips in which a person might mention a neighbor's misdeed. Linklater had a lifelong sympathy for the underdog, the hard pressed; he did not write up kids or folks he thought didn't know better or those who were in need, unless their actions were egregious. When he did apprehend someone, most folks assumed it was for good cause. His method of apprehending someone, or watching them for some time, took away any doubt about their activities or the scope of their actions. His demeanor also helped him, as he was calm, kept his thoughts to himself, and did not raise his voice. Indeed, his method of surprising an illegal trapper had a singular effect in downplaying what could become a charged incident. He just appeared when someone was skinning a beaver, for example.[58] Linklater worked to decrease any ambiguity that might arise in these situations and was always mindful in reporting any arrest or fine to Hanson. Consciously or not, he maintained a spotless reputation that offset any power imbalance in an Indian arresting a White man.[59]

Was Linklater tokenized as an Indian game warden? Yes, in the sense of being one of a kind in a workforce of non-Indian men and two women. But his qualifications for the job, his woodcraft, were unequaled. There is no evidence he was paid less or his status was different from other wardens. Linklater developed strong relationships that went beyond polite tolerance with several of them and even with the commissioner.[60] Many wardens sought him out to learn from him, and many who worked with him fondly called him "Link." His ability to get along with anybody was real, not a forced trait. He had close friends in both the White and Indian worlds.

John Linklater with three associates, 1920s. *From left:* Sam Wirta, son-in-law and a trapper-warden; Linklater; William Hanson, warden supervisor and co-owner of fishery; and Joe Hoffman, Linklater's neighbor at Jackfish Bay. Photograph from Warner Wirta. Courtesy of Isle Royale National Park.

While Linklater was known as a "legendary" game warden, one of his greatest contributions was what he taught and inspired in others. He was interested in general scientific knowledge, or as another put it, he was "cautiously analytical." His mind "always asked the whys and where-fores."[61] Linklater had keen observational skills and a near photographic memory, able to notice faint animal tracks in dry leaves and moose behaving strangely (walking in circles to the right).[62] Sigurd Olson documented another remarkable example of Linklater's observational skills:

> Jack Linklater told me that the coyote den on Jack Fish Bay shows every evidence of the pups playing around and dragging bones, rabbit skins and other offal in and out of the den, using the entrance and the surrounding few rods as a playground. He states that by the middle of June the pups begin to sally forth with their mother hunting mice and cotton tails and from that time on their residence in the den is more or less of a temporary affair. In bad weather they may come back but if the weather is dry and sunny they might stay away indefinitely. Usually by the end of July or August the den is permanently deserted, the family taking up its abode wherever it happens to find itself. By Sept and Oct the pups are usually as large as the parents and in some cases young males have been caught which are larger than many small females several years of age. The new family pack can easily distinguish when hunting by the difference in the howl of the pups and the adults, The pups often bark and howl in excitement when on the trail of a rabbit or deer and trappers state that it is not hard to tell their high pitched untrained voices from the steadier deeper calls of the parents.[63]

Olson and many others admired Linklater's observational skills, which were integral to his success as a game warden. In one instance, they led to an unsettling discovery. In spring 1928, while on Isle Royale, Linklater discovered the victims of the *Kamloops* shipwreck who made it to shore only to die of exposure. He first saw candy wrappers, shoes, torn clothing, and small wreckage and followed this trail of debris into the woods, where he found the frozen bodies of seven crew members in a makeshift lean-to.[64] The Canadian authorities had been looking for the ship and its crew for five months. Despite the electrifying news of the discovery, Linklater was quiet about it. Tellingly, he wanted no credit or even an association with finding the bodies. Instead, he enlisted a neighboring commercial fisherman to talk to the newspapers.[65]

When writing a master's thesis on wolves and coyotes, Sigurd Olson's ace in the hole was Linklater. Olson cited him more times than any other contributor by far.[66] Indeed, Olson, who came up with the first "scientific" population estimates of wolves and coyotes in the boundary waters, was heavily reliant on Linklater's input to reach his conclusions, as well as on information from Hanson and Forest Service ranger Tom Denley. Olson wrote in his thesis notes, "ask Jack [Linklater] and Bill [Hanson] about their observations." Olson's thesis papers contain two maps of animal density and pack territories that Linklater drew for him for his work.[67] Olson went on to publish two academic articles from this research, but revealingly he acknowledged Linklater only as "a trapper and game warden and formerly in the employ of the Hudson Bay Company."[68] Not able to escape the pervasive biases of the time, Olson did not mention he was an Indian, possibly thinking it would undermine the credibility of Linklater's information.

Linklater shared his knowledge and observations with those who might consider them. For example, John consoled a late-fall city transplant to the north woods, telling him that splitting wood in cold weather has its advantages as "it would split better when full of frost."[69] Another time, Linklater told canoeists that one rock art panel was drawn by different tribal artists—both "Siouan and Ojibway."[70] Sharing his knowledge freely meant that many learned of his abilities. One friend asserted that Linklater "knew the biology and botany of the woods better than most biologists and botanists."[71] His knowledge and willingness to share, coupled with his guiding skills, made him in high demand among academics. Professors at the Universities of Illinois, Michigan, and Minnesota sought

Sigurd Olson *(far left)* travels by dogsled, as Jack Linklater, with large pack *(far right)*, breaks trail and leads the dog team, 1927. Wisconsin Historical Society collection, 74111.

his assistance. Aldo Leopold wanted him to guide his family deer hunt with bows. Sigurd Olson befriended him, traveled with him, and conversed with him about subjects ranging from wolves, moose, deer, and spirits inhabiting the woods to his family's connections to the Hudson's Bay Company.

A good example of Linklater's scientific collaboration occurred with University of Minnesota ornithologist Walter Breckenridge. Breckenridge wrote of one experience working with Linklater on spruce grouse:

> The only time I have heard the call [of a northern saw-whet owl] was while camping on the trail of the spruce grouse with the late Jack Linklater, a Chippewa half-breed whose woods-abilities and experience made him seem to be a voyageur of old set down in our Arrowhead Country a couple of centuries late. Sitting outside the cabin one evening about mid-May, we heard this monotonously regular

call come from across the Kawishiwi River and Jack remarked that this was unusually late for the call and that late March and April was when it was usually heard. Later, I found the well-known ornithologist, Frank Chapman, confirmed these dates and I was then even more impressed by the accuracy of Linklater's observations.[72]

In a similar conversation Linklater described the drumming of a spruce grouse to a Michigan newspaper friend unfamiliar with this grouse found primarily in Canada:

The bird's favorite drumming place is on a log, deep in the swamps, Linklater says. He poses at one end, lifts himself vertically into the air and drums as he rises to a perch six or eight feet above the log. A moment's pause and he slants downward toward the opposite end of the log, rolling forth his thunderous wing music as he goes.

A spruce grouse drums in the woods near Winton, 1931. Photograph by Walter Breckenridge. Courtesy of University Archives, University of Minnesota, Twin Cities.

From his new station he again rises vertically to a convenient perch, then tilts obliquely back to the end of the log from which he first started, still drumming on the wing. The same performance is repeated over and over. Linklater says, the vertical rise, the slant down from perch to log, and all the while the bird beats out his strange song of pride and ardor![73]

Linklater's time as a game warden and his time on Isle Royale overlapped. He continued to guide on the mainland and at the island, and he assisted scientific research and conservation efforts in Minnesota and Michigan. His game warden work was not full-time until after 1930; hence he could either take a leave of absence or, when not employed in the late-summer months, go to Isle Royale as a handyman and guide for Frank and Alice Warren. He appears to have first gone to Isle Royale in 1911, more than ten years before his game warden position began. In the 1920s, he went every year, staying in an outbuilding of the Warrens at Rock Harbor.

In May 1927, John and Tchi-Ki-Wis first opened the Birch Island fishery in McCargoe Cove. They fished the summer months into the fall from 1927 through 1930. Even while commercial fishing, John continued to guide VIPs, such as Frank Oastler.[74] Their fishery in McCargoe Cove provided easy access to the island interior for guiding trips as well as close access to the open waters of Lake Superior and its excellent fishing grounds. Most days when the Linklaters tended their nets outside McCargoe Cove, looming in the distance across the lake was the backside of the Sleeping Giant, or Nanabushu—the Anishinaabeg trickster. Here, too, they lived in a storied Anishinaabeg landscape. They would have known the story of Captain McCargoe hiding his vessel at the head of the cove to avoid being found by the Americans during the War of 1812.[75]

In spring 1929, the Michigan Legislature passed an act and provided funds for a survey of Isle Royale. The University of Michigan was designated to conduct the broad survey of island resources including those in the fields of archaeology, botany, geology, geography, and zoology. From 1929 thru 1931, scientists went to Isle Royale to do research, a majority of whom eventually made their way to Linklater's Birch Island doorstep.[76] Linklater helped find prehistoric objects in several locations, and even assisted archaeologist Carl Guthe with a dig near his house, where they uncovered more potsherds and a chipped point. Another archaeologist, Fred Dustin, visited with Linklater.[77] In a number of cases Linklater invited scientists or they asked to stay on Birch Island. This increased their conversation and collaboration, often after a welcome dinner of freshly caught whitefish.

Birch Island Fishery just prior to purchase by the Hansons and Linklaters, circa 1926. Captain Francis stands on the dock with two hired men. The main residence cabin is behind the net reel on the left; the forty-foot vessel Superior is on the right. Frank M. Warren photograph. Courtesy of University of Minnesota Duluth, Archives and Special Collections.

John Linklater with pipe and waders poling a boat slide across Snug Harbor, Isle Royale, 1925. The dock to the left is for large vessels that came to Rock Harbor. Frank M. Warren photograph. Courtesy of University of Minnesota Duluth, Archives and Special Collections.

Three botanists collected nineteen specimens on or nearby Birch Island, one even from "front of house—site of garden." Geologist George Stanley, for whom Stanley Ridge on Isle Royale is named, paid Linklater seventy dollars in November 1930 for use of a boat, gas, oil, and smoked meat. Perhaps the Michigan scientist who connected most with Linklater was ornithologist Norman Wood, who stayed at Birch Island and developed a real fondness for the Linklaters. Upon leaving Birch Island, Wood wrote in his diary:

> am about ready to say goodbye to Birch Id. It is a beautiful spot and I shall always hold it as a great privilege that I was allowed 3 weeks on it. The family here John Linklater and wife, (grand)son, Father in law are all fine folks and I have enjoyed them all—It would have been perfect if Lillian (wife) had been here.

Linklater collected four warblers for Wood, while grandson Frank brought in a "fine turtle" (likely a western painted turtle), which quickly became a specimen. Moose biologist Adolph Murie also stopped at Birch Island, later observing and shooting a number of moose for specimens at the head of McCargoe Cove.[78] Linklater's hospitality to the Michigan scientists is exemplified by the fine brown smoked whitefish sent to Ann Arbor for the director of the museum, Norman Wood, and his family and museum staff.[79]

UNINTENTIONALLY Linklater became enmeshed in two public disputes about moose in the late 1920s. The issue on the mainland was alarming; moose were dying from engorged ticks and the eruption of a new disease that made them behave strangely and become emaciated. While as yet few moose had died from this mystery disease, its novelty was worrying. The alarm bells about the new disease (which we now know to be brainworm) were rung dramatically when warden Leo Chosa hauled a moose carcass by dogsled that died of a "strange malady" to be shipped to the University of Minnesota.[80] Linklater and other wardens reported that dying moose were behaving erratically, stumbling, walking in circles, or appearing partially paralyzed or unusually tame. Linklater noticed that moose more often had paralysis on the right side, or "they run toward the right, with the head drawn toward the right shoulder, clockwise."[81] Linklater and Hanson wondered if the worms they saw in other animals were to blame. Veterinarians, biologists, and game wardens struggled to diagnose the disease, first pronounced as hemorrhagic septicemia, later more generally "distempers." While research was ongoing, so were moose deaths:

> During the spring of 1931 and 1932 we made investigations of the disease conditions affecting moose. The State Game and Fish Department, the State Live Stock Sanitary Board and the University of Minnesota cooperate in this work. John Linklater, a warden, was detailed as guide and it was through his knowledge of the habits of the moose that we were able to observe this animal at exceedingly close range. In observing the moose there seems to be two conditions affecting them, one type being extreme emaciation and weakness; and, the second form causing the animal to walk or run in circles.

John guided several research trips in which ill moose were located, dispatched, and autopsied—all internal organs, stomach contents, and the head were collected, blood smears were drawn, and the moose's temperature was taken immediately at death. The university veterinarians tried to isolate the cause but were unable to do so. Not until the 1960s and 1970s did brainworm begin to be understood.[82]

The dying moose begged the question, why?[83] Initially, some scientists thought the eruption of ticks on moose and the "strange malady" were related. Linklater noted that "ticks had been observed on moose in Minnesota since 1903," indirectly suggesting the malady was different and "new."[84] Further, he observed that the engorged ticks on mainland moose were not appearing on Isle Royale moose. This made Linklater speculate that it was habitat change from wholesale logging on the mainland that caused the sickness. He further thought the habitat change might be related to dietary changes, making the mainland moose more prone to

John Linklater *(left)* with waders, Frank Warren *(right)*, and an unidentified man, circa 1927. Linklater and Warren are holding camera gear for their studies of moose on Isle Royale. Frank M. Warren photograph. Courtesy of University of Minnesota Duluth, Archives and Special Collections.

disease. His thoughts, absent the knowledge of brainworm, drew attention from others, and an article about Linklater's idea is found in Aldo Leopold's files on moose.[85] Because of Linklater's acknowledged expertise on moose and his many connections with scientists, his views and ideas were quoted in area newspapers. For Linklater, too, "thinking moose" with scientists must have been fulfilling as he was able to learn from and test his ideas on others. In many ways it was a reciprocal relationship, which must have pleased him.

While Minnesota conservationists were alarmed with the decline in moose numbers, the inverse problem of supposedly too many moose was plaguing Isle Royale. The question of moose numbers on Isle Royale was complicated by a lack of a systematic way to count them and the observers' motives, particularly hunters.[86] From 1925 on, sportsmen sought to hunt on Isle Royale to reduce moose numbers.[87] Linklater's response to the "sport" of this idea was classic: "There would be just as much sport in shooting these moose as there would in walking into a farmer's barnyard and shooting his cattle."[88] Sportsmen's evidence of overpopulation was mostly wishful thinking in the 1920s. Those with slightly more knowledge and a great deal more experience disputed these claims. Frank Warren, Linklater, newspaper man Ben East, and Frank Oastler—a physician who had the job of investigating Isle Royale to see if it was of national park caliber—disagreed. So, too, did University of Michigan biologist Adolph Murie in May 1930.[89]

To investigate, Warren and Linklater set out to document moose numbers, the condition of moose, and their food supply. For a couple weeks each summer of 1924, 1926, 1927, and 1929, Frank and Alice Warren, Linklater, and occasionally his grandsons Frank Nelson and Victor Wirta camped at locations with high moose numbers (Lake Ritchie, McCargoe Cove, Hidden Lake) to study and particularly to photograph them. Frank

Frank Warren in the bow and Jack Linklater in the stern of the canoe, testing the health of a moose by driving it to shore at Isle Royale, circa 1925. Unknown photographer. Warren Collection photograph. Courtesy of University of Minnesota Duluth, Archives and Special Collections.

Aquatic plants collected by John Linklater and Frank Warren that were presumably eaten by Isle Royale moose in the 1920s. Plants were sent to the University of Minnesota for identification as part of their moose study. Frank M. Warren photograph. Courtesy of University of Minnesota Duluth, Archives and Special Collections.

Warren's diaries, though sparse in detail, recount the effort. In 1926, they counted and charted more than three hundred different sightings. In his canoe, Linklater once got within ten feet of the moose before it spooked. To test the health of the moose, Linklater and Alice went out in a canoe and slowly drove the moose toward Frank, who was secreted in a brush blind on the shore with a movie camera. Linklater quietly paddled toward the moose when its head was under the water (Alice seemed mostly to have watched), then stopped when it surfaced, and repeatedly got close to the moose before it swam or strode away toward Frank with his camera.[90] They repeated this technique over and over. Occasionally the roles were reversed, Frank marveling at Linklater's ability to shoot first-rate film. Warren and Linklater even collected underwater plants the moose were eating and had them identified at the University of Minnesota.

Warren's diary entries are intriguing. On June 23, 1927, they saw "a plain caribou track" in the sand, one of the last such observations of these animals before they became extirpated. On August 20, 1924, Frank and Alice slept under an improvised fly made into a "tent," while John slept under the canoe (as did his voyageur ancestors). Warren noted that John frequently spoke in "moose" or called the moose. On August 30, 1927, Frank Warren "reloaded the 2nd movie with f3.3 telephoto and Alice remained at the portage while Frankie and I went west along the N shore to get picture of the big bull N.W. of Burnt Id, then we found John who had been talking with the bull." Of course, research required "fuel," and John the scientist became the cook. They regularly ate "a good bannock," voyageur fare of a quick flat bread, or a more robust meal: "We returned to camp and had supper of whitefish, boiled potatoes, coffee and blueberries and sugar with cookies and more coffee for dessert."[91]

An important question regarding whether there were "too many moose" was if there was enough winter browse to get them through a harsh winter. At that time, scientific knowledge of what moose ate in the winter was rudimentary. An argument ensued on whether moose ate balsam fir (common on Isle Royale), and if they could repeatedly eat balsam fir twigs year after year. Warren, Linklater, and others said they could and did. Warren was so adamant about this that he asked Linklater back in Minnesota one winter to clip samples of balsam fir that had been repeatedly browsed by moose and to send them to him quickly as evidence.[92] Linklater assisted biologist Murie, who shot three moose and then examined their stomach contents to see what they were eating. Linklater noted their diets consisted of a "low species of honeysuckle that grows in profusion," a finding that added a more nuanced view of food availability than others at the time.[93] Warren and Isle Royale's game warden, Bill Lively, also thought that brush wolves (coyotes) were killing many young moose.[94]

The issue of whether there were "too many moose" was a loaded question: those who initially said yes wanted to hunt them, while those who

Frank Warren photographs a moose at close range during their Isle Royale moose studies, circa 1927. John Linklater likely took this photograph. Courtesy of University of Minnesota Duluth, Archives and Special Collections.

said no were strong advocates for making Isle Royale into a national park without a hunting preserve. In 1930 the State of Michigan renewed the game refuge status of Isle Royale, prohibiting moose hunting. And when the Isle Royale National Park legislation was passed in Congress the following year, the threat of a moose hunting preserve was further quashed. A couple years later, a new public outcry arose when evidence of starving moose was brought to the public's attention. Linklater did not go to the island after 1930, and he missed contributing to this chapter of the debate. He was not there to see the overbrowsing conditions that set in motion an emergency effort to do something about "too many moose." A year after Linklater's death, Adolph Murie's *The Moose of Isle Royale* (1934) concluded that the moose population was above the island's carrying capacity and had to be reduced.[95] In subsequent years a moose translocation effort was begun, and the 1936 forest fire changed and later improved moose browse in one-fifth of Isle Royale.

JOHN LINKLATER'S SCIENTIFIC COLLABORATORS

University of Michigan
Norman Wood, ornithology
Fred Dustin and Carl Guthe, archaeology
Clair Brown and Carl Grassl, botany
Adolph Murie, wildlife biology
George Stanley, geology
Walter Koelz, fisheries

University of Minnesota
Ruel Fenstermacher, veterinary science and wildlife
William L. Jellison, parasitology
Walter Breckenridge, ornithology

University of Illinois
Al Cahn, wildlife, parasitology
Sigurd Olson, wildlife biology

U.S. Biological Survey
Stokley Ligon, predator control
unknown, waterfowl survey

U.S. Department of the Interior
Dr. Frank Oastler, park recommendation for Isle Royale

Archaeology research (privately funded)
Eugene McDonald and Burt Massee Expedition

Moose studies (privately funded)
Frank M. Warren

Province of Ontario (unconfirmed)
two expeditions or surveys

A NUMBER OF CONSERVATIONISTS enjoyed talking with Linklater and were inspired by him, and in a few cases, he challenged their thinking. Among those involved in establishing Isle Royale as a national park were Frank Warren, newspaperman Ben East, and park investigator Frank Oastler.[96] East was one of two newspapermen, the other being Albert Stoll, who led the public crusade to create a national park. East's articles in downstate Michigan newspapers often covered the unusual or seldom-seen parts of Isle Royale. For example, he wrote about "Teddy Roosevelt," a young Isle Royale bull moose captured and displayed at fairs in Michigan before ending up at a Grand Rapids zoo. East wrote about witnessing a rare event of two cow moose battling in his article "Just an Affair between Two Ladies."[97] East eventually became enamored with Linklater and wrote a series of articles about him, one virtually a biography. East touted Linklater's expertise:

> This is John Linklater, Indian guide and dog musher living on Birch Island on the north shore of Isle Royale. Linklater was born in Canada on the north shore of Lake Superior and has lived all his life in moose country. That he is an exceptional woodsman and a clear thinker is evidenced by the fact that he spends his winters as a game warden.

After affirming Linklater's knowledge, East then asked him questions that became the basis of other articles: How many moose are on Isle Royale? Do bull moose charge people? To this last question, Linklater responded that a moose that has not been harassed, cornered, or wounded did not charge people. Others disagreed, though none assumed as Linklater that you approach moose with care, even respect.[98] To back up Linklater's experience with moose, East wrote, "Linklater has succeeded in decoying monster bulls within five feet of his hiding place in the alders. When they come too close you put the [moose] horn down and call under your hat," he explained. "That sends the sound along the ground and confuses them. They can't locate it and they tramp around, searching for the cow."[99] Linklater's answers to East's questions came from firsthand experience. To East and presumably his readership, Linklater was a striking individual:

> If you pay a visit to Isle Royale and fail to get acquainted with this quiet woodsman who knows the wilderness as only those with the blood of wilderness children in their veins know it, then you have missed one of the most interesting experiences to be had on that lonely, rock-girt frontier of Michigan. . . . And when you have landed on John Linklater's dock on lovely Birch Island and seen the spic-and-span cabin that John and his Chippewa wife prize above any city home, when you have listened until late at night to his tales of the north country, you will find it hard to believe you are still on Michigan soil.[100]

East developed a friendship with Linklater such that even in the Linklaters' absence from Isle Royale in 1931, East stayed at their place on Birch Island.[101]

One incident East did not write fully about is illustrative of Linklater's guiding skills, dexterity, and tact. In summer 1930, there was an osprey nest on Monument Rock that was active and had chicks. A few people had climbed the rocky spire to photograph or merely observe the chicks. East, learning of this, wanted to climb the spire and take pictures of them. Leading him, the sixty-year-old Linklater made it to the top, but the young

Ben East did not. Instead, Linklater lowered the chicks in his hat down to East so he could photograph the birds. Then Linklater placed the chicks back on the nest. He never spoke of this. And East never admitted to his readers that he did not make it to the top.[102]

In the midst of scientists, newspapermen, and tourists visiting Birch Island, Linklater and Bill Hanson were trying to fish commercially in Lake Superior. The first summer on Birch Island, a wealthy land-owning family, the Rumelys, had two of their children, Scott and Mary, stay with the Linklaters and Hansons. Scott was nine years old, and he remembered the Hansons "kept a big round barrel of pancake dough starter and ate pancakes all the time. . . . [he then] . . . ate whitefish with the Linklaters till he could stand it no more then he would go over to the [Hansons] and eat pancakes." His older sister remembered that "the old Indian Grandma [Tchi-Ki-Wis] was wonderful."[103] Tchi-Ki-Wis ran the household at Birch

Isle Royale picnic among Tobin Harbor and Rock Harbor cottagers, mid-1920s. Linklater *(far right)* holds a stick that extends the frying pan for cooking pancakes or bannock. Frank M. Warren photograph. Courtesy of University of Minnesota Duluth, Archives and Special Collections.

Island, cooking for many and collecting reindeer moss to stuff the "pleasantly hard" mattresses in the four cabins.[104]

The Hansons, perhaps with help from the Warrens and the Linklaters, bought the fishery in December 1926 from the elderly Captain Francis, who had homesteaded the property. Linklater may have worked for Francis earlier, and he was familiar with the operation.[105] But it was William Hanson's name on the deed, with John Linklater as witness. The purchase price was one dollar, so the real transaction did not appear on the legal description. A number of Isle Royale old-timers assumed that the Warrens bought it for the Linklaters, and Frank Warren did take interest in the property and its value in his diary.[106] "They purchased a large fishing outfit with 6 pound nets, herring, whitefish and 20 trout nets; a forty foot vessel *Superior*, a 23 foot gas boat *U Dine*, and a handful of small boats."[107] The next season, the Linklaters arrived first and got the cabins tidy, hired a couple of men who had previously worked for Francis, worked on the boats (the larger two were pulled up on Indian Point for storage), mended nets, and set them in the water. Bill and Ellen Hanson, newlyweds at the time, arrived in late June. Unlike most island commercial fishermen, they had pound nets, which required a scow and a steam-powered pile driver to thrust poles into the lake bottom.

The pound net wings were hung on the poles, acting as a fence to direct fish toward a "pot" from which they could not escape. Further, their territory included valuable whitefish spawning grounds, rare on the island. Bill and Ellen came to Birch Island only one year, as his game warden position became full-time and their child needed extra care found only on the mainland.[108] The Linklaters, John Robinson, and grandsons ran the fishery through 1930, when Linklater realized he had to work year-round as a game warden or lose his position. His monthly salary in 1933 was $150 a month, a reliable and valuable wage for the time. Converted to today's value, it had the purchasing power of $3,005.[109] With the Depression grinding on, Linklater (coached by Frank Warren, whether he wanted it or not) understood that leaving his game warden job was too much of a financial gamble, particularly as prices for fish had dropped. Linklater did

Two men lift a pound net near McCargoe Cove, circa 1926. John Linklater is in the dory in the background. The Birch Island fishery was unusual among Isle Royale operations in its use of pound nets as well as the more common gillnets. Frank M. Warren photograph. Courtesy of University of Minnesota Duluth, Archives and Special Collections.

not fish again—which he fancied, despite having one incident in which four feet of the bottom of his gas boat opened up while on the Big Lake.[110] In absentia, Hanson held on to the property until the park commission began buying private lots in the mid-1930s (by which time both John and Tchi-Ki-Wis had died).

Even while running the fishery, Linklater became Dr. Frank Oastler's guide on Isle Royale. Oastler's inspection of Isle Royale began in June and July 1929. Through a connection with Mrs. Farmer at Rock Harbor Lodge and Frank Warren, Oastler was paired with Linklater as they camped around the island, at Lake Ritchie, Tobin Harbor, Mud Lake, Raspberry Island, Greenstone Island, and Birch Island, McCargoe Cove. Mrs. Oastler also came along, and Warren sometimes joined them. For more than ten days they traveled around the island, seeing things such as a trap with three or four toes from a brush wolf.[111] Oastler learned of an island dare, to ride a swimming moose, but Linklater declined to do so. In a canoe, Linklater got Oastler close enough to pat a moose on its back, but there was no riding.[112]

John Linklater on a "sea stack" on Isle Royale, 1929. Linklater climbed the sea stack for Dr. Frank Oastler, who was investigating the suitability of Isle Royale as a national park. Courtesy of National Park Service, Isle Royale National Park.

On a successive trip three years later, when Linklater was working as a game warden in the summertime on the mainland, Oastler convinced guide Milford Johnson to ride a moose for fifty dollars. Milford got paid for the harrowing act but stated afterward, "I never want to earn fifty dollars like that again. My hair stuck straight up from my head." They used the Linklater canoe on their trip, and at one point Milford saw it "abused" and how it responded.

> Mrs. Linklater made that [the canoe] for John Linklater. It was pretty when it was new. . . . Anyway, when they unloaded that off the steamer *America* . . . where Pete [Edisen] lives there now. And the Indian [passenger? deckhand?] . . . the front gangway to the water must have been nine feet to the water. They put it in the water and he jumped from the gangway right into the middle of the canoe and it just bobbed right up and down. Boy, if I had done that I would have gone right through it [laughter]. It never took a drop of water in it.[113]

Oastler's report affirmed that Isle Royale was appropriate for national park status. After his time with Linklater and Warren, he became an advocate for their view, saving the archipelago from a moose hunting preserve or being a target for cutting timber. Oastler concluded that the moose were one of the main attractions (and he linked the claim of insufficient food to those interested in hunting).[114]

Perhaps Linklater's greatest contribution to American conservation and wilderness advocacy was his deep influence on Sigurd Olson. Linklater's assistance to Olson in his moose, wolf, and coyote research was but one example of their connection and friendship. They traveled together on at least six camping trips, and they interacted regularly; Olson's Border Lakes Outfitting Company and the Game and Fish station were only one block apart in Winton. Olson's clients sometimes walked down to the station and saw or heard the sled dogs in Linklater's care. Few people knew of Linklater's involvement with Olson's academic endeavors,

Sigurd Olson's Border Lakes Outfitting Company at Winton, Minnesota, circa 1930. The outfitter was located only blocks from the state Game and Fish Station where Linklater worked. Olson Family Collection. Courtesy of David Backes.

but twenty years later Linklater reappeared in Olson's popular writings. Linklater was dead, but Olson brought his memory back in "Wilderness Music," a keystone essay in Olson's first book, *The Singing Wilderness*.[115] Olson mentions Linklater in six of his nine books. For Olson, Linklater was a living bridge to the fur trade past replete with trappers, Indians, voyageurs, clerks, far-flung posts, and canoe travel. Olson wrote in his essay "Immortality" that Linklater "forged a link between me and a nebulous background I had not been aware of," and when Linklater drowned, Olson was "bereft."[116] Olson was also nostalgic and thoughtful about the more recent past. On a canoe trip with his son, they passed Camp 25 on Newfound Lake. Olson recalled being with Linklater and Bill Hanson at the cabin: "How bright that lantern used to be, and how warm and friendly the cabin after a day in the bush."[117]

Olson had a deep appreciation for Linklater's traditional ecological knowledge. Linklater's assistance to Olson in his scientific endeavors was expanded on in his more popular writings. In *Open Horizons,* Olson wrote more dramatically about what he had learned:

Jack Linklater, son of a Scotch factor of Hudson's Bay post and a Cree woman and one of the finest woodsmen I have ever known, felt different.

"In all my life," he told me one night, "I've never known a single instance where a wolf has killed a man. One whiff of our scent and they're gone."

The huskies of our dog team stirred and tugged at their chains. For some reason they were restless.

"The dogs know when they're around," Jack said, looking at the spring moon. "They're close tonight. With all that wolf blood in 'em they can't forget."[118]

Linklater's most significant effect on Olson was as a premier example of someone who was fully attuned to nature and "heard" a more resonant nature than most of us might. The essay "Wilderness Music" centers when Linklater heard spirits "talking" and tried to share that epiphany with Olson:

Last night I followed a ski trail. . . . Breathless after my run, I stopped to rest and listen. . . .

As I stood there leaning on my sticks, I thought of Jack Linklater, A Scotch-Cree of the Hudson's Bay Company. In such a place he would have heard the music, for he had a feeling for the "wee" people and for many things others did not understand. Sometimes when we were on the trail together he would ask me to stop and listen, and when I could not hear he would laugh. Once in a stand of quaking aspen in a high place when the air was full of their whispering, he dropped his pack and stood there, a strange and happy light in his

eyes. Another time, during the harvesting of wild rice when the dusk
was redolent with the parching fires on the shores of Hula Lake, he
called me to him, for he felt that somehow I must hear the music too.
"Can't you hear it now?" he said. "It's very plain tonight."
"I stood there with him and listened, but heard nothing. . . ."
One night we were camped on the Maligne River in the Quetico
on a portage trail used for centuries by Indians and voyageurs. The
moon was full, and the bowl below the falls was silver with mist. As
we sat listening to the roar of Twin Falls, there seemed to be a sound
of voices of a large party making the carry. The sound ebbed and
swelled in volume with the ebb and flow of the plunging water. That
night I thought I heard them, too, and Jack was pleased.[119]

Four times Olson witnessed Linklater hearing something transcendent or
what Olson assumed were spirits talking. Linklater tried to share these
moments with fellow game wardens as well, but like Olson they were
skeptical. Still, Linklater's woodcraft, trust and respect, great experience,
and earnestness swayed Olson and the wardens to listen and try to hear.
Linklater was aware that these non-Indigenous men were skeptical, but
pressed on wanting them to hear it, too. Finally, at Twin Falls, Olson was
tentatively able to share the mystery with Linklater.[120] For Olson, the
experience opened doors for him to consider nature being more than
he might first perceive. Olson was, at minimum, affirming the evocative
power of sounds in woods and how they might transport one's thoughts
and feelings to a different time and place. Linklater, here and elsewhere,
was Olson's guide.

Olson, in turn, sought to explain this experience and Linklater's. His
penchant for seeking spiritual meaning in nature harmonized with this
experience. But he narrowly interpreted it, as to him these spirits were
more like ghosts of people from the past, such as the voyageurs making
the carry at Twin Falls Portage. Olson admitted, in a reach for him, that
the spirits might be of the "wee people" of the Indians, but he did not
know. These experiences and his inclination to question his religious

background, stemming from his childhood with his strict Baptist minister father, challenged him to consider spiritual matters beyond orthodox Christian beliefs.[121] But he did not take this too far.

Even with Olson's empathy toward and interest in what Linklater heard and knew, he was not able to pursue the question of what it was that Linklater was hearing. The question that was beyond Olson's reach was, Which spirits was Linklater hearing? And could they be telling us something that we should heed? Linklater heard the spirits talking in the air, in the rustle of leaves, in rapids, and near an Anishinaabeg camp. It was most likely that Linklater was hearing different spirits.[122] Likely sensing he had pushed Olson far enough, Linklater did not provide greater details about the spirits nearby.[123] The main point Linklater wanted to convey to Olson may have been that nature—including extraordinary places, rocks, plants, waters, and air—was literally alive, and if you could listen, they could talk. A spirit might aid, or hurt, or advise you. Being with Linklater encouraged Olson to reflect about nature, not just understand it. As a "spiritual seeker" Olson acutely pondered what Linklater heard, how he went in the woods, and what he could learn from him.

In his other writings, Olson would come to this same precipice of belief, at least for him. In *Listening Point*, he reported that older Cree Indians believed in *Mannegishi*, or little people.[124] In this specific case, these spirits were seen as well as heard. In his essay "Intuition," Olson went as far as to say, "there is an interplay between the mind of man and inanimate objects."[125] In contrast, for Linklater and traditionally raised Tchi-Ki-Wis, the world was both animate and inanimate. Spirits resided among them. The natural and supernatural worlds were intermingled. Animals in particular had the ability to shape-shift from natural to supernatural and even return to an earlier time and talk to humans. For Olson, notable places, such as Darky Lake, had a palatable character, almost a spirit that would be felt by Linklater and others with heightened sensitivities. Olson was drawn to think about "places that always speak of the unknown."[126] For Olson, this unexplainable yet looming different belief system functioned more as a stimulant to consider a deeper, different nature, rather than one specific to an Anishinaabeg worldview. It served as a push to consider that there might be an unseen and yet undescribed character to nature—a topic frequently explored in his writings. It fit Olson's search "for more" in nature. This experience and familiarity with an Anishinaabeg worldview sharpened his questions and enhanced his readings of contemporary Western philosophers and thinkers. His readings are widely acknowledged. But his attempt to understand the impact of Anishinaabeg belief via his experiences with Linklater also played a significant role in the belief system he was consciously constructing and is evident in his writings.[127]

There is no doubt that Olson felt a closeness to Linklater to the degree that they talked about his family and planned a future trip. Olson wrote: "He had asked me to go with him to visit his mother's people, but something had always interfered." Linklater must have trusted Olson and felt close enough to have broached the idea of visiting his relatives together. Years later, Olson's memory of Linklater was haunting enough that he wrote about a Pelican Narrows Cree leader named Linklater he had met on a canoe trip in the "Lonely Land," and he had "the same bold features, good eyes with a flash of humor."[128] Olson's admiration for Linklater is most evident in two actions: first, Olson gave the eulogy at Linklater's funeral, and second, Olson proposed that the new Izaak Walton League Ely Chapter be named the John Linklater Chapter.[129] Olson believed that naming the new Ike chapter after Linklater was appropriate, but he likely also felt that others did as well. Olson must have further guessed that Linklater's memory was an asset in working to preserve wilderness in canoe country. Linklater's good name was deemed helpful for the cause and perhaps even won the hearts of a few more locals.

EXTRICATING WHAT LINKLATER THOUGHT about nature, animals, lands, and waters is tricky. One clue not yet considered is what little he wrote for public consumption, an essay titled, "An Old Indian Prophecy," published in 1924 in the Minnesota Department of Conservation magazine (the full essay is reprinted following chapter 5 of this volume). Linklater wrote with an archaic style that is very expressive:

The old fellow had a peculiar way of squinting his eyes and looking out over the water as though trying to penetrate the future. I had often noticed this peculiarity. Whether he was trying to arrive at conclusions based on what we might call history handed down by tradition; or whether he was just making a guess at the future, I could never tell.[130]

Evidence from within the story suggests that the "old Indian friend" likely told the prophecy to Linklater before 1900, or more than twenty-four years before the essay was published.[131] At the time of its telling, moose were plentiful in the area, and beaver were quite rare. Thus, his prophecy that moose would disappear and beaver would take their place was predicting a reversal of conditions from when this prophecy was made. In the short term, Linklater's friend was correct; after recovering, moose numbers dropped, and beaver numbers rebounded in the 1920s.[132] As Linklater wrote, "Truly, the old Indian's prophecy is being fulfilled. The moose are vanishing." Prophecies were traditionally used in times of hunger, poor hunting, and community stress. And traditionally elders would be turned to for advice if a problem arose or strange phenomena were encountered, as they were "libraries of the knowledge" for the Anishinaabeg.

"An Old Indian Prophecy" is a window into traditional Anishinaabeg thought and belief, particularly concerning "natural" fluctuation or ecological cycles in populations of animals. The elder left aside for the moment consideration of human impacts; instead he asserted that nature is dynamic too and in this instance does not persist in some equilibrium. Nature fluctuates on its own, populations go up and down, and not just because of the "agency of man." Nature also adapts to change; hence so must humans.

The elder also states that moose will go "to the place whence they came," likely a reference to where moose spirits dwell. This is a very slight, glancing nod to an Anishinaabeg belief: the spirit owners of moose may be calling the moose spirits home, thus depriving the empirical world, the visible world, of moose. The prophecy, as related through Linklater's pen, does not make this later point explicitly. By mentioning human agency, Linklater is referencing the growing belief (among the magazine's readership) in the impacts and changes caused by humans. Neither the elder nor Linklater takes this very far, leaving aside an alternative and traditional idea that human disrespect toward moose—for example, not treating them with care in hunting custom and ritual—might also have the same effect of causing them to disappear from whence they came.[133] But the reader is not left with a feeling of "what went wrong"; instead Linklater closes hopefully with "the moose are vanishing, so let us encourage the species that has come in their place." Linklater is celebrating the return of the beaver "in spite of the most greedy prosecution that any species of wild animal life has known." Ironically, here, as far as his family is concerned, the elder is pointing his finger at fur trade people like the Linklaters as contributing to the wide decimation of beaver in North America.

A beaver dam on the Stuart River, photographed by Walter Breckenridge in 1931. After near decimation during the fur trade, beaver populations in northern Minnesota began rebounding in the 1920s. Courtesy of University Archives, University of Minnesota, Twin Cities.

Linklater, too, was a storyteller of traditional subjects and of his experiences. When tourists came to Birch Island, "Around the campfire he tells them stories of the island; the Indian legends, which inhabited the island with spirits of 'wendigoes' and the speculations of archeologists who have tried to prove that the early miners were Norsemen, who came up the Great Lakes to mine the copper."[134] Linklater had once guided newspaperman and amateur archaeologist William Ferguson, who made an outlandish claim that a Stone Age city was located off Siskiwit Bay, Isle Royale.[135] Linklater mixed the telling of Ferguson's wild tale with what most Whites might think was an equally wild tale—of wendigoes, or Anishinaabeg ice-in-their-heart monsters from the depth of winter that threatened starving men, women, and children. Linklater told other Anishinaabeg and Métis stories, such as that Isle Royale, or Minong, was a floating island that should be approached only properly and respectfully.[136] Non-Indians seized on the "utterly absurd" claim literally and dismissed the legend, yet loved to hear it.[137] Further, he could add personal touches to his stories: As a child, Tchi-Ki-Wis and her grandmother and family paddled across the Big Lake to Minong after ceremonies to appease lake spirits that might make the crossing dangerous, deadly, or calm. He told stories of the trickster Nanabushu behaving outlandishly and irreverently.

In telling these stories to a rapt audience of White listeners, Linklater was acting as a cultural broker, an intermediary, bringing Anishinaabeg legends, beliefs, and artistry to their attention and, he hoped, to their appreciation. It is not clear what they might have learned, but those who reported on the experience were swept away by their enchanting introduction to a different world. Linklater was working as an educator, bringing Anishinaabeg and Métis culture in the most sympathetic fashion to those who knew little about it. In a similar effort, Linklater appealed to readers in a *Fins, Feathers, and Fur* article to protect the Hegman Lake pictographs, asking "that travelers thru this country treat the remaining monument of his people with the respect due their antiquity." Essentially, he argued, even if you don't understand what the pictures on the cliff mean, their antiquity and their connections with "the legends of his race" make them worthy of preservation.[138] Here, Linklater was taking on a familiar role as a cultural educator of newcomers, much like he did with Sigurd Olson.

Linklater was equally at home learning science from professors, thinking about how things are the way they are, and absorbing *aadizookan* (sacred stories) from Anishinaabeg elders. He was intensely curious, with a near photographic memory. His way of knowing about the environment, about grouse and porcupines and how to shoot rapids, was a mix of experience and traditional beliefs from his Métis, Anishinaabeg, and Cree forebears with empiricism akin to science. His penchant for inquiry and his skill in noting natural phenomena were intermixed with knowledge gained from his Indigenous worldview. Thus, for the Linklaters, objects such as the copper found on the Minong Ridge (not far from Birch Island) were alive and had a particular and potent spirit. But to understand copper's physical properties and its presence in rock formations, he was also willing to talk with geologists. What then was this particular suite of knowledge, of reading nature, Linklater was endowed with? What was this traditional ecological knowledge? As one scholar puts it, traditional ecological knowledge is "a cumulative body of knowledge, practice, and belief, evolving by adaptive processes and handed down through generations by cultural transmission, about the relationship of living beings (including humans) with one another and with their environment."[139] Linklater's traditional ecological knowledge was born out of his and his ancestors' long experience in nature. One example of this knowledge was described by one of the people he guided on Isle Royale: "The saplings in many places were trimmed for twelve or fifteen feet above the ground, which Mr. Linklater explained was caused by the moose that in the winter season straddle the tree, push it down, and eat its tender branches. When the weight is removed, the tree straightens up. He also informed us that moose would invariably appropriate a newly blazed trail to their own use."[140]

But his traditional ecological knowledge was not just an addendum to Western science. His knowledge was lodged in a particular way of understanding the world nested in Métis and Anishinaabeg culture. Linklater may have accepted an Anishinaabeg belief that an animal knows when it is being hunted and behaves differently.[141] Unfortunately we have only a snapshot of Linklater's belief system and personal experience, but we do have many examples of his traditional ecological knowledge. For example, when observing a moose eating submerged plants in deep water with "his ears laid back along his head . . . John will tell you that is the way he shut the ear canal and keeps the water out."[142] From a brushy blind, he knew how to call moose in and then "converse" with them close-up.[143] How did he know they wouldn't locate and charge him? He approached moose with Anishinaabeg values of humility and respectful behavior (refusing to harass a swimming moose by riding it). And he did not feel the need to build a barrier to protect him from the moose he was calling, as many with less knowledge might.

Linklater's long experience with moose hunting is demonstrated in another story:

> Among Jack's many admirers is Dr. Fenstermacher, veterinarian at the University Farm, whom we often assisted in securing specimens of animals for laboratory examinations. A story he delights to tell is about a sick moose they had located. Jack got out his rifle and one cartridge, the only one he had. The Doctor suggested going back to town to get more ammunition. Jack nonchalantly asked, "You want only one moose, don't you?"—and so it was.[144]

Stories about Linklater often have a heroic bent, sometimes to the point of incredibility. Still, his friends liked to tell about his surprising strength and steadfastness. His care and concern for Tchi-Ki-Wis is illustrated in a favorite story about him:

> The two were camped one winter at an Indian village up on Poplar Lake, not far from the old Gunflint trail. As an aftermath of child-birth, an abscess formed on his wife's breast. It was an ugly sore, larger than an egg. It was bitter cold, and the closest medical attention was at Grand Marais, 40 miles away.

John Linklater near Winton, Minnesota, spring 1931. Photograph by Walter Breckenridge. Courtesy of University Archives, University of Minnesota, Twin Cities.

Over a campfire, Linklater heated his hunting knife enough to sterilize the blade. He operated on the abscess. Then over the fire, he heated a nail red hot. He cauterized the wound.

On snowshoes they trekked the forty miles to Grand Marais and the doctor. John reportedly carried Tchi-Ki-Wis during the trek when she was unable to walk by snowshoe herself. It was a two day trip.[145] The same story retold in *Earth Never Tires* highlights other points, such as Tchi-Ki-Wis's trust in John's expert way with a knife, her refusal to let a White doctor operate on her breast, and intervention by spirits to guide a successful operation.[146] The story affirmed White progressives' belief that because Indians lived in the "wilds," they developed great strength and indeed were natural athletes.[147]

Unlike so many other Linklater stories, I have found only one version of the following story, recounted in his obituary in the *Minneapolis Tribune*:

The Hudson's Bay Company liked the young half-breed. For some years he worked for them, buying furs up under the Arctic Circle.

So did the provincial authorities, who trusted his honesty and his bravery. Up in Canada, the Indians were being paid off by the government in dollar bills. They paid them that way so they wouldn't spend all their money in a single fling. A bill, to an Indian, was a bill and no more—whether its denomination was $20 or $1.

To John provincial authorities delegated the task of packing the bills to the paymasters, a job not without danger from outlaws. But to him, nothing could happen—unless it was "his day."[148]

Besides expressing the racism of the day (that Indians were incapable of understanding money), the story projects a good deal about Linklater's character: honest and stalwart. The obituary added that "he always made good money, with open generosity, he gave it away . . . if a 'tenderfoot' admired any possession of his—a pair of moccasins, a pair of snowshoes, a parka he was likely to be embarrassed by the persistence with which Jack Linklater insisted upon his accepting it as a gift." With his generosity he affirmed a strongly held Anishinaabeg value.

A favorite story about Linklater was his impromptu Christmas trip to Lac La Croix. A heavy snowstorm impeded travel for several days. Linklater worried that the Lac La Croix kids would miss their Christmas gifts. So he hitched up his dogs, trotted in front of the team, and made it to Lac La Croix to deliver small presents and candy. In one version, he made the trip from Winton to Lac La Croix in one day.[149] While some of the elements to these stories may indeed have been exaggerated, they illustrate the community's admiration for Linklater. The Christmas story is like so many others about him; they were told in a way that non-Indian friends could appreciate, but they leave unsaid and unknown Linklater's connections to Anishinaabeg communities, in this case to Lac La Croix. He was graciously delivering presents to children whom he treasured but also to children to whom he was related. The story captivated two disparate audiences—a fitting measure of Linklater's life.

CHAPTER 5

Making the Carry

JOHN LINKLATER'S LIFE invited stories. And veteran Ely newspaper editor
and storyteller "Jackpine Bob" Cary took up that mantle and ran with it.
Cary wrote a column about strange experiences during the blowdown in
1999 in the Boundary Waters Canoe Area Wilderness, when straight-line
winds crumpled a vast swath of trees from Ely toward Grand Portage.
Cary was inspired by what he knew of Linklater though he had never
met him. Ironically, the blowdown area was largely Linklater's old game
warden territory.[1] The tale begins when an out-of-town newspaper man
writing about the blowdown contacts the seen-it-all Ely newspaper editor.
The young St. Paul newspaper man, looking for a new slant on the blowdown, decides to follow up on the personal side of the event, that no one
was killed, though there were many close calls. Over coffee, while discussing the event with the older editor, the cub reporter says:

> "One thing that kind of struck me during my interview [with campers]
> was that a state conservation officer apparently saved several people
> from disaster . . . but I can't locate the conservation officer."
>
> "You can't?" Charlie [the older editor] focused on the face across
> the table.
>
> "No. There were three different groups who said they were warned
> about the storm by a conservation officer. It was a half hour before
> the storm hit, they all said. Two of the groups were paddling down
> Basswood Lake and this lone canoe man in uniform came up and told

them there was this big storm coming, and they had better head for shore and take cover."

"They said that?"

"Yeah. And the other party . . . let's see . . . it was a guy, his wife and two kids who were coming across the portage into Basswood Lake . . . Prairie Portage. They said this conservation officer told them they had best not go out on the lake but take cover on the shore because a terrible storm was coming. They said they got their canoe and gear down to the beach in front of the Canadian ranger cabin when the storm hit, and the ranger stuck his head out of the door and waved them to come in. They rode out the storm inside the ranger cabin. Said the conservation officer probably kept them from drowning."

Charlie motioned the waitress for a refill. "What can I do for you?" he asked Brewer.

"Well, I can't find that conservation officer. I thought it would be a terrific angle for my article . . . like how did he know the storm was coming when nobody else did."

"Did you check with the Department of Natural Resources?"

"Sure did. Drove out to the D.N.R. office on Route 88. They said they didn't have anybody patrolling Basswood Lake the day of the storm."

"It all happened on Basswood?"

"Sure. Just like I said. The people I talked to say the conservation officer was a dark, wiry guy, medium height, with a clipped black mustache. Maybe fifty-six years old."

"I don't know any officer like that." Charlie scratched his chin. "Did they get his name?"

"Yeah, wait a minute." Brewer glanced at his notes. "They said he had a brass name tag over the pocket of his uniform with the name 'J. Linklater' on it."

Charlie felt a tingle shoot down his neck and sat bolt upright. "You sure?"

"Sure I'm sure. I wrote it down in my notes . . . right here."

"Did they say where the conservation officer went?"

"That was another funny thing," Brewer frowned. "The people paddling down the lake didn't see him coming. All of a sudden he caught up with them, and after he warned them about the storm he sort of vanished."

"Vanished?"

"Well, they didn't see where he went. Same for the family coming over the portage. They talked with him maybe a minute, and then it was like he wasn't there anymore."

"And another thing." Brewer added. "When I mentioned this to staff out at the Natural Resources office, they looked at each other kind of funny. Said they never heard of an officer by that name. You ever hear of him?"

"Uh huh," Charlie said, draining his coffee cup. "Yeah, I heard of him."

"You know where I can find him?"

"No, not right now."

After promising the rookie reporter he would contact him if he located Linklater, the editor goes back to his office, looks through his old files, and finds one labeled "Linklater, Jack." The file contains letters from Jack's colleagues and basic biographical information.

The final entry, on a worn sheet of paper, was a coroner's report signed by Robert Opel, Winton, MN: "Jack Linklater, age 67, died July 8, 1933, when his canoe overturned in a windstorm on Basswood Lake." There was an attached note which said, "Old Ojibwe people on Lac La Croix have a superstition that the spirit of Jack Linklater still roams the border lakes."

The editor, reading this last bit of information, thinks of the young reporter and his promise to contact him, shrugs, tears up the contact information, and drops it into the wastebasket.

While taking more than a few factual liberties, Cary's story captures a number of essential truths about Linklater, all the while concluding that the young newspaper man wouldn't get it, wouldn't understand. Cary's portrayal is accurate: Linklater was concerned and helpful to others in the woods. He could read nature's "signs" like few others, and he often appeared unannounced among poachers. Even in his death, he was part of Basswood Lake and the canoe country. And he was intimately linked to the Lac La Croix people. The fact that no one was killed by the blow-down was about as miraculous to Cary as the spirit of Linklater aiding area campers.

Linklater's death, inexplicable to many who knew him, inspired different theories of what may have happened on Jackfish Bay, midday, July 8, 1933. The official coroner's report concluded he died of "accidental drowning."[2] That part was obvious; what caused the drowning was not. His death, by a canoe mishap—albeit a canoe with a motor but not far offshore—was unthinkable to his friends. Some believed he must have had a heart attack prior to the canoe capsizing. Others thought his canoe hit a deadhead (a submerged log) that caused the boat to overturn. Others blamed it on high seas and/or an overloaded canoe. Only one timidly blamed it on Linklater taking a chance in the rough water.[3] Many accounts suggest Linklater, like many Indians at the time, did not know how to swim, making this the take-home point for those who might read or hear of his death. In a few accounts, while in the water, Linklater had the presence of mind to tell Tchi-Ki-Wis to swim for shore.[4] One of the two most credible accounts, by Mary Anderson, who stayed with Tchi-Ki-Wis after the drowning and surely talked to her about it, reported that "he hit a deadhead."[5] And since Anderson was a fluent Anishinaabemowin speaker staying with Tchi-Ki-Wis, this is virtually a firsthand account.

The other highly credible account was by Joe Brickner, who was traveling with the Linklaters earlier that day and saw Tchi-Ki-Wis soon after the tragedy. Eleven years after the event he wrote that the three were traveling together:

.

[We] continued our trip over Fall Lake. Jack's wife was with us, on her way home to their cabin on Basswood Lake. While packing the canoe over the Newton Lake portage, I slipped and seriously injured my back. At Pipestone Falls Jack insisted that I remain there and rest my injury. He would take his wife home and return for me. It was noon and he waved a farewell from the canoe—that is vivid in my memory. Afternoon passed slowly. About six o'clock a canoe party came over the portage. The guide told me of an over-turned canoe he thought belonged to our department. I secured a boat and motor and soon found the canoe. At the Linklater cabin some miles down the lake I found Mrs. Linklater. I learned the tragic story of the canoe over-turning a short distance from shore. She said Jack appeared stunned and she helped him take hold of the canoe. He told her to make for shore but when she reached shore Jack had disappeared. When the body was found, there was a bruise on the forehead and I am inclined to believe it was caused by the motor striking him while over-turning and stunning him, as Mrs. Linklater had suggested.[6]

Linklater's friend and boss Bill Hanson led efforts to recover the body. And even in this sad endeavor, Linklater was prescient. According to family lore, Linklater had once told his son-in-law, "if I drown, don't look for me for three or four days."[7] The body was recovered days after the drowning not far from where the tragedy took place. Hanson was staggered by his friend's death and would later remark: "I never thought John would get into a condition where he couldn't take care of himself." He added, "I'm not sure what exactly happened but something went wrong someplace and he couldn't recover himself."[8]

Hanson's sentiment was near universal. Linklater's untimely death did not make sense to most people. How could such a wiry and nimble canoe man die so unexpectedly?[9] Linklater could expertly handle canoes, traveled in all kinds of conditions while pursuing grizzled and threatening poachers, and dealt with fights among his mushing dogs: why couldn't he have saved himself from a canoe flipping so close to shore?

SEVERAL OF HIS WHITE FRIENDS thought Linklater's belief in fate, as they understood it, was the key to understanding his death. Further, they would add, that belief in fate stemmed from Linklater's Indigenous belief in dreams, particularly taught to him by his mother. So they would report what Linklater said to them; it either was or wasn't "his day" to die.[10] Linklater's friends called this belief "fatalism" and cited it as one source of his courage to confront an illegal trapper with a gun pointed at him or shoot a rapids alone. In this way of thinking, the when and how of Linklater's death was out of his hands, nor did it seem that he could fight to prevent it. But they also noted he wasn't reckless: while on the water, "the long way and the safe way was his."[11] He did not customarily expose himself to undue risk.

While visions or dreams likely informed Linklater's life, we know little about them. The fragmentary accounts presumed Linklater dreamed of his impending death. But Anishinaabeg dreams can be a warning, or advisory. They are not understood as setting fate; rather the dreamer may be given a momentary window to see future events. And some events foreseen in dreams did not necessarily happen if they were held off by ritual or a personal guardian spirit (generally originating in a vision quest). Thus, some events foretold in bad dreams were not inevitable; they were not fated.[12] Complicating understanding is Linklater's great reluctance to speak openly of his dreams, as was Anishinaabeg custom. Absent this knowledge of Anishinaabeg culture, his White friends wondered whether Linklater knew he was meeting his day. Is that why, when in the water, he had the presence of mind to tell Tchi-Ki-Wis to swim for shore, telling her he was safe but really knowing he would die? These same friends also thought that Linklater's dreams—and his Indian heritage bestowed on him by his mother—gave him extra powers.

More likely than any strict fatalism (absent in Anishinaabeg and Métis belief systems), Linklater accepted death in a way that was foreign to his White friends. From his life, he knew from death (such as properly hunting moose or lifting a gillnet of writhing whitefish) came life. Honoring life as Linklater did was to accept death. His dreams, understood in an Anishinaabeg context, may have taught him to be comfortable with his eventual death. And ultimately, his dreams and cardinal beliefs were Anishinaabeg/ Métis beliefs, particularly if a spirit guardian was part of how Linklater understood and operated in the world. His vision was not accessible to his non-Indian friends, but Linklater's actions speak more to central Anishinaabeg values and beliefs than fatalism. Bravery, humility, and respect are three of the seven Anishinaabe grandfather teachings. Linklater's friends' prescription of fatalism was more of a guess about Linklater's motivations and actions, which were unfathomable to them, just as the spirits he heard in the winds at dusk were beyond what Sigurd Olson could hear or understand. However sympathetic his non-Indigenous friends were to him, they could not fully contemplate or understand his beliefs. To paraphrase what newspaperman Ben East once said about Linklater, while he thought in English, his beliefs and his real perception of the world were Indigenous—intrinsically spiritual but also empirically based and rational.[13] How Linklater combined his tendency to seek out "whys"— why moose on the mainland were behaving differently than those on Isle Royale, for example—with animistic perspectives stumped his White friends. But this mix was not unique to Linklater and is inherent in a Cree hunter who seeks prey in a traditional fashion.

While his friends tried to make sense of his death, the shock of it spread widely. The news was carried by the associated press and published in at least twenty-two newspapers across the country.[14] A typical announcement came from an Alabama newspaper:

Famous Guide Dies . . . WINTON, Minn. (AP)—Jack Linklater was on the Great Portage Tuesday; a portage across the Great Divide whence none return. The north woods most noted guide, woodsman and game warden, drowned in Jackfish Bay near here Sunday. His sturdy wife, a full-blooded Chippewa Indian, swam to shore after a squall upset their canoe. Sixty-seven years ago Linklater was born, the son of a Scotch father of Hudson Bay and a Cree woman. For the last 10 years he had been a state game warden.[15]

His funeral service in a one-room Winton church was packed with mourners. State wardens served as pallbearers, and Sigurd Olson gave a eulogy. He was buried in the Ely Cemetery, according to some, the first Indian to be buried there. A month after his death, the *Minneapolis Sunday Tribune*, at the insistence of his many well-to-do friends, ran a full-page obituary.

Less well known, prior to Linklater's death in 1933 and Tchi-Ki-Wis's death in 1934, was the fact that they had both been ill. Linklater had been weakened by pneumonia in the winter.[16] He had also suffered from rheumatism for some time.[17] Tchi-Ki-Wis had been ill the winter before, and she had even temporarily moved from Jackfish Bay to her daughter Clara's home in Embarrass, Minnesota, for some of late winter 1932. Tchi-Ki-Wis also had some undiagnosed chronic illness that made her uncomfortable.[18] John Robinson, Tchi-Ki-Wis's father, had also been ill during fall 1932.[19] All of them had lived a vigorous, physical life, sometimes with little lag or recuperative time. By the early 1930s, their health had caused them all to slow down.

JOHN'S DEATH hit Tchi-Ki-Wis hard. While efforts were ongoing to recover his body, she was heard keeping a vigil with a "death chant." A chant for a traditionalist like Tchi-Ki-Wis was to "ritually sing the soul over to the next cycle of existence."[20] According to some, Tchi-Ki-Wis never got over his death. She even remarked to Mary Anderson, a younger Anishinaabe woman, that losing her husband was the worst thing to happen to her.[21] Sixteen months after Linklater's death, she collapsed at their Jackfish Bay home and die of myocarditis, or "organic heart disease."[22] Anderson reflected that Tchi-Ki-Wis "died of a broken heart." Only six months later, John Robinson, Tchi-Ki-Wis's father, died in a "poor house" in Duluth. Clara Linklater Wirta died soon thereafter in November 1935 of a heart ailment. Grandson Frankie Nelson moved to Michigan in the Depression, then joined the service to fight in World War II. He eventually settled in Texas. John's sister, Alice Wakemup, lived on but was distanced from surviving members of John's family. In a matter of three years, four generations of the family had walked on or were effectively gone. The era of Linklaters who lived and knew Jackfish Bay intimately was over. And for the young Wirta kids, this meant they were cut off from their Indian past. This rupture in family history likely led to a number of the spurious family stories, such as John's father having a second wife and family, that William went home to Scotland, and that John was born in North Dakota.[23]

The passing of the Linklaters is also a marker of the end of a tradition of Anishinaabeg going to Minong and living on the island, largely on their terms. Today Grand Portage Anishinaabeg continue to go to Isle Royale to fish and gather plants, or to work on the ferries, but few stay there long. As it turns out, 1933 was the watershed year of change for Indian use of the island. John had died, and Tchi-Ki-Wis could not make it to Minong. Across the "Indian Portages" on the south-central part of the island, Adam Roach LaPlante, a Grand Portage Band member and hired man at the Holger Johnson fishery and resort, drowned in May 1933. Adam Roach and his grandmother, Mary LaPlante, had worked for the Johnsons' mom-and-pop resort on Chippewa Harbor, teaching the Johnson kids how to make birch-bark items to sell to tourists.[24] The end of the era of Anishinaabeg residence on the island is paralleled by the end of woodland caribou on Minong. Linklater noted in 1930, his final year on the island, that "the last caribou is gone from Isle Royale."[25]

Ben East's articles go as far as asserting the Linklaters' "Indianness" was a fundamental part of Isle Royale's character. East documented Tchi-Ki-Wis's craft work and in a *National Geographic* article included a photograph of the Linklaters in front of their Birch Island fishery. For East, there was a connection between the Indian prehistoric past and the Linklaters. This link assumes a historic presence of "Chippewa" on the island. East made this clear in his photograph caption: "An Isle Royaler and his Chippewa Wife."[26] Sadly, once the park was established, the National Park Service (NPS) did not see or endorse this historic presence. After the Linklaters' deaths, their place was abandoned and well used by Civilian Conservation Corps men and strangers. Under management by the NPS, no maintenance work protected the cabins. Eventually, the NPS deemed these "trappers' cabins," in dilapidated shape, were not important enough to maintain. One park official wrote: "The structure is of dubious value in interpreting the history of the park."[27] In 1967, after the cabins were struck from the inventory of historic structures, they were burned.[28] The lack of knowledge that the Linklaters were Native Americans and about the use of Minong by modern Anishinaabeg meant the last visible signs of Indian use of Isle Royale were destroyed. The Linklater home on Jackfish Bay did not fare any better. In the early 1950s, the Hoffman/Cook family buildings were burned (to keep illegal trappers from using them), and the Linklater place was dismantled and left to rot.[29] The idea, in both protected areas, that the Anishinaabeg had a home place in the wilderness was a concept beyond the conceptual reach of most government conservation officials.[30] The result was that evidence of the Linklaters' presence in these areas was effectively erased.[31]

Bob Cary wrote so that the Linklaters would be remembered. His story works in great part because of the mystery of Linklater's death and the marvel of his life. Still, there is so much we don't know that might help us understand the Linklaters. There are, too, what could provisionally be called "maybe stories," or those that were told but cannot yet be veri-fied.[32] For example, one abbreviated story was that Linklater came to the border country from farther north, the Albany River country. This was symbolically true as he came from Lac Seul, though it is not part of the Albany River watershed. But did he temporarily work for the HBC on the Albany, the old stomping grounds of his grandparents?[33] This leads to another question: how connected was Linklater to his mother's family at Lac Seul? He was connected enough that he had planned to canoe there with Sigurd Olson long after his mother had passed on.

According to a stray comment from friend Ben East, Linklater guided and served as an interpreter on two expeditions into "Cree country."[34] No definitive confirmation has yet been found, but the claim is credible. One possible expedition was a six-month timber and geologic survey of northwestern Ontario for the province in 1900—about the right time. The expedition ended so late, the men had to pull their canoes across

The Linklaters in front of their Birch Island fishery with a model canoe made by Tchi-Ki-Wis. A similar photograph was published in Ben East's *National Geographic* article about Isle Royale, December 1931. Courtesy of the Wirta family.

frozen lakes. The expedition cook and guide was a John James Linklater, most often just called Linklater in the published reports; he was a boon to the endeavor.[35] However, the expedition was organized in Kenora/Rat Portage, where a second John James Linklater (also a woods-wise Métis) lived at the time. Which J. J. Linklater was along on this expedition? The signatures on payroll notes appear to match Linklater's handwriting. If it was Linklater, it gave him another opportunity to travel the waterways of his mother, grandfather, father, and their families.

The most central event to the Linklaters' lives that we know little about is their young daughter Maggie's death. The tragedy still begs questions. Why is there no documentation of her death? Why didn't Linklater's powerful White friends help if there was something nefarious about it? Or did those relationships bloom after this tragedy, and thus they were not available to assist John and Tchi-Ki-Wis at the time? Did this experience reinforce Tchi-Ki-Wis's reticence and her carefully maintained distance from White neighbors?[36] Most important, how did this tragedy, when Maggie was only twenty years old, shape their lives? How did it affect their relationship, their communications? It clearly did not break or diminish their devotion to one another, but there is little evidence to say more.

The circumstances around Maggie's death demonstrate the ever-present prejudice toward Indians at the time. A White teenager's death in Winton would have been recorded and the subject of a newspaper article or obituary. Friend Mary Anderson stated: "I don't think Linklater would have gotten the job as a game warden . . . in the early days [in the Ely area]."[37] Mary, having lived through this era, was alluding to the widespread bias against Indians at the time. This is another way of noting Bill Hanson's exceptional confidence in Linklater. But aside from that confidence Hanson had in him, Linklater must have felt an added pressure to get things right, as he was further scrutinized as an Indian. And he was as good as or better than his game warden peers, all the while being helpful and collegial with them.

Some of Linklater's "surprising" talents, at least to those who knew him at the time, such as being adept with a camera, contain an implicit con-

John Linklater holds an improvised ladder set up for Frank Warren to photograph chicks in a nest on Isle Royale, 1925. Frank M. Warren photograph. Courtesy of University of Minnesota Duluth, Archives and Special Collections.

trast about his "Indianness." While it is hard to know which of the Frank Warren photographs and movies Linklater took, Warren often credited him. Warren paid for their development and had copies made to aid in his conservation interests. And the Linklaters' relative comfort with Warren led to some candid photographs at Birch Island—where Tchi-Ki-Wis and her father are shown fooling around and laughing.[38] Linklater being both "traditional" and a handy camera man astounded newspaper man East, the implicit assumption being that Indians could not do both or be that "advanced." Echoing the social Darwinism of the day, East noted that Linklater evolved from the bow and arrow of his youth, to guns, to a camera. Again, implicit was the question, how could such an individual "evolve" so quickly? Not acknowledged was that Linklater was a quick learner, for example, that he became a safe and knowledgeable boat pilot on the rough waters of Lake Superior in a short time.[39]

Both John and Tchi-Ki-Wis were typically judged through the lens of whether they were "good," "bad," or "real" Indians. In some ways they did not conform to society's expectation of "good" Indians. Early in their marriage they lived a nomadic life of hunting and gathering and were thus perceived as uncivilized. They were not agriculturalists; they did not work the land. Ironically, they were "landed," attached to Jackfish Bay, deeply knowing and appreciating its landscape and bounty. But they were rarely thought to be equal to White folks, Tchi-Ki-Wis especially. Tchi-Ki-Wis was more often seen as a "real Indian," as her appearance more closely matched the expectations of Whites at the time.[40]

The Warrens' relationship with the Linklaters, and especially with John, who they spent much more time with, is complicated. The Warrens appreciated Linklater, in part, for his loyalty and steadfastness, hard work, and outdoor know-how. Frank Warren's relationship with him was one of both a supposed superior and a friend. Frank's paternalism toward Linklater was both selfless (getting him life insurance and looking after Tchi-Ki-Wis after John's death) and selfish (demanding Linklater guide them rather than Rock Harbor Lodge guests). For example, Tchi-Ki-Wis assisted the wife of a man who died of a heart attack. The Stellwagens were friends of the Warrens, prompting Frank to write to John. "Tell Tchee-keewis that I think she is a splendid, brave woman and that we were very proud of her. I send a little present to her in this letter."[41] Warren felt compelled to make a positive judgment of Tchi-Ki-Wis's actions with the grief-stricken Mrs. Stellwagen. But Frank also thought of Linklater as his best friend.[42] And in a well-cared-for Warren family album devoted to their distinguished forbearers (all White and well-to-do) there is a large print of Tchi-Ki-Wis. The iron mine titleholder and "Indian" became good friends despite their far-reaching differences in wealth and cultural background. Frank loved to tell the story about when Linklater was in Minneapolis and the Warrens took him to their church, the Plymouth Congregational Church with its gothic arches, cut-stone walls, and heavy wooden beams. When the offering plate was passed around, Warren put money in and then passed the collection plate to Linklater. He reached into his wallet and pulled out a five-dollar bill and put it in the plate. Then he reached in and took four dollars in change. Clearly Linklater understood the offering custom, but he had a stronger sense of what was appropriate for him and unabashedly did it in the presence of the Warrens and any other elite churchgoers who might see.[43]

SIMILAR TO THE COURSE of many people's lives, a whole sequence of events contributed to John Linklater eventually making his way to Lac La Croix and meeting Tchi-Ki-Wis. John's great-grandfather coming to James Bay and the HBC is an essential part of John's story. Those tough times propelled William Linklater I to leave his homeland and family for a hoped-for better future. John's grandfather William Linklater II's rise in the HBC ranks was atypical, but his drowning death was not. The young family then sought a restart in Red River at the worst of times—food was scant, and the Métis Rebellion was palpable. The tragedy of John's grandmother's pregnancy and her death was but one event that hastened the dispersal of his uncles and aunts from Red River country. The economic, political, social, and military put-down and disenfranchisement of the Red River Métis added further reason to leave Red River. Away, in the bush and small settlements, the Linklater siblings gathered, often in pairs with their spouses and families. William Thomas Linklater, John's father, and his sibling closest in age, auntie Margaret, or Maggie Swampy, now a member of Fort Alexander First Nation, saw a good deal of one another. The family's experience in many distant places and among many people equipped John with linguistic skills and a geographic base of knowledge to draw on in his adulthood.

Both John and his uncle Charlie were mere toddlers on their first long canoe trips—what we today might consider "epic" trips. Every year of his life he was in a canoe traveling throughout the North Country. In all the photographs of him, he is always in the stern of the canoe, the position which steers the canoe. He was a sternman, a position that acknowledged his mastery of a life defined by canoes and canoe waters. He truly was the son of a canoe man and an Anishinaabe mother fluent in their culture and use. John's maternal side endowed him with Anishinaabeg heritage of which he was deeply appreciative. It also gave him a love of place of their homeland on the Canadian Shield. He absorbed Anishinaabeg lifeways and traditional ecological knowledge; he was curious, learning day by day, and he excelled at getting along in the bush. He was uncomfortable in cities and content in the boreal forest. He and Tchi-Ki-Wis did not want to live on the reserve at Lac La Croix. Given a choice, they preferred to live away from modernity—boomtowns, money and banks, Indian agents, legal arrangements. They appear to have minimized the boarding school experience of their children and Frank Nelson. For example, in 1918, seven-year-old Frankie had not yet attended school, nor did he attend in 1919–20.[44] When they had to, on occasion they rented a place in Winton, bought a car, and wrote letters to friends, though John never had a "street" address other than where he worked.[45] John most commonly rode the railway to Duluth to take a lake vessel to Isle Royale, rather than paddle to the North Shore to catch the ship in Grand Marais or Grand Portage. But whenever they could, they resorted to their life on Jackfish Bay, close to plentiful fish, game, and wild rice, close to other Anishinaabeg friends and families, and away from the prejudice of White society.

Linklater's many affluent White friends saw him as a romantic hero. Further, they thought, they might never meet people like the Linklaters again, as they were the embodiment of vanishing, authentic Indians.[46] He was inspiring, different from them, but safe to the degree of being approachable and overtly loyal. They trusted him. Frank Warren believed that if need be, Linklater would have gladly given up his life for him.[47] They hung on Linklater's sparse words, such as when he called the northern lights the "Breath of the Great Spirit."[48] Ultimately, Linklater as a romantic, one-of-a-kind figure had perhaps his strongest appeal to conservationists such as Sigurd Olson, Ben East, Dr. Frank Oastler, and Frank Warren. He was interesting to travel with and to learn from, whether about nature, Anishinaabeg and Métis language, or lore.

Linklater's keen observational skills, interest in learning from elders, curiosity about nature, and lifetime thinking about plants, animals, waters, and terrain produced a deep well of traditional ecological knowledge that was widely recognized by others. His friend Bill Hanson plainly stated: "He had a hunting instinct. . . . He could read signs [even] on beaver dams."[49] Linklater had a long view of animal cycles, ups and downs, for a time span beginning before his birth, evident in his writing.[50] Listening to elders added depth of time but also conferred a historical and cultural context

John Linklater and an unidentified woman (likely a Warren family member) in front of a Ford Model T, late 1910s. John is formally dressed and appears to be the driver of the car. Frank M. Warren photograph. Courtesy of University of Minnesota Duluth, Archives and Special Collections.

to biological knowledge.[51] Animals and plants were not just objects to be used; they were teachers and gifts. He assumed these animals, plants, rocks, and waters existed in relationships that are best understood and respected.[52] Even the different Anishinaabemowin names for plants and animals—a language weighted toward verbs—often pointed out relationships. But Linklater was also a great believer in direct observation and questioning—were moose eating balsam fir for winter browse on Isle Royale?—and then testing by repeated observations, or essentially trial and error.[53] Linklater's traditional ecological knowledge was not static or just an accumulation of facts. Changes, such as the northward movement of caribou out of Minnesota and from Isle Royale, begged further questions, observations, and testing out responsive explanations. Traditional ecological knowledge was a method of appreciating the plants, animals, and the specific place that he chose to make his home.

LIKE THEIR ANISHINAABEG and Métis relatives and friends, the Linklaters were swept into a torrent of change. In their lifetimes they faced the coming of railroads and railroad men, Dawson Trail laborers and soldiers, Métis disenfranchisement and diaspora from Red River, and the increasing habitation of northern towns by non-Natives. They lived through the power, whims, and alienating reality of nearby Indian agents, treaty annuities, enforcement of reserves and reservations, and the international border. Indians were told to stay on the reservations, whether American or Canadian, and give up their traditional religion. All around them, the cutting of the white and red pine stripped the landscape of fragrant, shaggy, and towering trees. Linklater, needing work to raise his family, worked in dangerous jobs getting logs to the hungry sawmills at Winton. In courtrooms and formal hearings, lumber baron Edward Backus schemed of damming much of the western boundary water lakes to float more trees to market. If the dams had been permitted and built, the backed-up waters on Lac La Croix, for example, would have been raised eighteen feet.[54] Dams would have inundated the portages, lakeshores, and Anishinaabeg villages, much of what the Linklaters loved, knew, and had assumed would stay the same. Cataclysmic change, such as the threat of flooding by dams and the Métis struggles at Red River, are a constant backdrop to the Linklaters' lives.

Part of this sweeping tide of contemporary forces was the rise of conservation as it was applied to the North Country. It was a double-edged sword for the Linklaters. Like all other border lakes Anishinaabeg, they were powerless to stop this idea, which in its most extreme form led to the eviction of the Sturgeon Bay, or Kawawaigamok, people from Quetico Provincial Park and extinguishment of their Reserve #24C.[55] Tchi-Ki-Wis's relatives and friends were forced from their winter camp in the center of Quetico. The advent of the park meant the Kawawaigamok and Lac La Croix people's way of life, honed through centuries of living in this place, was deemed of little importance, and their traditional movements to harvest plants and animals were no longer acceptable. An Indian agent similarly removed a number of Basswood Lake Anishinaabeg, making

sure they returned to reservations and reserve lands, as the living wilderness was to be emptied of people.[56] Misguided conservation measures
such as trapping and poisoning wolves for bounty (thus supposedly protecting deer and moose) were put into effect. Making do, like so many
others in the North Country, Linklater trapped wolves for their bounty.
He likely was relieved when he learned a faction of scientists, including
his friend Sigurd Olson, disputed the wisdom of poisoning and trapping
wolves.[57] But he also likely learned conservationists could be as fickle as
their theories.

How did Linklater reconcile the brutal eviction of the Kawawaigamok and extinguishment of their reserve with conservation ideals and
his efforts? To be sure, he took no part in this cruel expulsion, but as a
game warden he was enforcing laws shaped in good measure by powerful
sportsmen and often at the expense of Indians. This was a deeply personal
question for him; it was not, however, for the well-to-do Euro-American
conservationists such as Frank Warren. For the Linklaters, it was also a
pressing question, linked with having food to eat and money to live on.
One small way Linklater could exercise his conservation ideals and human
sympathies was in the discretion given to him as a game warden. Linklater
did not arrest those who were struggling, those who were hungry. He knew
about hunger and large unrelenting forces on people, Indian and Métis
people in particular. He participated in efforts to establish a protected Isle
Royale because it had the promise of safeguarding moose, plants, and a
unique place. Moose were threatened on the mainland with sickness and
ticks, so protecting them on the island made sense. Whether a grandiose
park idea motivated him, we don't know, but there is no evidence that he
engaged in related political battles. For his non-Native friends, the discussion of the park idea was more abstract and divorced from the world Linklater experienced and knew. Conservation was a battleground of elites,
but many of those same elites often deferred to his biological knowledge.
He thrived in wild places, but like many whom he guided, he did not
forsake people—Anishinaabeg—who lived in and were an integral part
of those places. At the same time, he and Tchi-Ki-Wis cared deeply about

moose, healthy wildlife, and a diversity of plants, as a welcome presence in the country and as an anchor to their culture. Isle Royale's diversity of plants was a boon to their way of life, as Tchi-Ki-Wis gathered roots to dye cedar mats and to make medicine. John must have listened to professors talk of then nascent scientific concepts about ecological processes, but he already knew and felt the relationships of plants, animals, and people. He once talked of the not easily seen interrelationship of deep snow, porcupines, cedar, deer, and bobcat to one White conservationist.[58]

Linklater's long association with powerful Whites such as the Warrens, professors, and the Minnesota Game and Fish commissioner protected him and his family in indirect ways. Those friendships and his competence helped him keep his job when the Depression ground on. And the Warrens paid Linklater relatively well when he was with them. While we will never know for sure, those friendships (and his mixed ancestry) were likely a factor in the Linklaters and Hoffmans being left alone on Jackfish Bay, unlike several of their Anishinaabeg neighbors. But there were limits and trade-offs to those friendships and associations. After the Linklaters stopped coming to their fishery, John's influential friends did not keep their Birch Island possessions from being thrown out into a swamp and their fishing boats and equipment from being vandalized.[59] Nor were these friends able to protect a teenage Margaret Linklater from an unscrupulous White logger who impregnated her, perhaps ill-treated her, and certainly abandoned her and her baby. The Linklaters' friendship with the Warrens and others could be exasperating at times when they became overbearing or patronizing.

Literally, the Superior National Forest and Quetico Forest Reserve were created around and on top of the Linklaters' chosen home. They felt the real impacts and limitations of this conservation effort. But as far as we can tell, it did not embitter them. Linklater still became a mentor to many. To Sigurd Olson and other area conservationists, Linklater was an inspiration. He knew more about being in the woods and on the water than anyone they had met (and he was a gifted camp cook). Linklater's keen observational skills were highly acclaimed and made him a sought-

Camp scene at Isle Royale with John Linklater holding a frying pan and Alice Warren in tent, circa 1924. Frank M. Warren photograph. Courtesy of University of Minnesota Duluth, Archives and Special Collections.

after guide—for Aldo Leopold, no less. Olson and others looked forward to spending time with Linklater. For Olson, Linklater was a living embodiment of border lakes history and lore, the traders, their epic voyages, and exploration. Talking or better yet traveling with Linklater was to be "embedded" with the past not in an anachronistic way but in a living, vivid, practical, and surprising sense. Linklater's influence was also quietly felt behind the efforts to create Isle Royale National Park as he boosted the knowledge base of park enthusiasts.

Linklater was more than fifty years old when he collaborated most with numerous scientists, and his trapping, trading, and logging days were behind him. He regularly assisted their scientific field work in the boundary waters and on Isle Royale, locating archaeological sites, ill moose, rare plants, birds, and animals. He provided information on animal behavior and distribution of animals and plants. For Olson, he charted hundreds

of miles of wolf trails and annotated a map with comments, such as that
the Nina Moose and Little Indian Sioux country was "Best wolf country
also best moose country" (Plate 16).[60] Linklater's estimates on wolf density
in the boundary waters were indirectly affirmed later by one of Olson's
students, biologist Milt Stenlund. In his memoir, Stenlund noted "how
remarkable his [Olson's] estimates were, despite the lack of specific census
techniques, airplanes, and radio telemetry."[61] But Olson's estimates were
not his alone; he was heavily dependent on Linklater's freely given knowledge. As so often was the case, Linklater's scientific contributions were
unrecognized and a surprise to those who did not know him.

While assisting in scientific fieldwork, Linklater and his companions
discussed research ideas as they solved pressing problems. The Linklaters
regularly hosted scientists by providing food, gear, and shelter. Generally,
they looked out for their well-being. Linklater also provided geographical

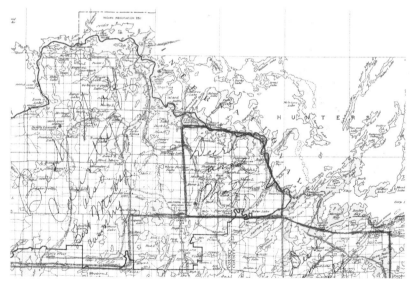

Detail of a map showing wolf trails and areas of high concentrations of moose and deer
in the boundary waters, circa 1927. Linklater mapped these trails and areas for Sigurd
Olson. Courtesy of the Minnesota Historical Society.

help and transportation in navigating the surrounding woods and waters. On an initial research trip of University of Minnesota veterinarians, Linklater drove them to a remote camp and helped get them ready, piloted them with a dog team to Ensign Lake, and later guided them on a canoe trip. Having Linklater along ensured a high level of comfort and competence for the often young and inexperienced scientists.

Because of the adversity he and Tchi-Ki-Wis faced, John was grateful for being treated equally, and thus he possessed "a deep appreciation for any favor, regardless of how trivial."[62] Further, this appreciation and strong belief in reciprocity among people was congruent with his similarly strong respect for nonhuman beings.

THE LINKLATERS lived remarkably productive lives, despite facing a crush of change and threats to their way of life. They persevered. Tchi-Ki-Wis continued to make beautiful, geometric cedar mats and well-crafted and necessary objects like dog harnesses and moccasins. She and John likely introduced parkas to the Ely area. They practiced cardinal Anishinaabeg values, such as generosity to others, even if it left them short of a parka or meant sharing their last wild rice while on trail. It was their resiliency in the face of threats, changes, and pressures that stands out. John was also resilient as a teacher—about fish, moose, traveling, the natural world, and Anishinaabeg and Métis lifeways. But few friends and acquaintances wholly understood his teachings about Indigenous lifeways or even accurately captured his words.[63] He felt a deep drive to communicate about the dignity of Indigenous people and how they lived, and to offer a glimpse into what they thought. John and Tchi-Ki-Wis were remarkable in their humility, each finding a way to teach or assist others without drawing attention to their efforts. For years, John routinely mushed the perimeter of the boundary waters with a dog team, doing warden work that is barely noted in records. And before dog teams were common in the Ely–Winton area, Linklater ran two teams, his family's and the Minnesota Game and Fish team.[64]

John was born during the last days of the self-governing (and short-lived) Métis Republic in Manitoba. Despite his Métis origins, he did not live around many Métis people in his adult life. He would not hear the "lilting cadence" of Métis language often in Winton or Jackfish Bay. Instead, in Minnesota, he and his sister Alice intermingled and lived with Anishinaabeg people. Only for short periods of time in Red River, Kenora, and Fort Alexander did John live among Métis communities. Many of his immediate family married Indigenous spouses: his father, his sister, his auntie Margaret, and uncle Archie in the Yukon. About half of his uncles and aunts married Métis spouses: Barbara, James, John (twice), and Charlie. No one married a White person.

Linklater's experience, as others viewed him, exemplifies how arbitrary government-defined racial categories are. He began life among proud Métis, an identity reinforced through his visits to Red River and to his uncles and aunts. But his mother, whom he also identified with, was a Lac Seul First Nation Anishinaabe. His August 7, 1870, birth missed the deadline to apply for Métis scrip by three weeks, which would have confirmed Canadian recognition as a Métis.[65] Instead, as a young adult, he moved to Minnesota and became, in the eyes of the U.S. government, a non-status Indian. Or, in effect, an Indian without a home. He is conspicuously absent from the 1901 and 1911 Canadian census from Lac La Croix, in which all his family are documented and which were combined with treaty payments. For Linklater, it was better not to risk the Canadian Indian agent recording him as a White man, which would mean Tchi-Ki-Wis and his daughters would lose their status as Indians. At the beginning of World War I, Linklater was required to come forward to the U.S. government and was officially deemed an "alien." In the "miscellaneous remarks" column, the examiner added: "Halfbreed but not ward of U.S. nor Canada."[66] Officially, then, he was not even a dependent of Canada or the United States, leaving open the question of what he would be if he was not deemed an alien. Racially, he was neither White nor Indian. His more knowledgeable friends did not have a polite category to put him in, even in his obituary. It was his character more than his blood that defied arbitrary racial and national origin categories. Linklater's life rebuffed the binary categorization of Indian or White, "civilized" or "savage."

John and Tchee-Kee-Wis Guide Campers

A publicity photograph for a Northern Pacific Railroad brochure taken on the trail as the Linklaters guided guests from Brady Cove to Daisy Farm, Isle Royale, 1930. Photograph from William Lehr Koffel Papers, Bentley Historical Library, University of Michigan.

Despite this ambiguity about what category the two governments might place him in, there is no evidence that he focused much attention on it. He did not feel exiled from Canada or his official Métis status; rather he moved to places in which he was comfortable. He was at home in the lakes, rivers, and rocky terrain of the canoe country and the remote archipelago of Isle Royale. Linklater was told he was different from those around him in multiple and insensitive ways. When John and Tchi-Ki-Wis were asked to participate in a Northern Pacific Railway tourist brochure about Isle Royale, they had no idea of what would result. Following a full-page photograph of the Linklaters leading a hike—in newer clothing and Tchi-Ki-Wis holding a lovely white hat—the next page of the brochure was an invitation to "explore" a prehistoric ossuary full of Native American bones.[67] Running these pages consecutively was both an act of privileged indifference and promise of desecration. John and Tchi-Ki-Wis knew what insensitivity was, what discrimination felt like. As a means of self-protection, John did not publicly talk about it and was reticent about his heritage and family. He did not publicly assert being Métis, White, or Indian. He did not need to, as ultimately he was comfortable with who he was, proud of his strong way of being. To paraphrase what one misunderstood Montana Métis once said, which Linklater might have voiced: "It doesn't matter what you call me, I know who I am."[68]

John and Tchi-Ki-Wis, like their home Métis and Anishinaabeg communities, cherished family, kin, elders, and children. This is illustrated through many examples, such as naming conventions. John's Lac Seul grandfather's name, Ochee, is yet used today to denote a family line (Ocheewasawan).[69] Daughter Maggie Linklater was named after John's aunt, and Clara Linklater after John's deceased sister, following English language naming custom. But both had their own Anishinaabemowin names, thus following both Indigenous and Scottish/Métis naming customs. John's father, grandfather, and great-grandfather were all named William Linklater. Only after this run on William as a given name for the first-born male was there an exception: John was named after his uncle. John and Tchi-Ki-Wis lived in a multigenerational family, with Tchi-Ki-Wis's sister (in an Anishinaabeg sense) and brother-in-law and parents nearby. And they essentially raised their grandson, Frankie Nelson. Linklater expressed a loving fondness for his granddaughter in their letters to one another, evident in part by the nicknames they used. He, too, enjoyed being with and speaking to young people—Boy Scouts and children of friends.

People's admiration of John forestalled questions of what "category" he should be placed in. Few of his friends thought of him as an outsider, and no one thought of him as a threatening alien, though he never became a U.S. citizen. But few knew of this because of the Linklaters' penchant for privacy. John and Tchi-Ki-Wis did not own their place on Jackfish Bay, nor are we sure of the legal arrangement they had with the Hansons and Warrens for Birch Island in McCargoe Cove. At the time, Isle Royale was, like Jackfish Bay, a "backwater," away from the brighter lights and scrutiny of towns and well-trafficked places. Commercial fishing in a remote place like Birch Island was closely related to the subsistence fishing the Linklaters did at Jackfish Bay. Both levels of fishing permitted them to maintain a more traditional lifestyle. Living at these remote places delayed and buffered their immersion in the change brought from afar. At the same time, in John's and Tchi-Ki-Wis's lives, the remoteness of Jackfish Bay was undercut by the actions of U.S. and Canadian Indian agents and the creation of the Quetico and Superior National Forest. John was like so many Métis in Canada; he was both landless in a legal sense but deeply landed in another. Living remotely suited them, but it was also a quiet "resistance from the crush of assimilation and colonization."[70] By not purchasing property, they never abandoned the concept of communally held land. Though they chose to live on the edges of government influence and White communities, that influence and presence had grown.[71]

Linklater's full-page obituary in the *Minneapolis Tribune* exemplifies the struggle among his friends to find a "racial category" they felt fit him:

> But in him was something other than the Indian. Courage he had inherited from both his father and mother. Stout Scotch honesty, he had from his father. And from the Cree woman came open-handed generosity and patience—and the fatalism of "when it's my time. . . ."
>
> But the elements were mixed in him. On the one hand, the traits of the red man. On the other, the traits of the white.
>
> Perhaps this is why John Linklater died when he did and the way he did.
>
> The man who learned to build canoes like the Indian, and to ride the stormy lakes and rushing, rocky streams on the frail craft he could make "do anything but talk" added a white man's contrivance— a motor.
>
> With an outboard motor on their canoe, Tcheekeewis and John started across Jackfish bay near Winton, on July 8. John usually distrusted too many such appliances. A motor upset the delicate balance. His canoes were built as the red men built them.[72]

For his friends who provided information for this celebratory obituary, his ancestry was a conundrum. People of mixed ancestry were then believed to be unstable and debased, the very antithesis of Linklater. The conventional wisdom and now discredited scientific theory asserted that mixing these worlds and races led to undesirable results, and some thought of it as an outright threat to society.[73] In their mind's eye, the worlds were too far apart to be broached, with one being dominant and the other receding, one being better, the other inferior. Mixing these worlds led to tragic results, except there was the exemplar John Linklater.[74]

The same friends, and indeed virtually all Americans at the time, were unfamiliar with the idea that out of two worlds, through time, struggle, inventiveness, and engagement, might come another, a new people. This is the base idea of ethnogenesis, the originating process from which Métis people came. John was Métis born, like his father, uncles, and aunts. As "Métis" had not been formally or informally recognized in Minnesota or the United States at that time, there wasn't a "category" for his friends to place him in.[75] Nor is it legally recognized today, as it is in Canada. At that time, most Whites thought Indians that had "changed" weren't "authentic," that they were a shadow of "real Indians." Conventional thought posited that "blood mixture" disqualified Indians from being genuine and bolstered the view that true Indians were "vanishing."[76] Sensing he was neither of the binary choices (Indian or White), Linklater's obituary tried to identify a category to place him in: "But in him was something other than Indian." It was Linklater's Métis-ness, though then unnamed, that was an amicable enigma to many of his friends.

THROUGHOUT THEIR LIVES, John and Tchi-Ki-Wis regularly "made the carry," crossing social, cultural, and economic borders. For John, his crossings made him an intermediary, following a long tradition among his Métis forbearers, who as traders lived in two different worlds.[77] Instead of mediating between Indian trappers and traders, like his father, uncles, and grandfathers had, he lived well among Indian people and various nearby White communities.

John Linklater cooks pancakes on Isle Royale while guiding Frank and Alice Warren on a camping excursion, circa 1929. Frank M. Warren photograph. Courtesy of University of Minnesota Duluth, Archives and Special Collections.

John and Tchi-Ki-Wis regularly mixed Indigenous traditions with the ways of their White neighbors. Tchi-Ki-Wis made a variety of traditional objects and sold them to White collectors. John regularly "crossed over"— made the carry—from traditional ecological knowledge into science. He found himself living between Anishinaabeg and Métis lifeways and those of conservationists and cottagers on Isle Royale. He could broach the differences between an "Indian guide" and a wealthy White recreationalist, and explain traditional ecological knowledge to a scientist. John was a realist; he attended church when nearby and held deeply traditional spiritual beliefs. He and Tchi-Ki-Wis ate both a traditional diet of wild rice, fish, moose, deer, and berries and store-bought food.

The Linklaters regularly mixed lifeways that made sense to them. They were not simply traditionalists, unthinkingly doing as their ancestors had done. John wore the wool clothing preferred by White outdoorsmen of the time, used motors, took photographs, and wrote daily in the state game warden log. And yet they preferred to wear moccasins (Tchi-Ki-Wis more often), and John innovated with his dog team, delivering messages between mine captains before a phone system was in place. Both adapted to changing circumstances.[78] Tchi-Ki-Wis was inventive in finding a new, lucrative function for her cedar mats while the craft was being left behind by most of her contemporaries. The mats were traditionally used as a functional and portable flooring by Anishinaabeg, but she wove and sold them as art. Parka designs borrowed from John's Métis and Cree ancestors were sewn for his game warden colleagues, but when used by others, were also an expression of an esteemed Anishinaabeg value of generosity. Perhaps most emblematic of her creativity and adaptability was the building of a birch-bark *jiiman*, or canoe, and then covering it with canvas and tacking the canvas edges into gunnels with nails. This technique mixed that of wood-and-canvas canoe building that had become fashionable in the 1920s with Anishinaabeg methods. Tchi-Ki-Wis was not unconsciously following custom; she was alert to new ideas and creatively adapted traditions to better her family's condition.

John, too, married traditional ecological knowledge and skills with new scientific thought. His curiosity and near photographic memory helped him see patterns in animal behavior, recognize wolf pack boundaries, identify the location of rare plants, and know how to read the rapids to know what route to take in a canoe. His life was delineated by the thoughtful interplay of and respect for tradition with a cautious but open attitude toward change. This is not to say that John's curiosity and thoughtfulness and the adaptability of both Linklaters made them any less Indigenous in their creative response to new and challenging circumstances. In making the carry, as in all things, they made their own way.

It is fitting to close this biography with words Ellen and Bill Hanson carefully chose to describe John Linklater. Having worked alongside him for ten years, Ellen and Bill became revered friends, and Ellen had remarkably sharp and fond memories of Tchi-Ki-Wis and John:

Jack Linklater was a unique individual. He was proud of his Indian heritage. He was loyal to the laws of nature and worshiped all creation. Jack was of strong stature . . . he also embraced the ways and laws of the White man too. A true conservationist and true to his fellow man. He was an Indian but he could relate to the White man. He was just wonderful. He was something! Very soft spoken, I never heard Jack raise his voice. And he held your attention. . . . He was a commanding man but also dignified. Jack was dignified . . . and you were comfortable around him.[79]

Or as Bill Hanson put it more simply: "He was a masterpiece."[80]

"AN OLD INDIAN PROPHECY" (1924)

John Linklater

JUST AFTER JOHN LINKLATER became a game warden, he was asked to contribute an article to the Minnesota Department of Conservation magazine, *Fins, Feathers, and Fur*. Reluctantly he complied, writing it out in longhand, and then stenographer Ellen Hanson typed it at the Game and Fish Station. Written for Minnesota sportsmen of the day and titled "An Old Indian Prophecy," Linklater's essay described a conversation he had long ago with an Anishinaabe elder and "best friend" while on Basswood Lake. John clearly admired the "old Indian's prophecy," but he would not have been surprised if it were greeted by the magazine's readers with the same skepticism as his hearing spirits. Still, Linklater wanted to share this with White sportsmen so they might marvel at its foretelling, and he hoped his readers might reconsider what an "Old Indian" might know.

Both Indigenous men had observed long- and short-term cycles of nature. Snowshoe hare, grouse, lynx, and wild rice have relatively short cycles in population abundance, then decline, then rebound. This elder also witnessed long-term cycles in numbers of caribou and moose and of predators, such as snowy owls. The "old fellow" likely bore witness to radical change in beaver numbers, even local extirpations and comebacks. The old Indian and Linklater had seen beaver wiped out of the Quetico, and then they came back from the east side of the park.[1] Both men lived in a time of "the fine stands of timber everywhere, no logging camps, few white men and no deer or moose, nothing but caribou for big game."[2] All had changed. And from the vantage point of today, one hundred years later, the Anishinaabe elder's prophecy of declining moose is prescient. The beaver population has recovered from its historic low numbers of the early 1900s (and the fur trade era before) to today, when their houses now speckle the shallow waterways of canoe country. The old fellow reminds us that nature is dynamic, even without the machinations of people.

Linklater wanted the readers to appreciate another way of thinking about nature than what they knew or were accustomed to.

❋ ❋ ❋

Often I recall a prophecy that was made by an old Indian friend of mine some years ago. This old Indian was, perhaps, the best friend I ever had. Many an interesting evening I spent beside his camp fire listening to story, many of which were handed down for generations and made doubly interesting by the natural love for my people.

On this particular evening I recall so plainly, we were seated beside the camp fire as usual, which was on one of the many beautiful islands on Basswood lake, when suddenly, just across the island, we heard a splash which was caused by a cow moose and her calf. Evidently they had swam across the lake to the island and had left the water and walked across the island within a few rods of our camp without in any way betraying their presence, and I doubt very much we would have heard them if they had not made the splash which undoubtedly was cause by a stumble or a loose rock.

The moose at that time were very plentiful. The country was full of them. There were moose, moose everywhere. In every stream and in every bay that afforded any feed whatever, moose could be seen at all hours of day and night.

But getting back to the old Indian and his prophecy: At the time we saw the cow moose and the calf, which startled us, I remarked to the old fellow that the moose were getting more and more plentiful every year and asked him whether he thought they would continue to be as plentiful in the future.

The old fellow had a peculiar way of squinting his eyes and looking out over the water as though trying to penetrate the future. I had often noticed this peculiarity. Whether he was trying to arrive at conclusions based on what we might call history handed down by traditions; or whether he was just making a guess at the future, I could never tell.

Slowly he shook his head and said: "No, my son; the moose will not be with us very long. Perhaps in your time, but I am sure not in mine, as I am too old; if you will live to be an old man, you will see that the moose will have disappeared from this country entirely. They will have returned to the place from whence they came, and that—no man knows. In their stead will come the beaver. They will populate this part of the country very thickly. They will be more numerous than the muskrats. Every lake and stream will be inhabited by beaver. And, when that time comes, the moose will have gone to return, no man knows when."

About a year after, that old fellow started out on his last trail over the big divide to the "Happy Hunting Ground," and I am alive today to see his prophecy coming true.

It was perhaps ten years after the old fellow died that I first noticed the moose had begun to dwindle away. In places where we used to see ten or fifteen in an evening, there would be but two or three. In the winter time the tracks were more scarce, until today, they are all but a thing of the past.

Contrary to the popular belief, the scarcity of moose has not been brought about by human agency, but, as the old Indian said, they are returning "to the place from whence they came, and that—no man knows." I have lived to see the beaver increase in that region from a few scattered colonies until they inhabit most of the lakes and streams, not only in northern Minnesota, but in Canada as well; and they have multiplied in spite of the most greedy prosecution that any species of wild animal life has known.

Truly, the old Indian's prophecy is being fulfilled. The moose are vanishing, so let us encourage the species that has come in their place.

ACKNOWLEDGMENTS

MY DEBTS TO OTHERS who assisted me in writing this book are hefty. If this writing effort is described with a canoeing metaphor, then this was a portage with heavy and lumpy packs and multiple trips to get from one side to the other. Lots of people helped me pack, gave me tips to find an unmarked portage, and helped me make the carry. It was a group effort, bugs not included, and without good maps. The willing and timely assistance of friends, scholars, and strangers meant more to me than the gifts of information. Their help was a continuous affirmation that this project mattered to them and thus bolstered my efforts. Thank you.

After the sudden deaths of John and Tchi-Ki-Wis Linklater, much family history was lost. Their grandson, Warner Wirta, knew little about them, as he had been cut off from knowing much. The Linklaters had walked on before Warner and his siblings might have talked with them or known them well. His mother and great-grandfather died in successive years, leaving Warner and others to be raised by his Finnish immigrant stepmother and father. This vacuum of knowledge prompted an older Warner to seek out others to learn about John and Tchi-Ki-Wis Linklater; many were happy to oblige. Warner enlisted the help of Sister Noemi Weygant, who wrote a short biography of John Linklater that was published in 1987.

Several of the Linklaters' contemporaries documented their lives. A game warden colleague of John, who was with Linklater the morning of his death, wrote a four-page biography ten years later. Joe Brickner emotionally blamed himself for his friend's death, though he was miles away. A WCCO radio personality and author, Darragh Aldrich, wrote a novel about her and her husband's relationship with John and Tchi-Ki-Wis titled *Earth Never Tires*. It includes precious details about them, but Aldrich also took a number of liberties, such as writing that John died of a heart attack after fighting a forest fire. Later Shirley Peruniak, the thoughtful naturalist for Quetico Provincial Park, started collecting information about the Linklaters, most of it unique and rarely dubious. I am deeply indebted to all of them.

This effort is built on the prior work of Warner Wirta. Anna Wirta Kosobuski encouraged me and trusted my efforts. She shared the tapes, letters, and documents her late father assembled on his grandfather and grandmother. Family members of people crucial to this work included Robert Maki, nephew of Ellen and Bill Hanson, who genially and repeatedly came to my aid. Bob and son Rob Maki even boated me into the Linklater homesite on Jackfish Bay. The long-ago friendship of Ellen and Bill Hanson with the Linklaters, and thus their memories, made this work possible. The late Elaine Chadney, a Linklater family descendant, puzzled through the family genealogy with me and corrected me when I went astray. Frank and Alice Warren's nieces, Jean Anderson and the late Cornelia O'Neill, assisted and encouraged me. Research fortuitously led me to converse with Milt and Alice Powell, who graciously shared information about the Powell family and wondered with me how exactly Tchi-Ki-Wis was related to them. The late Gilbert Caribou generously shared his knowledge of the connections between the Caribou and Robinson families at Lac La Croix. Thank you for all your help; in Cree, Mîkwêc, and in Anishinaabemowin, Miigwetch.

One of the most enjoyable parts of writing this book was forays into subjects of which I knew very little (e.g., Cree and Métis heritage and history, Bungee language, cedar-bark mats, Orkney Island history, logging in the boundary waters). Learning about these topics means, of course, reading about them, and just as often it means finding an expert to talk with who is mercifully willing to answer elementary questions and gently correct mistakes. Quite a number of people answered my questions, the results of which fill the pages of this book. They include artist Carl Gawboy; Fraser Stuart and Rob Sarginson for help on Red River; Dr. David Backes, biographer of Sigurd Olson; linguist John D. Nichols; Lynn Laitala, Debbie Sessions, Marcia Anderson, Gilbert White, Jon Nelson, Bruce Casselton, John and Wendy Grace of the resort The Old Post on the site of the HBC Osnaburgh Post; Bethany Waite, Dryden, Ontario; Murat Vardar, Toronto; and Meredith Vasta and Katherine Meyers Satriano at the Peabody Museum, Harvard University. A contingent in Ely shared information and more: canoe builder Jeanne Bourquin; Paul Schurke of Wintergreen; Steffi O'Brien of the Listening Point Foundation; and Kris Trygg Kidd, who provided a wonderful "Historic Map of Basswood Lake Area" that sparked conversations with numerous area residents.

Former colleagues and friends were invaluable and often leaned upon. At Isle Royale the caretakers of the Linklaters' history are Seth DePasqual and Elizabeth Valencia; they are enthusiasts as well. Dave and Sarah Trigg made my stay on the island editing the manuscript more enjoyable and productive. Curator Penelope Yocum, archivist Jeremiah Mason, and Brett Sander assisted me with difficult collection questions and never-ending requests. Thanks to Steve Veit at Grand Portage National Monument, a dedicated and considerate custodian of a remarkable cedar mat collection, and Lee Johnson, archaeologist at the Superior National Forest, who enjoyed talking about Linklater with me and was also generous with contextual information. The creators of the gem of a collection at the Ridley Library of Quetico Provincial Park, the late Shirley Peruniak and her successor Andrea Allison, deserve acclaim for their efforts. Tom Theissen, retired archaeologist of the National Park Service and collector of Dawson Route historical documents, has a sharing instinct, from which I have greatly benefited. Numerous archivists at the Hudson's Bay Company Archives at the Manitoba Provincial Archives, including James Gorton, Laura Elsie Garinger, Chris Kotecki, and Marie Reidke, were instrumental to this work.

Erik Redix read an early draft and aided me immeasurably on grammar, content, and organization. Thank you to Linda LeGarde Grover, Nicole St-Onge, and one anonymous reviewer, who made invaluable suggestions to improve the clarity and analysis of this work. Conversations with the University of Minnesota Press staff, particularly editor Kristian Tvedten with his unflagging enthusiasm and good counsel, spurred me on and grew into a constructive collaboration. Copy editor Mary Keirstead has saved me, again, from too many grammatical and typographical errors. Travis Novitsky generously provided stunning photographs of Tchi-Ki-Wis's cedar mats. Thanks to Rhys Davies, who created the exquisite maps.

Thank you to the many archivists and librarians in the region who have been delightfully helpful: Stacy McNally at the Saginaw, Michigan, Public Library; Emily Riippa at Michigan Technological University; Trudy Russo at Lakehead University; Annakathryn Welch at the Archives of Michigan; Laurel Parson, General Synod Archives of the Anglican Church of Canada; Judy McIvor and Gloria Romaniuk of the Anglican Diocese of Rupert's Land; Christopher Welter, Iron Range Research Center; Carrie Johnson of Cook County Historical Society; Steve Harsin and Amanda St. John, Grand Marais Public Library; Julie Reid at the Centre du Patrimoine, Saint-Boniface, Manitoba; Rebecca Toov at the University of Minnesota; Sara Szakaly, archivist for U.S. Animal and Plant Health Inspection Service; Hailey Urilyon at the Treaty and Aboriginal Rights Research Centre of Manitoba; Margaret Sweet, Ely–Winton Historical Society; Charlie Iverson at the Science Museum of Minnesota; Braden Murray at the Lake of Woods Museum; Elizabeth Burnes, National Archives and Record Administration; Aimee Brown at the University of Minnesota Duluth Archives and Special Collections.

I appreciate the efforts of reference librarians at three institutions, who shared my inquiries among staff members at the Minnesota Historical Society, the Library and Archives Canada, and the Bentley Library, University of Michigan. Membership in the Orkney Family History Society provided much needed background on Orcadian history and genealogy. Thank you to the State of Minnesota's Legacy Fund, Arts and Cultural Heritage Funding, which was a great boon to researching Linklater's sway on Sigurd Olson.

John Linklater's influence on others did not stop with his and Tchi-Ki-Wis's (and their friends') deaths. Rather, it has just been layered over with time, made unrecognizable. As a Minnesota teen, canoeing in the summer, I, too, was "infected" with the romance of "going to the [Hudson] Bay." If going "north" is a Minnesotan's summer custom, going to the Bay is even better. If I inherited this desire from the magic of the canoe country and the writings of Sig Olson, many others were also aspirationally downstream from Sig, as he was of Linklater.

Thanks to my family: Madaline Cochrane (and then puppy Rainy), who paddled the Albany River with me and learned how to make a great bannock; Andy, an adventurer who thrives on sharing trips with others; Cory, who keeps me rethinking about power differences and justice in society; Rebekah, who calmly rekindles conversations in our family about what is important; Kenna, who kept me from writing and indeed sleeping. Mîkwêc to Jeannie, who patiently listened and sometimes asked a question, all of which helped me articulate my thoughts. This book is dedicated to my three older brothers, Pete, Steve, and Jamie, who taught me many things, some of which are useful.

NOTES

Preface

1. I was an enthusiastic student of Joseph Epes Brown, an inspiring Native American scholar. Brown (1920–2000) was a comparative religion scholar who sought out and recorded Lakota religious traditions from Oglala elder Black Elk. Brown wrote *The Sacred Pipe* (1953) and *The Spiritual Legacy of the American Indian* (1982). He lived with Black Elk and others he studied, making his knowledge deeply heartfelt. His teaching was moving to me, and we learned to respect all religions, particularly Indigenous religious traditions.

2. I had the good fortune to initially learn of bioregionalism from poet Gary Snyder, who taught at the Round River Experiment at the University of Montana one spring. The Round River Experiment was a short-lived, experientially based environmental learning program. This unstructured educational experience was fundamental to me both personally and academically, and its effects are layered throughout this work.

3. As the final product of this 1989 grant for the American Association for State and Local History, I wrote "Minong: An Ojibwa Sanctuary," which foreshadows much of what I wrote twenty years later in *Minong—the Good Place: Ojibwe and Isle Royale* (East Lansing: Michigan State University Press, 2009). The Linklaters are subjects in both works.

Introduction

1. Arnold Aslakson, "Jack Linklater: Son of Nature Whose 'Day' Came at 67: Half Cree and Half Scot, Noted Woodsman Had Fatalistic Conception to Meet Death," *Minneapolis Sunday Tribune*, August 18, 1933, 9.

2. Joe Brickner, "Jack Linklater as I Knew Him," *Conservation Volunteer* 6, no. 34 (July 1943): 40.

3. Sigurd F. Olson, *The Singing Wilderness* (New York: Knopf, 1971; reprint, Minneapolis: University of Minnesota Press, 1997), 199. Olson wrote of Indians and voyageurs making the carry at Twin Falls Portage on the Maligne River. It is a reference both purposefully historical and yet also about his remarkable experience with Jack Linklater at that moment. Some residents of Ely, Minnesota, believe that Olson gave John Linklater the nickname Jack. This is likely an apocryphal story but rightly suggests a warm friendship between the men.

4. Paul Schurke, Ely, Minn., personal communication, February 16, 2021.
5. See "gabadoo" and "gakiiwenige" in "The Ojibwe People's Dictionary," https://ojibwe.lib.umn.edu/. For those of us who are not Anishinaabemowin speakers, this dictionary often provides a handy recording of how to properly say Anishinaabemowin words.
6. My daughter Maddy and I were fortunate to see gillnets "stashed" in trees on a historic portage on the Albany River. They were modern nylon nets, but their presence suggests a traditional practice. John Linklater's grandfather William Linklater was a Hudson's Bay Company postmaster (a type of clerk) and traded with the same Miskeegogamang people, whose descendants cached the gillnets we saw. In William Linklater's day they would have been known by English speakers as the Osnaburgh House Band, named after the HBC post.
7. The Linklaters' fishery at Isle Royale that they operated in the late 1920s also has an expansive view, down the fjord-like McCargoe Cove, to the quiet waters of Brady Cove, and through a narrow opening to open water of Lake Superior. While speculative, it appears the Linklaters were drawn to homesites that were both environmentally protected and advantageous but also were pleasing to the eye.
8. Kalvin Ottertail and Margaret Ottertail, "Lac La Croix First Nation, Quetico's Traditional Lake Names," March 2000, unpublished, Ridley Library, Quetico Provincial Park, Atikokan, Ontario, 7.
9. Milt Stenlund, *Burntside Lake—The Early Days 1880–1920* (Ely: Ely–Winton Historical Society, 1986), 2, 5.
10. Richard Rhodes and Evelyn Todd, "Subarctic Algonquian Languages," in *Subarctic,* ed. June Helm, vol. 6, *The Handbook of North American Indians,* ed. William C. Sturtevant (Washington, D.C.: Smithsonian Institution, 1981), 54.
11. Ottertail and Ottertail, "Lac La Croix First Nation, Quetico's Traditional Lake Names," 8. The Ottertails describe the natural phenomenon that gave the lake its name: "The pines around Lac La Croix were once the biggest and tallest trees around. These pines were one of the earliest to be cut down during the logging days. Trees like the ones we had on Lac La Croix are rarely seen today."
12. The spelling of "Mandaquabeek" comes from the 1901 Canadian Census for Lac La Croix. Indian agents spelled the name of the head *ogimaa* for Lac La Croix "Indian" numerous ways, such as Macatanassin, Macatarassin, Muckadaysin, or Magatewasin. He was also known as Chief Blackstone in English. Indian Affairs, Treaty Annuity Paylists for Treaty 3, Lac La Croix, 1874, 1877, and 1885, Record Group 10, Library and Archives Canada, Ottawa, Ontario. I am using the spelling for Blackstone, Magatewasin, provided by Lac La

Croix resident Mary Jourdain, June 8, 1981, in Blackstone File, Ridley Library, Quetico Provincial Park.

13. Lac La Croix, 1881 Annual Report, Indian Affairs, Library and Archives Canada, Ottawa.

14. The Orkney Islands is an archipelago of about seventy islands northeast of the mainland of Scotland. It has a long history, with remarkably large prehistoric settlements.

15. A "factory" was a large fur trade post, often on Hudson Bay, where furs were accumulated to ship to England. On the return voyage supplies and men came to North American to trade for furs. A "factor" was a fur trader, but a manager of a large post or factory.

16. One of the hurdles in researching and writing this biography is the number of William Linklaters and John Linklaters in the historic record in Canada and in their Orkney Islands home. "Linklater" is one of the most common surnames in Orkney. There are dozens of "Williams" and enough "Johns," including one virtually the same as "our" John Linklater, as to confuse the historical trail. Indeed, I "followed" the "wrong" William and John Linklater for quite some time. As it turns out there are six William Linklater biographical sheets in the Hudson's Bay Company archives. William Linklater (a) is John Linklater's great-grandfather; William Linklater (b) is his grandfather; William Linklater (e) is his father. Hudson's Bay Company Archives (HBCA), Provincial Archives of Manitoba, Winnipeg.

17. William P. L. Thomson, *The New History of Orkney*, 3rd ed. (Edinburgh: Birlinn, 2008), 372.

18. Marriage "solemnized at Lac Seul," between William Linklater and Eliza Fly, May 7, 1869, Rev. Robert Phair, Lansdowne, in the Diocese of Rupert's Land, General Synod Archives, Anglican Church of Canada, Toronto, Ontario.

19. When John was on a guiding trip with Frank and Alice Warren on Isle Royale, as a lark they jumped on a commercial fisherman's scale. John weighed 149 pounds (the lightest of the three). Frank M. and Alice Rockwell Warren Papers, Archives and Special Collections, University of Minnesota Duluth, Duluth. *Ely Miner*, October 15, 1984. Pete Trygg, Arthur Johnson, and Robert Maki, taped interviews by Warner Wirta, undated, Ely, Minn., Warner Wirta Collection, Duluth, Minn. Ellen Hanson, taped interview by Sister Noemi Weygant, August 30, 1982, Floodwood, Minn. Art Knutsen, interview by Warner Wirta, November 22, 1983, Ely, Minn., Wirta Collection. Warren Photograph Collection, Album 4, Isle Royale National Park, Houghton, Mich. The Warner Wirta Collection is a collection of letters, cassette oral history tapes, memorabilia, Christmas cards, and receipts that

Warner collected about his grandparents. Warner's daughter, Anna Wirta Kosobuski, is the keeper of this collection and kindly let me read and use it for this manuscript.

20. Brickner, "Jack Linklater as I Knew Him," 37; Knutsen, interview; Frank M. Warren, letter to A. A. Webster, July 24, 1933, Wirta Collection.

21. Ellen Hanson, interview; C. L. Gilman, "Going In by Gasoline," *Outing* 68 (April–September 1916): 308.

22. Knutsen, interview, Wirta Collection.

23. Art Johnson, interview by Warner Wirta, July 30, 1982, Babbitt, Minn., Wirta Collection.

24. Ibid. Darragh Aldrich, who knew Tchi-Ki-Wis well, said in her fictional portrayal of her that "I doubt if you get her to talk much, though she understands English perfectly." Darragh Aldrich, *Earth Never Tires* (New York: Kinsey, 1936), 37. Mary Ottertail, or Aquayweaskeik, a contemporary and distant relation to Tchi-Ki-Wis, "never spoke English, though she understood it very well." Dorothy Powell, *It Happened: True Indian Stories as Told to Me* (Grand Marais, Minn., privately printed, 1988), 24.

25. Warren Photograph Collection, Isle Royale National Park. Dr. R. Fenstermacher, letter to John Linklater, November 28, 1932, Wirta Collection; subscription to *Sports Afield*, Wirta Collection; Knutsen, interview.

26. Read today, some historical language is insulting and demeaning, though it was the language then used. To fully tell the "Linklater story," it is informative to present and reflect on that language, with the few exceptions where its reuse is too repugnant.

27. Jacqueline Peterson, "Red River Redux: Metis Ethnogenesis and the Great Lakes Region," in *Contours of a People: Metis Family, Mobility, and History*, ed. Nicole St-Onge, Carolyn Podruchny, and Brenda Macdougall (Norman: University of Oklahoma Press, 2012), 25–27.

28. "Finding the Fiddle in the Yukon," https://whatsupyukon.com, December 13, 2012. "In Old Crow [Yukon], fiddles have been popular since Archie Linklater, a Scot from Manitoba, came to the Yukon and married a Gwitch'in woman." One of the tunes that directly recognizes him is called "Archie Linklater's Handkerchief Dance."

29. Jennifer S. H. Brown, "Metis, Halfbreeds, and Other Real People: Challenging Cultures and Categories," *The History Teacher* 27, no. 1 (November 1993): 20.

30. There was a third John Linklater in the area, five years younger than the John Linklater who is the subject of this book. The younger John was also Métis, lived in Kenora, and sometimes translated for the area Indian agent. 1881 Canada Census for Lake Winnipeg, 1901 and 1921, Canada Census, Kenora,

Ontario; John James Linklater, Métis scrip, Library and Archives Canada, Ottawa, Ontario.

31. The North West Company (NWC) was a bitter fur trade rival of the Hudson's Bay Company. Based out of Montreal with a summer headquarters in Grand Portage and then Fort William, the NWC had more than one hundred posts as far west as the Rocky Mountains. It was heavily dependent on a long canoe transportation route through the upper Great Lakes and into western Canada. It was a consortium of business concerns that at one time outcompeted the HBC. Begun in 1779, the NWC merged with the HBC in 1821, with the HBC keeping its name, but the workforce was then dominated by NWC men.

32. Eleanor Blain, "The Bungee Dialect of the Red River Settlement" (master's thesis, University of Manitoba, 1989), 143; Dr. Elaine Gold, personal communication, May 10, 2020, University of Toronto, Ontario; Douglas Anderson, personal communication, May 12, 2020, Toronto, Ontario. Anderson is a Métis descendant originally from Manitoba. Mark Abley, "How's Your Michif and Bungi?" *Montreal Gazette*, April 13, 2013.

There is a debate about whether Bungee was a dialect or distinct language, with Cree syntax and English, Anishinaabemowin, and a few Gaelic loan words. Like Cree, for example, Bungee did not make a grammatical distinction between masculine and feminine, such as "he" and "she." The Linklaters would have first heard Bungee at Moose Factory, then likely spoke it at Red River. However, Bungee is now an extinct language. Its extinction as a living language came in great part because of the prejudice against it, as it was assumed to be a substandard language. Manitoba elites thought it to be a language of "hicks" and Indians with different syntax than English. Bungee speakers were embarrassed to use it publicly, and it "died" not long ago for lack of validated use.

33. Fred Dustin, "Isle Royale Place Names," *Michigan History* 30 (1946): 717.

34. Ben East, "Hunts Moose Only with His Camera," *Saginaw (Mich.) Sunday News*, September 14, 1930.

35. Peterson, "Red River Redux," 22.

36. Alice Mary (née Linklater) Morrisseau, Métis scrip, Library and Archives of Canada, Ottawa, Ontario; Alice Wakemup, "Allotment No. 701," Bois Forte Band, Wirta Collection.

37. For example, Ellen Linklater, Métis scrip, Library and Archives Canada, Ottawa, Canada. In this scrip, completed after Ellen's death by her sister Nancy Brown, Mrs. Brown made an affidavit about Ellen's children. This legal record clarifies who were her children, or for our purposes, all the uncles and aunts of John Linklater on his paternal side.

38. Lee Brownell, interview by Warner Wirta, no date, Ely, Minn., Wirta Collection.
39. Timothy Roufs, ed., *Gabe-bines: "Forever Flying Bird," Teachings from Paul Peter Buffalo* (Minneapolis: Wise Ink, 2019), 54.
40. Generosity, or sharing with others, was, and is, a highly esteemed Anishinaabeg value. It was "acting appropriately" to share food, clothing, and needed objects, which as a consequence created a network of friends, strong kinship bonds, and a safety measure in a harsh environment. Alternately, "hoarding" or only looking out for oneself, was frowned upon. Gifting created networks in families, as did diplomatic gestures among larger groups. The Linklaters were noted for gift giving, especially to "tenderfeet" or newcomers. Aslakson, "Jack Linklater."
41. "Club Notes," *Minneapolis Morning Tribune*, November 30, 1947.
42. Aldrich, *Earth Never Tires*, 200–1.
43. Al Evans, "Hitting the Snowshoe Trail," *Fins, Feathers, and Fur* 37 (March 1924): 149.
44. Frank Warren was a mining engineer and financier who lived in Minneapolis. The Warrens would spend extended periods of the summer at Isle Royale.
45. Sigurd Olson, letter to Aldo Leopold, fall 1931, Aldo Leopold Correspondence, University of Wisconsin Digital Collections, Madison.
46. Statute 3282, "Sale to Indians," and Statute 6471, "Trespasses," General Statutes of Minnesota, 1923, Minnesota State Archives, St. Paul.
47. 1921 Circular, Canadian Department of Indian Affairs, "Lac La Croix file," Northern Studies Centre, Lakehead University, Thunder Bay, Ontario.
48. Bruce G. Steelman, "Voyageur Describes Border Canoe Trip," *Minneapolis Sunday Tribune*, August 18, 1912.
49. Biennial Report of the State Game and Fish Commissioner, Biennial Period Ending July 31, 1916, (Minneapolis: Syndicate, 1916), 20. The full photo caption reads: "Good Types of Indian Trappers and Hunters—Such Experienced Men Are Commissioned to Trap and Hunt in the Superior Game Refuge."
50. Dustin, "Isle Royale Place Names," 717.
51. Evans, "Hitting the Snowshoe Trail," 151. The photograph is reused in the February 1932 edition of *Fins, Feathers, and Furs* as an intriguing reminder to resubscribe with the heading: "When the Bannock Bakes." Ironically, bannock, which is similar to Indian fry bread, was a common Métis food. Later, the photograph was reused by game warden and author Woody Schermann with the caption: "Game Wardens Jack Linklater and Leo Chosa having their lunch. Both Wardens were part Indian. Chosa later was fired and bragged the Wardens could never catch him. Linklater did." Hilary W. Schermann, *Minnesota Game Warden: A History 1887–1987* (privately printed, 1987), 111.

52. James C. Scott, *Domination and the Arts of Resistance: Hidden Transcripts* (New Haven, Conn.: Yale University Press, 1990), xii, 17, 173. Scott writes: "hidden transcript is typically expressed openly—albeit in a disguised form."
53. Robert F. Berkhofer Jr., "White Conceptions of Indians," in *History of Indian-White Relations,* ed. Wilcomb E. Washburn, vol. 4, *The Handbook of North American Indians* (Washington, D.C.: Smithsonian Institution, 1988), 528–29.
54. Elaine Chadney, Linklater family genealogist, provided me a picture of Charles Linklater's medal for participating in the 1885 Métis Rebellion as part of the Ninety-Fifth Winnipeg Regiment. Charles Linklater, uncle to John Linklater, fought to suppress the rebellion of fellow Métis and their Aboriginal supporters. Most of the Métis rebelling were French-Canadian-Oijbwe descendants who were often Catholics, not the "Scotch" Métis. Elaine Chadney, personal communication, Winnipeg, Manitoba, January 18, 2019. The commemorative medal has Charles Linklater's name engraved on it.
55. Reuben Hill, who as a young man knew the Linklaters on Isle Royale, wrote: "Mrs. Linklater had spoken to John that as a young girl she was there with her grandmother." Reuben Hill, letter to Carol Maass, February 16, 1984, Isle Royale National Park, Houghton, Mich. In "Centennial Notes," *Michigan History Magazine* 19 (1935): 455, Linklater "states that his wife's grandmother and his own grandfather remembered the going of the Chippewas to Isle Royale. The latter recalled the gathering on the Canadian shore and the ceremonies, dance and appeal to the spirits deemed necessary before the trip could be made."
    Another record implies that Linklater's grandfather also made the paddle to Minong. I believe this is an inexact rendering of the statement above in which Linklater's grandfather observed the ceremonies and the start of a family group crossing to Isle Royale but did not participate in the voyage. George R. Fox, "Isle Royale Expedition," *Michigan History* 13, no. 2 (1929): 317, 319.
56. Jean Morrison, *Superior Rendezvous-Place: Fort William in the Canadian Fur Trade* (Toronto: Natural Heritage Books, 2001), 138; Thomas Richards and Ellen Richards Linklater, Métis scrip, Library and Archives of Canada, Ottawa, Ontario.
57. Clifford Ahlgren and Isabel Ahlgren, *Lob Trees in the Wilderness* (Minneapolis: University of Minnesota Press, 1984), 102.
58. Company employees would sometimes jest that "HBC" stood for "Here Before Christ," denoting its antiquity and even stodginess. Of late, Indigenous commentators have a pointedly different take for HBC, or "Here Before the Company," reacting to the comment about the antiquity of the company and underscoring their history and primacy in the north, not the HBC's.

59. This paper was found in the Frank M. and Alice Rockwell Warren Papers. It was written after March 1927, as that is the latest recorded date. About this time, Frank Warren convinced John to start a life insurance policy, and Warren repeatedly urged John to not forget to pay its premiums. Warren's niece, Jean Anderson, an archivist, is certain the handwriting is not of her uncle or aunt, nor is it in John's hand. It is simply titled "John J. Linklater."
60. Aslakson, "Jack Linklater."

1. Out of the North

1. This imagined scene relies on information reported by ethnographer David Bushnell in 1899: "[Ojibway] children as soon as they are able to stand alone are taught to stand in the forward of a bark canoe, and with a small paddle, not over thirty inches in length, to keep stroke with those who are propelling the craft." While at Osnaburgh House, Charlie grew up around HBC boatmen and kids from the Mishkeegogamang Band, all of whom used canoes daily. David I. Bushnell, "An Account of a Trip to Hunter's Island, Canada: Made during the Autumn of 1899," Bushnell Collection, Library and Archives Canada, Ottawa.
2. One HBC factor wrote about Linklater's death: "I am sorry to have to report the death by drowning last July of Wm Linklater postmaster of Osnaburgh while visiting his nets. The body was recovered a few hours after the accident." A. McDonald, letter to G. Dallas, September 9, 1864, Moose Factory, B.3/b/95, Hudson's Bay Company Archives (HBCA), Provincial Archives of Manitoba, Winnipeg. Six months after the drowning, one HBC clerk at Lake Nipigon wrote to another in Montreal: "The Indian Reports that Post Master W Linglatre [sic] of Osnaburgh was drowned setting nets." L. D. Delaronde, Lake Nipigon, to E. M. Hopkins, February 24, 1865, B.135/c/97, HBCA.
3. Philip Goldring, "Labour Records of the Hudson's Bay Company, 1821–1870," *Archivaria* 11 (Winter 1980/81): 69.
4. Charles A. Bishop, *The Northern Ojibwa and the Fur Trade* (Toronto: Holt, Rinehart and Winston, 1974), 203.
5. Sylvia M. Van Kirk, "The Role of Women in the Fur Trade Society of the Canadian West, 1700–1850," (PhD dissertation, University of London, 1975), 232.
6. David Anderson, *The Net in the Bay, or, Journal of a Visit to Moose and Albany* (London: Hatchford, 1854), 3ff. Bishop Anderson gives an account of the same trip in 1852, albeit his canoe was traveling west to east, from Red River to Fort Albany. We do not know any details about the specific trip of the Linklater family. As a general rule the HBC encouraged families to move

from the "interior" to Red River so as not to become a burden on the meager resources of smaller posts such as Osnaburgh. We do not know if the Linklater family traveled with an HBC canoe(s) delivering "mail" to Red River, but it is quite likely. Since William Linklater was recognized as a "clerk" and no longer a lowly servant, the HBC was more likely to make accommodations to assist the family.

7. *Nor'Wester* (Winnipeg), October 1, 1864. News of William Linklater II's drowning was slow to reach officials from such a distant post. This tragic news fit with the *Nor'Wester* editor's bias against the HBC.

8. Osnaburgh House, July 1, 1868, B.155/a/82, HBCA.

9. William P. L. Thomson, *Orkney Land and People* (Kirkwall, Orkney: The Orcadian Limited, 2008), 202.

10. Edith I. Burley, *Servants of the Honourable Company: Work, Discipline, and Conflict in Hudson's Bay Company, 1770–1870* (Toronto: Oxford University Press, 1997), 69.

11. Fort Albany, 1816–1817, B.3/a/120, HBCA. I am summarizing from a year's worth of entries in the post journal.

12. Fort Albany, Angus Bethune, letter to Thomas Vincent, Chief Factor, Moose, from Albany, March 31, 1823, B.3/6/51, HBCA.

13. William Linklater and Eleanor Thomas were formally married long after their country marriage began. Indeed, their marriage on July 19, 1840, in Moose Factory occurred seven days after all of their children but their oldest son, William, were baptized on July 12, 1840 (Benjamin, Archibald, James, Catherine, Mary, and George). They lived much of their adult lives in Albany, rather than Moose Factory, which appears to have had a few more ministers passing through to formalize a marriage. Moose Factory, Church Records Collection, Archives of Ontario, Toronto.

14. Jennifer S. H. Brown, *Strangers in Blood: Fur Trade Company Families in Indian Country* (Vancouver: University of British Columbia Press, 1980), 206.

15. Goldring, "Labour Records of the Hudson's Bay Company," 55–56.

16. I am using the spelling Alice (née Linklater) Morrisseau Wakemup used for her mother, in Alice's application for a Bois Forte allotment. "Allotment no. 701," Bois Forte Band, no date, circa 1910, Warner Wirta Collection.

17. Records for John Linklater's birth year vary from as early as 1865 to as late as 1870. I have not found a birth record to confirm this August 7, 1870; however, I am confident this is correct. His birthday, August 7, is not in dispute, but the year is. There are two reasons I believe he was born in 1870. First, the 1881 Canada census, with information potentially drawn from both his father and mother, places him at eleven years old, or born in 1870. Second, if he had

been born only a couple weeks earlier (before July 15, 1870), he would have been eligible to apply for the first Métis scrip for money or land. His father, William Thomas, and his older sister, Alice, applied for Métis scrip and received it. John did not apply for scrip, nor did his father do so on his behalf, and hence he did not receive it.

In a too-good-to-be-true moment of historical irony, in the Warner Wirta Collection is a letter from the director of the Division of Game and Fish of the Minnesota Department of Conservation to John Linklater, which says: "Dear Mr. Linklater: On the recent examination for Game Wardens you failed to give the date of your birth. Kindly give us the date of your birth, giving month, day and year." It is possible that John was not quite sure of his birth year. William Stewart, St. Paul, to John Linklater, February 4, 1932, Wirta Collection.

18. "John J. Linklater," Frank M. and Alice Rockwell Warren Papers.

19. Burley, *Servants of the Honourable Company*, 131.

20. Savanne Post Inspection Report for 1891, E. K. Beeston, October 26–28, 1891, B.343/e/2, HBCA.

21. Eliza likely died in a remote location, certainly not at Lac Seul or Wabigoon, where her death would have been noted by the Indian agent in the Treaty Paylists (as no payment to her would have then been made). Instead, uncertainty about her pervades in the 1890 and 1891 Treaty Paylist for Lac Seul and Wabigoon. Her name is listed after her mother, but the entry for Eliza, or "No. 135," recording whether she received treaty payment is left blank. If present, as the male head of the household, William, not Eliza, would have received the annual treaty payment of five dollars for his wife. Canada, Department of Indian Affairs, Lac Seul Treaty Paylists, microfilm reels: C-7135 and C-7136, for the years 1875 to 1893 accessed at www.heritage.canadiana.ca. The originals are held at the Library and Archives Canada, Ottawa.

22. I am calculating her age at her death from what was given in the 1881 Canada Census (in which she is listed at thirty-four years of age). Her daughter, Alice Linklater Morrisseau Wakemup, in her allotment application to the U.S. government, says her mother was a "full blood." Interestingly, Alice or her unknown scribe spelled Linklater "Linglighter." Alice Wakemup, "Allotment no. 701," Wirta Collection.

23. I have been unable to translate her name. An aggravating problem may be that the transcription of her name may be inexact.

24. Lac Seul Treaty Paylists, 1875–93.

25. Long after the Linklaters and Ah-zhe-day-ge-she-gake were gone, a dam was built on the western outlet of Lac Seul and raised the waters approximately

ten feet higher. Thus, "the 1930s hydro development at Ear Falls resulted in massive flooding of the traditional territory of the people. This forced many families to relocate to higher ground." Lac Seul First Nation, History, http://lacseulfn.org/about/history.

26. Canada, Indian Affairs, Sessional Paper No. 15, second session, Parliament of Canada, for the year ended December 31, 1892.

27. Canada, Indian Affairs, Annual Report, and Treaty Paylist, microfilm roll, C-7136 for the years 1881 and 1884.

28. Ibid., Annual Report, 1881.

29. Ibid.

30. Mary Ellen Snodgrass, *World Epidemics: A Cultural Chronology of Disease from Prehistory to the Era of Zika* (Jefferson, N.C.: McFarland and Company, 2017), 130; Paul Hackett, *A Very Remarkable Sickness: Epidemics in the Petit Nord, 1670–1846* (Winnipeg: University of Manitoba Press, 2002), 144.

31. "Surveyor's Report of Exploration Survey Party #10," Sessional Papers, Legislature of the Province of Ontario, vol. 33, part 9, fourth session, Ninth Legislature, 1901, 258; Bishop, *The Northern Ojibwe and the Fur Trade*, 116.

32. Bill Straight, "An Historic Review of the Presence and Abundance of Lake Sturgeon in the Upper Reaches of the Winnipeg River, Fall/Winter 2010/11," www.cgrf.ca/wp-content/uploads/2017/Historic-Review_sm_2PDF; Tim E. Holzkamm, Victor P. Lytwyn, and Leo G. Waisberg, "Rainy River Sturgeon: An Ojibway Resource in the Fur Trade," *Canadian Geographer* 32, no. 3 (September 1988): 194–205.

33. Osnaburgh House, September 14 and 25, 1857, B.155/a/70, HBCA.

34. For clarity's sake, I am denominating the three William Linklaters as William I, William II, and William III. The documentary record does not record them as such, adding to the genealogical confusion. William continued to be a common name among the descendants of these three, further clouding matters.

35. I am indebted to the late Elaine Chadney of Winnipeg, a Linklater family descendant, who toiled hard to dispel some of the misleading genealogical claims (particularly if William II was born on Hudson Bay with Cree and Flotta roots, or was a different William from Stromness, Orkney). This later genealogical assertion is common on family trees posted on the internet, the problem being multiple William Linklaters with sketchy biographical information on both sides of the Atlantic. Some William Linklaters have similar birth dates, while a few do not have any recorded birth date, particularly if they were born at a remote HBC post, where such recordings were not customary. Family genealogists have favored reusing existing family trees, often

populated with information "ripe" for use, and they less frequently investigate individuals with less clear (and not recorded) birth or death dates.

36. When at Moose Factory, William I wrote frequently of what was needed on the sloop he commanded. For example, he wrote an extremely detailed memo to his superiors about what gear and repairs were needed for the sloop in the coming year. Moose Factory Miscellaneous, February 17, 1851, memorandum, B.1/ z/1, HBCA.

37. Beginning on September 7, 1856, through 1857, William "held [Sunday] prayers with my men at the Post." Osnaburgh House, September 7, 1856, B.155/a/69, HBCA. He was very attentive when traveling ministers came to Osnaburgh, such as the Reverend John Horden in August 1856, and the Reverend Thomas Vincent in March 1863.

38. In a memorandum given to him when departing for Osnaburgh, his superior wrote: "I understand your grandmother [Catherine Best Thomas] is [to] accompany you inland. She is an annuitant and as a certificate of her being alive on the 1st June is necessary each year, while she lives. I give you a certificate copy of the forms, three of which are necessary annually." "Memo for P.[ostmaster], Mr. Wm Linklater, Albany, 16th July, [1856] on his leaving for Osnaburgh," James Nutt, Osnaburgh House Miscellaneous Document, B.155/z/1, HBCA. Indeed, the next year, 1857, William Linklater II filled out a "Certificate of Widow Thomas Being Alive, June 1857"; ibid.

39. John S. Long, " 'Shaganash': Early Protestant Missionaries and the Adoption of Christianity by the Western James Bay Cree, 1840–1893" (PhD dissertation, University of Toronto, 1986), 69.

40. William Linklater, Osnaburgh Census for 1858, B.155/z/1, HBCA.

41. Osnaburgh House, November 18, 1857, B.155/a/70, HBCA.

42. Osnaburgh House, May 20, 1859, B.155/a/71, HBCA.

43. Osnaburgh House, October 18, 1861, through July 24, 1862, B.155/a/75 and 76, HBCA.

44. Fur traders never called Osnaburgh House "Oz." Contemporary Anishinaabeg of the Mishkeegogamang Ojibway Nation, formerly known as the Osnaburgh House Band, call it "Oz" today.

45. Ronald Fritz, Roger Suffling, and Thomas Ajit Younger, "Influence of Fur Trade, Famine, and Forest Fires on Moose and Woodland Caribou Populations in Northwestern Ontario from 1786 to 1911," *Environmental Management* 17, no. 4 (1993): 477–89.

46. Moose Factory Miscellaneous, 1854, B.3/z/3, HBCA. For example, in 1959 after receiving a higher wage of forty-five pounds sterling, William II still owed the Moose Factory Sale Shop twenty-seven pounds. The next year

William II owed the HBC twenty-three pounds. Indeed, the records for both William II and III document they were always in debt to the HBC, although the debt diminished as both of them received higher wages. Moose Factory, Miscellaneous, B.3/z/3, HBCA, William Linklater contracts 1856 and 1859, A.32/38, HBCA. For a record of wages and debts for William Linklater III, see "William Linklater," in Servants/Winterers records, 1879–1891, B.235/g/10, 11, 12, 18, 19. In the last record for William Linklater III in 1891, his wage is 33.70, and his "book debt" is 26.76.

47. Bishop, *The Northern Ojibwa and the Fur Trade*, 157.

48. Fort Albany, "Returns of the Albany River District Posts, Outfit 1860" for Osnaburgh House, B.3/z/3, HBCA.

49. Helena and Ellen were alternately used as her given name. Ellen was more commonly used, particularly by English speakers; hence my use of Ellen rather than Helena in the text.

50. Long, "'Shaganash': Early Protestant Missionaries and the Adoption of Christianity by James Bay Cree," 84.

51. 1870 Manitoba Census, St. Andrews Parish, Library and Archives Canada; 1881 Canada for Manitoba, Library and Archives Canada; Métis scrip for John Brown, Nancy (née Richards) Brown, and John Turner (Brown's adopted son), Library and Archives Canada, Ottawa.

52. Donald Gunn, *History of Manitoba from the Earliest Settlement to 1835* (Ottawa: MacLean, Roger and Co.: 1880), 318.

53. Robert Coutts, "'By a Union of Effort We Effect a Great Deal': The English-Speaking Métis and the Anglican Mission at St. Andrew's Park, Red River," accessed November 7, 2012, http://www.ecclectica.ca/issues/2003/2/coutts .asp.

54. Dale Gibson, *Law, Life, and Government at Red River*, vol. 1 (Montreal: McGill-Queen's University Press, 2015), 204.

55. *Beyond the Gates—1880–1981* (St. Andrews Centennial Book, 1981), 174; *Dictionary of Canadian Biography*, s.v. "Alfred Boyd," by John L. Finlay, accessed October 25, 2016, http://www.biographi.ca/en/bio/boyd_alfred _13Ehtml.

56. "James Gunn," Red River Ancestry.ca, http://redriverancestry.ca/GUNN -JAMES-1824.php; "William Bolland (1757–1804) and Penachequay (fl.1800–1810)," Denney Collection, Glenbow Museum, Calgary, Alberta.

57. Distinctions were made not just on "race and colour" of British versus Métis women but also on their education, knowledge of "civilized arts," and whether their parents' marriage was properly Christian. Sylvia Van Kirk, *"Many Tender Ties": Women in Fur-Trade Society, 1670–1870* (Winnipeg:

Watson and Dryer, 1980), 7; Jennifer S. H. Brown, *Strangers in Blood: Fur Trade Company Families in Indian Country* (Vancouver: University of British Columbia Press, 1980), 212.

58. "The Queen versus Ellen Linklater," Court of Assiniboia, Charge of Infanticide, August 16, 1866, records held in the Provincial Archive of Manitoba, Winnipeg. From 1844 to 1872 five infanticide charges were brought to the HBC-run provincial court. All were found guilty. Ellen received the shortest sentence of the five. To see these records, also consult Dale Gibson, ed., *Law, Life, and Government at Red River,* vol. 2: *General Quarterly Court of Assiniboia Annotated Records, 1844–1872* (Montreal: McGill-Queen's University Press, 2015). Complicating the court case was one chilling fact: infant deaths were quite common in this time period. Infanticide was uncommon in Cree cultural tradition, although it did occur in incestuous relationships. The circumstances surrounding Ellen Linklater's charge are unspecified, making it difficult to determine what might really have happened. Coutts, "By a Union of Effort," 8; *Ellen Smallboy: Glimpse of a Cree Woman's Life* (Montreal: McGill-Queen's University Press, 1995), 32.

59. Sarah Ballenden, a high-status Métis woman at Red River a decade before Ellen Linklater "paid the price" of any peccadillo, real or imaginary. "Gossip and innuendo were enough to convict her," Van Kirk, *"Many Tender Ties,"* 229, 207; Brown, *Strangers in Blood,* 215.

60. Pierre Swampy and Margaret Linklater, marriage, June 19, 1871, St. Boniface Parish, Centre du Patrimonine, Saint-Boniface, Manitoba.

61. William Linklater (e), Biographical Sheet, HBCA, and Alice Mary (née Linklater) Morrisseau Métis Scrip, Library and Archives Canada, Ottawa and Osnaburgh House, July 1, 1868, B.155/a/82, HBCA.

62. Gunn, *History of Manitoba,* 324.

63. Coutts, "By a Union of Effort," 9.

64. At this time, "Rupert's Land" was a vast region mostly in what is now Canada for which the HBC had exclusive trading rights—a monopoly on trade. Named after Prince Rupert, cousin to King Charles II, it was a region defined by watersheds that empty into Hudson Bay. The region also included a small portion of extreme northern Minnesota, that is, before the international boundary was agreed on by the fledgling United States and Great Britain.

65. Gunn, *History of Manitoba,* 320–23.

66. Lawrence Barkwell, "Legislative Assembly of Assiniboia," 2010, Louis Riel Institute, Winnipeg, Manitoba.

67. Ibid.; "Manitoba's Provisional Government of 1870: The Convention of Forty," no date, Louis Riel Institute.

68. John Tait, as quoted in Coutts, "By a Union of Effort," 11.
69. Robert Watson, *Lower Fort Garry* (Winnipeg: Hudson's Bay Company, 1928), 34.
70. Ibid., 37.
71. Rev. Dr. G. Bryce, "Intrusive Ethnological Types in Rupert's Land," *The Transactions of the Royal Society of Canada*, vol. 9 (1903–1904), 148.
72. D. N. Sprague and R. R. Frye, compilers, *The Genealogy of the First Metis Nation* (Winnipeg: Pemmican Publications, 1983), 28.
73. Métis scrip for Barbara Linklater Knott, Alexander Knott, and their children: Sarah, Thomas, Annie, Jessie, John, and Patrick. Library and Archives of Canada, Ottawa; "List of Grantees of Lands in Assiniboia under the Earl of Selkirk and Hudson's Bay Company from 1812 to July 15, 1870," in *Beyond the Gates of Lower Fort Garry: A Sequel*, ed. Barbara Gessner (R. M. of St. Andrews, 2000), 167.
74. Brad Milne, "Manitoba History: The Historiography of Métis Land Dispersal, 1870–1890," https://www.mhs.mb.ca/docs/mb_history/30/Metisland dispersal.shtml (also available in *Manitoba History* 30 [Autumn 1995]).
75. Sprague and Frye, *The Genealogy of the First Metis Nation*, no pagination.
76. Reverend Cochrane was apparently a well-liked Métis pastor, who experienced more personal tragedy than he could bear. He took to drink and only four days after John was baptized, was suspended. His parishioners did not perceive his drinking to be a significant cause of concern, but the church hierarchy did. Derek Whitehouse-Strong, "Reverend Henry Cochrane: 'Excellent Native Preacher,' 'Bad Example,' and 'Innocent Victim of European Clerical Jealousy,'" *Historical Papers*, Canadian Society of Church History, 2004, https://churchhistcanfiles.wordpress.com/2013/05/2004–5-strong -article.pdf.
77. *Manitoba Free Press*, April 26, 1873. Ellen died at the age of forty-eight, having spent thirty-one years at Moose Factory, eight years at Osnaburgh House, and her last nine years at St. Andrews.
78. *Manitoban and Northwest Herald*, April 26, 1873.
79. Métis scrip for William and Ellen Linklater's children: William, Margaret, Barbara, John, James, Archibald, and Charles, Library and Archives Canada, Ottawa; 1881 Census for Manitoba. The Browns also adopted three children. Métis scrip for John, Alex, and Joseph Turner, Library and Archives of Canada, Ottawa.
80. According to stories John told his friends, he was sent to live with his grandmother to attend school. Nancy Brown was technically John's great-aunt, but by Indigenous custom he would have called her his grandmother. When

at Red River, he would have been fully immersed in Métis culture, language, food, dress, and customs. Sister Noemi Weygant, *John (Jack) Linklater: Legendary Indian Game Warden* (Duluth, Minn.: Priory Books, 1987), 2; Aslakson, "Jack Linklater."

81. O. R. Tripp, "Hunting Moose with a Camera," *Minneapolis Journal*, June 1930.

82. Alice M. Johnson, "James Bay Artist, William Richards," *The Beaver* 298 (Summer 1967): 4–10; *Dictionary of Canadian Biography*, s.v. "Richards, William," by Jennifer S. H. Brown, accessed July 6, 2019, http://www.biographic.ca/en/bio/richards_willliam_5E.html.

83. Donna G. Sutherland, "St. Jude's Anglican Church," July 2009, St. Clement's Heritage Advisory Designation Project, http://heritagemanitoba.ca/images/pdfs/featuredProjects/St_Judes_Church_Heritage_Designation_Heritage_MB.pdf.

84. John Linklater (uncle to John), "North-West Halfbreed Claims Commission," 1900, Library and Archives Canada, Ottawa. John traveled from his residence at St. Johns, North Dakota, to Swift Current, Saskatchewan, to "personally . . . appear" to make this claim for his children, John Henry and Flora Harriet Linklater.

85. "Archibald Linklater," in Servants/Winterers records, 1879–1890, B.235/g/10, 11, 12, 18, 19, HBCA. In 1878 in one of his first contracts with the HBC, Archibald lists his parish as St. Andrews; Northern Department servants' engagement registers, B.239/u/3, HBCA. The same year his brother William's parish is listed as "native"; that is, he did not have a home other than his HBC posts, and he was of Native blood; Servants/winterers, for 1880, B.235/g/5, HBCA.

86. Praxis Research, "Historic Métis in the Rainy River and Kenora Districts of Ontario: Fishing Practices and Off-Reserve Residence," 27, prepared for Native Affairs Unit, Ontario Ministry of Natural Resources, Peterborough, Ontario, 2002.

87. George Swampy and Pierre Swampy, Northern Department servants engagement registers, 1823–1895, B.239/u/3 #2160, HBCA.

88. Helen Swampy, baptism, May 25, 1882, Notre Dame du Portage Registres, Kenora, Diocese of Thunder Bay, Ontario; 1911 Canada Census, Fort Alexander, Manitoba. This census reports Pierre and Margaret Swampy as "Saulteau," or Anishinaabeg.

89. Margaret Swampy died on June 14, 1941, age ninety-six, on the Fort Alexander Reserve; Manitoba Vital Statistics, Winnipeg, Canada. The Indian Act (of Canada) defined an Indian as a male of Indian blood belonging to the tribe. His wife and children were also Indians. Thus, Margaret, a Métis,

married Pierre of the Fort Alexander Anishinaabeg tribe and thus legally became an Indian.

90. "Chiefs and Councilors," *www.oldcrow.ca/cc.htm*; Leonard Linklater, personal communication, Whitehorse, Yukon, May 9, 2016.

91. "Archie Linklater Real Pioneer," *Edmonton Journal*, August 21, 1921.

92. Arctic explorer Vilhjalmur Stefansson described Archie as "over 6 feet in height, powerfully built and used to the roughest kind of work. For years he had been a member of the Royal Mounted Police at Dawson, at which time he had gained a reputation as a traveler"; Vilhjalmur Stefansson, *Hunters of the Great North* (New York: Harcourt, Brace, 1922), 238; Clara Vyvyan, *The Ladies, The Gwich'in and the Rat: Travels on the Athabasca, Mackenzie, Rat, Porcupine and Yukon Rivers in 1926* (Edmonton: University of Alberta Press, 2015), 285.

93. Charles Linklater, Métis scrip, Library and Archives Canada; "Charlies P. Linklater," *Rod and Gun in Canada* 6 (June 1904): 39.

94. Charlie was the only one of the siblings who divorced, and he moved from Rat Portage to the greater Red River area. As was customary, he left his children with his ex-wife and soon-to-be new husband. He remarried, raised a second family, and often moved throughout central Manitoba.

95. "Modern Leather Stocking from Wilds of Far North," *Minneapolis Journal*, March 31, 1904; *Virginia (Minn.) Enterprise*, May 6, 1904. John, too, had a "run in" with a moose; having shot one, he was treed by another; "Game Warden Aid Makes Trip from Winton to See Explorer," *Minneapolis Tribune*, February 5, 1929.

96. Margaret Bemister, *The Windmaker: Thirty Indian Legends* (Toronto: Macmillan, 1912). Charles told five stories that appear in this volume under the heading of "The Adventures of Wesakchak."

97. "Private Frank Linklater, Died: April 24, 1915," Canadian Great War Project, http://canadiangreatwar project.com/searches/soldierDetail.asp?ID; "Linklater, William," Kenora Great War Project, http://kenoragreatwar project.ca/canadian-infantry/Linklater-william; John Linklater, Alien Registration and Declaration of Holdings, February 27, 1918, State of Minnesota, Minnesota Commission of Public Safety, Iron Range Research Center, Chisholm, Minn.

98. Simon J. Dawson, "The Red River Expedition of 1870," *Thunder Bay Sentinel*, September 21, 1882.

99. Alice Wakemup, "Allotment # 701," Wirta Collection.

100. Mae Wirta, letter to John Linklater, October 27, 1930, Embarrass, Minn., Wirta Collection.

101. Alice Morrison Wakemup, St. Louis County, Minnesota Vital Statistics death record, August 21, 1965. Alice's birth date, like John's, is listed differently through the years. Alice was likely born in 1869, the birth year both her parents provided the census taker in the 1881 Canada Census. Thus, Alice was ninety-six years old at her death. The Canadian spelling of Morrisseau (sometimes with one "s") is often rendered as Morrison in the United States.

102. In the 1891 Canada Census, Clara Linklater, John and Alice's younger sister, appears in two places at two different census takings. She is recorded as being both with her older sister at Lake of the Woods in April and with her father at Savanne, Ontario. William Linklater was recently widowed, and perhaps Clara went to live with her sister, as her father was traveling for his HBC job. There is no record of Clara after these census recordings, and she likely died not too long after this. Similarly, there is no record of Charles Edward after the 1881 census. Life insurance document, Frank M. and Alice Rockwell Warren Papers.

103. By the time of her March 1894 application for Métis scrip, Alice and Daniel Morrisseau had already lost three infants: William, Andrew, and Elizabeth. The first and last were named after her parents. Alice Mary (née Linklater) Morrisseau scrip, scrip number 4163, Library and Archives Canada, Ottawa.

104. April 9, 1894, letter from the inspector of Indian Agencies to the Manitoba Superintendency, Office of the Inspector to the Commissioner, Dominion Lands, Winnipeg, Manitoba, in Alice Mary (née Linklater) Morrisseau scrip claim file.

105. 1901 Canadian Census, Beaudro Fishery, Lake of the Woods.

106. Daniel Morriseau and Alice Linklater were married on August 11, 1887. Both Daniel and Alice list their ages as twenty. Alice Mary (née Linklater) Morrisseau, Métis scrip, Library and Archives Canada, Ottawa; Marriage of Alice Linklater and Daniel Morrisseau, Rat Portage, August 11, 1888, District of Rainy River, Rat Portage (Kenora), Ontario.

107. 1908 Census of the Bois Fort Chippewa Indians of Nett Lake, accessed at www.fold3. She is already listed as Mrs. Frank Wakemup.

108. Alice Wakemup, "Allotment #701," Wirta Collection.

109. John Linklater, "Alien Registration and Declaration of Holdings," 1918.

2. The Anishinaabeg Family and Artistry of Tchi-Ki-Wis

1. "John Linklater," "Alien Registration and Declaration of Holdings," Minnesota Commission of Public Safety, State of Minnesota, Iron Range Research Center, Chisholm; John Linklater and Helen Linklater, Morse Township, St. Louis County, Minn., 1930 Federal Census.

2. Bruce M. Littlejohn, "The Dawson Route: A Phase of Westward Expansion" (M.A. thesis, University of British Columbia, 1967), 9, 132, 133.

3. The Dawson Route dams were built for two reasons: to raise the water level around rapids, and to raise lake levels to improve navigation for the small fleet of steamboats scattered along the route. But raising the level of a lake, such as Pickerel, or "Kaogassikok," drowned out trees; as one traveler noted, "numbers of fine trees are now growing in the water, for, by damming up the outflow of the lakes to make the landing places, the water level has been raised and the shore trees have thus been submerged several feet." Rev. George M. Grant, *Ocean to Ocean: Sandford Fleming's Expedition through Canada in 1872* (Rutland, Vt.: Tuttle, 1967), 50. Raised water levels likely adversely impacted wild rice beds along the route.

4. Annual Reports for 1887, 1891, 1892, 1893, and 1894, Canada, Department of Indian Affairs, Library and Archives Canada, Ottawa.

5. James Trow, *A Trip to Manitoba* (Quebec: Marcotte, 1875), 17.

6. George F. G. Stanley, *Toil and Trouble: Military Expeditions to Red River* (Toronto: Dundurn Press, 1989), 143, 219, 236, and 246.

7. Littlejohn, "The Dawson Route," 241.

8. "Statement of Paul LaPlante Made at Grand Portage, April 20, 1931," Minnesota Historical Society, St. Paul. Warner Wirta, personal communication, March 27, 2006. Warner gave me a photograph of John Robinson posed with a number of other men. Warner annotated the photograph: "Great Grandfather John Robinson. He came up with the English Army before the 1900s from Sault Ste. Marie, Canada." John Robinson had arrived in the area roughly by 1870. The evidence, both direct and circumstantial, suggests he was not originally from Lac La Croix but from an Anishinaabeg community far to the east that had stronger French ties.

9. John Linklater file, William (Bill) Hanson, interview, Ridley Library, Quetico Provincial Park, Atikokan, Ontario; Frank M. Warren, letter to George Baggley, Superintendent, December 9, 1941, Isle Royale National Park, Houghton, Mich.; Ellen Hanson, interview by author, November 11, 1988, Floodwood, Minn. Ellen remembered John Robinson speaking French with a hired hand, Charlie Grandmaison, at the Linklater-Hanson fishery on Isle Royale.

10. "Inspection Report, Pine Portage Post, Lac La Pluie District," 1890, B.328/e/1, HBCA. Interestingly "Robson" owed a great deal of money to the HBC at the time but did not seem active as a trapper. Perhaps he was a temporary HBC employee?

11. "The Huronian Mine on Jackfish Lake was the first gold mine in northwestern Ontario. In the winter of 1870–71, two Indians working for the Hudson's

Bay Company found a gold vein, or 'free gold in the form of thick leaves.'" Walpole Roland, *Algoma West: Its Mines, Scenery and Industrial Resources* (Toronto: Warwick and Sons, 1887), 176–77.

12. Elizabeth Arthur, "Simon J. Dawson, C. E.," *Thunder Bay Historical Museum Society*, 1987, 18.

13. Grant, *Ocean to Ocean*, 51, 64. At one point, Blackstone along with his father effectively operated as toll takers along the Dawson Trail, each posted at the start of the central water route, or roughly in what is Quetico Provincial Park today. At the time Reverend Grant and his party traveled along the Dawson Route in summer 1872, they encountered Blackstone at the west end of the portage out of Lake Windegoostigwan (part of the French River watershed northeast of today's Quetico Provincial Park), and Blackstone's father where the Rainy River enters Lake of the Woods. Blackstone's father asked the party "for some return for our passage through it," and the Grant party provided food for him and his band.

14. "Rev. E. F. Wilson's Account of a Lake Superior Missionary Tour," *Algona Missionary News*, vol. 1, September 1, 1878, in *Thunder Bay District 1821–1892*, ed. Elizabeth Arthur (Toronto: The Champlain Society, 1973), 184; W. S. Piper, *The Eagle of Thunder Cape* (Thunder Bay, Ont.: Thunder Bay Historical Museum Society, 2001), 23. The late Milt Powell, an Anishinaabe man from Saganagon Lake and great-grandson of Chief Blackstone, thought this story was told to "sow discord" toward Blackstone, and he did not believe it. Milt Powell, personal communication, May 17 and 13, 2013, Grand Marais, Minn.

15. Annual Report for 1879, Indian Affairs, Ottawa.

16. Grant, *Ocean to Ocean*, 51.

17. Hon. Alexander Morris, *The Treaties of Canada with the Indians* (Toronto: Coles, 1979), 44.

18. There is a double irony in the names recorded in the Halfbreed Adhesion. This cannot be "our" John Linklater, as the John Linklater listed had eight children in 1871. Our John Linklater was one year old at this time, and his future wife, Tchi-Ki-Wis, was likely not yet born. Library and Archives Canada, Indian Affairs, RG 10, vol. 1675, "Dawson Route Paylists," October 17, 1871; "Treaty 3 between Her Majesty the Queen and the Saulteaux Tribe of the Ojibbeway Indians at the Northwest Angle on the Lake of the Woods with Adhesions," Aboriginal Affairs and Northern Development Canada, http://aadnc-aandc.ge.ca/eng/1100100028675/1100100028679, accessed October 5, 2012; Lawrence Barkwell, compiler, "Treaty Three Métis," Louis Riel Institute, no date, drawn from Library and Archives Canada, Indian Affairs, RG 10, vol. 3715, file 21, 809.

19. In the 1901 Canadian Census, the older namesake Tchi-Ki-Wis is identified as "Mary" Linklater. Many White friends believed that John had given Tchi-Ki-Wis her name.

20. Lac La Croix, Annual Report for 1881, Indian Affairs, Ottawa, Canada.

21. "Kawawaigamot Band," Annual Report for 1882, Indian Affairs, Ottawa, Canada.

22. Julia Charlotte Connors, birthplace Kawa Bay, 1900, Archives of the Roman Catholic Diocese of Thunder Bay, North of Lake Superior Missions, Father William Maurice Database, Thunder Bay, Ontario.

23. "Kawawaigamot Band," Annual Report for 1881, Indian Affairs, Ottawa, Canada.

24. "Kawawaigamot Band," Annual Report for 1883, Indian Affairs, Ottawa, Canada.

25. Lucy Eldersveld Murphy, *Great Lakes Creoles: A French-Indian Community on the Northern Borderlands, Prairie Du Chien, 1750–1860* (Cambridge: Cambridge University Press, 2014), 162; Lucy Eldersveld Murphy, "Women, Networks, and Colonization in the Nineteenth-Century Wisconsin," in *Contours of a People: Metis Family, Mobility, and History*, ed. Nicole St-Onge, Carolyn Podruchny, and Brenda Macdougall (Norman: University of Oklahoma Press, 2012), 232.

26. Period and contemporary accounts of "Chief Blackstone" sometimes confuse father with son. Blackstone the elder died in 1885. He guided the Lac La Croix First Nation through the travails of the Dawson Route and the early treaty period. He was immediately succeeded by his son, or John Blackstone. Blackstone the younger did not remain a leader long but was replaced in 1889, under the urging of the Canadian Indian agents. Shirley F. Peruniak, *An Illustrated History of Quetico Provincial Park* (Atikokan, Ont.: Friends of Quetico Park, 2000), 18; Blackstone file, Ridley Library, Quetico Provincial Park, Ont.

27. "Rev. Wilson's Account of a Lake Superior Missionary Tour," 183.

28. When the first train came through, Anishinaabeg from Kawa Bay and Lac La Croix met it, including Blackstone. More than three hundred Anishinaabeg greeted the train and its VIP passengers. "The First C.P.R. Train Arrives in Thunder Bay," *Port Arthur Weekly Herald*, July 8, 1882, in *Thunder Bay District, 1821–1892*, ed. Arthur, 128–30.

29. Annual Report for 1883 and 1888, Indian Affairs, Ottawa, Canada.

30. Annual Report for 1885, Canada, Indian Affairs, Ottawa, Canada.

31. Annual Report for 1890, Canada, Indian Affairs, Ottawa, Canada.

32. 1901 and 1911 Canadian Census for Lac La Croix; 1920 U.S. Census for Fall Lake (Winton), Minn.

33. Frank Warren, letter, December 9, 1941, Isle Royale National Park. Warren's letter describes the gifts he and his family were donating to Isle Royale National Park, including objects made by Tchi-Ki-Wis.

34. Shirley Peruniak, note, "Lac La Croix Family Clans," Ridley Library, Quetico Provincial Park, Atikokan, Ont.

35. Milt and Alice Powell, personal communication, May 17, 2013, Grand Marais, Minn. The Powell family also mentioned further information about the relationship between the Connors and Robinsons. O kee wak e ji qua ke, daughter of Blackstone, married Ed Connor and helped him run a small trading post on Pine Point, Basswood Lake. According to Sophie Conner Powell, her father, Ed Connor, and John Linklater came from the Albany River country (in the north) and married sisters. Ed married O kee wak e ji qua ke, and John married Tchi-Ki-Wis. John Linklater file, Ridley Library, Quetico Provincial Park, Atikokan, Ont. Ed Connor was originally from the Bad River area of Wisconsin.

36. Shawbegeezigoh was living at Kawa Bay when Simon Dawson came through and the Dawson Trail was constructed. Blackstone file, Shirley Peruniak, Ridley Library, Quetico Provincial Park, Atikokan, Ont.

37. Walter Caribou, interview by Jerre Pete, February 4, 1997, Grand Portage, Minn. This oral history interview is part of the Vermilion Lake Bois Forte Oral History Project, Minnesota Historical Society, St. Paul. Walter Caribou, interview by Warner Wirta, no date, Grand Portage, Minn., Wirta Collection. Lynn Laitala, personal communication with author, November 11, 2018, Lake Linden, Mich.

38. 1920 Census for Fall Lake (Winton), Minn.

39. John and Vi Sansted, interview by Warner Wirta, August 21, 1982, Winton, Minn. John Sansted was a respected canoe guide who began guiding in the 1920s and worked for four decades. Sansted knew the Linklaters well. Tauno Maki, *Since 1888 Ely* (Ely, Minn.: Ely Echo, 1988), 293–94.

40. It is more likely Helen Robinson/Tchi-Ki-Wis and Grandma Hoffman were "sisters" in terms of being close blood kin or sisters of the same clan. John and Susan Robinson have only one daughter (and two granddaughters) listed in the Lac La Croix treaty paylists, thus precluding the possibility that Grandma Hoffman and Tchi-Ki-Wis were true sisters. In the 1910 federal census for St. Louis County, Ma-Me No-a-go-shish/Grandma Hoffman is listed as forty years old; thus her birth year would be approximately 1870. In another census her birth year is 1860; hence her birth year can be only approximated, as is the case of many early census records for area Anishinaabeg.

41. Virtually all sources spell his name "Hoffman." His name is spelled "Charles

J. Hofmann" in the 1920 Census, and Charles Joseph Hofmann on his 1918 registration card for the World War I draft. Although a German immigrant, he was naturalized before World War I.

42. Margaret Sweet, *Winton: The Town That Lumber Built* (Ely, Minn.: Ely–Winton Historical Society), 59; Maki, *Since 1888 Ely*, 294.

43. Ibid.; Robert Maki, personal communication with author, July 5, 2019, and January 18, 2020, at Fall Lake and Ely, Minn.

44. Frank M. Warren, letter to Mrs. Joseph E. Pecore, July 11, 1933, Frank M. and Alice Rockwell Warren Papers.

45. Paul Caribou died on the Four Mile Railroad from Fall to Basswood Lakes in November 1923, leaving son Walter fatherless and at Grand Portage. John Kingfisher, living at Nett Lake at the time, went to Grand Portage and brought back young Walter Caribou with him. Gilbert Caribou, personal communication with author, May 10, 2005, Grand Portage, Minn. The Caribou family were also related to Blackstone, as was Tchi-Ki-Wis and her mother, Susan Robinson, or Mandaquabeek. Billy Blackwell, personal communication with author, March 31, 2016, Grand Portage, Minn.

46. Paul Caribou and John Linklater were together on Basswood Lake in 1916. Gilman, "Going In by Gasoline," 308.

47. Walter Caribou, interview.

48. U.S. Federal Census for 1920 and 1930, Fall Lake, Minn. In the 1930 Census, John Robinson is listed as a widower, and there is no mention of Susan. When "old man Robinson" was accompanying John and Tchi-Ki-Wis to Isle Royale in the mid-1920s, he was alone. It is most likely Susan Robinson died at Jackfish Bay and was interred in a grave house near the Linklater home. The grave houses were well known, but their occupants were not.

49. In an "early" HBC post document, Little Caribou, as early as 1829, was said to be from Lac des Bois Blanc (Basswood Lake). He was documented by the HBC clerk as coming both from Grand Portage a great deal and "inland" from Lake Superior, suggesting a lengthy familial connection between inland Anishinaabeg and Grand Portage. Fort William Post, September 30, 1829, B.231/a/9, HBCA.

50. Timothy Cochrane, *Minong—the Good Place: Ojibwe and Isle Royale* (East Lansing: Michigan State University Press, 2009), 130–32.

51. Ben East, "Hunts Moose Only with His Camera—Chippewa Guide on Isle Royale Has Lain Aside Bow and Rifle—Calls, Stalks Quarry," *Grand Rapids (Mich.) Press*, September 20, 1930; this article was syndicated in other newspapers. "Jack Linklater, Wilderness Guide and Warden, Drowns," *Minneapolis Journal*, July 10, 1933.

52. While it occurred earlier than the period I am discussing, Henry Gillman collected fourteen "Ojibway" objects on Isle Royale in 1873, but the makers are not identified. This is an illustration of the tendency to not see Indigenous people as (named) individuals and as a significant part of Isle Royale history. Three of the objects have a cultural affiliation of "Grande Portage," while the others' cultural affiliation is not identified. That summer, Gillman feverishly wrote of the ancient copper miners and their mysterious identity and efforts, but none of his public writings mention collecting "modern" Ojibway objects from Isle Royale. The catalog numbers for those objects are 76-19-10/10212–10223, Peabody Museum of Archaeology and Ethnology, Harvard University, Cambridge, Mass. Henry Gillman, "Ancient Works at Isle Royale, Michigan" *Appletons' Journal* 10, no. 229 (August 9, 1873): 173–75.

53. Ellen Hanson, personal communication with author, October 17, 1988, Floodwood, Minn.

54. Walter Caribou, statement, transcribed by niece Harriet Ottertail, Ridley Library, Quetico Provincial Park, Atikokan, Ont. The statement is undated; however, Walter lived at Nett Lake, with strong connection to Lac La Croix, until 1980, when he moved to Grand Portage. It is likely this was written before that move, or before 1980.

55. Ellen Hill married William, or Bill, Hanson on June 11, 1927, and immediately left for Birch Island, Isle Royale, for her honeymoon and Bill's partnership with John Linklater to conduct commercial fishing. Having worked as a stenographer for the Game and Fish Department in Winton alongside John and her not-as-yet husband Bill, Ellen Hanson knew Jack and Tchi-Ki-Wis better than any other non-Indigenous person. Ellen Hanson, interview by Warner Wirta, July 30, 1982, Floodwood, Minn., Wirta Collection; "Ellen Hanson," *Mesabi Daily News* (Virginia Minn.), September 18, 2010; Ellen Hanson, interview by Warner Wirta, March 23, 1984, Floodwood, Minn., Wirta Collection.

56. Mrs. Arthur Johnson (with her husband), interview by Sister Noemi Weygant, undated, Hoyt Lakes, Minn., Wirta Collection. As well as making clothing for herself and her sister, Maggie, Clara made dresses that she sold to Mrs. Johnson and others.

57. Ellen Hanson lived a long life, dying in 2010 at the age of 105. Her obituary noted: "Upon [high school] graduation she was hired as a clerk typist for the State Game and Fish Headquarters located in Winton—a position she held until 1935. She married chief warden Bill Hanson on June 11, 1927. They honeymooned at Isle Royale on property they owned jointly with fellow warden

Jack Linklater and his wife, Tchi-Ki-Wis. They teamed up with the Linklaters there and commercially fished until their return to Winton in September." *Mesabi Daily News* (Virginia, Minn.), September 18, 2010.

58. John Macfie and Basil Johnston, *Hudson Bay Watershed: A Photographic Memoir of the Ojibway, Cree, and Oji-Cree* (Toronto: Dundurn, 1991), 20, 33. The first photograph is of a parka but with a front zipper; the second is of a pullover parka. Alanson Skinner, "Notes on the Eastern Cree and Northern Saulteaux," Anthropological Papers of the American Museum of Natural History 9 (New York: American Museum of Natural History, 1912), 15–17.

59. Aldrich, *Earth Never Tires,* 116.

60. I had thought the Linklater canoe was the only surviving Indigenous-made canoe used on Isle Royale. However, I recently discovered a second canoe, both older and shorter, in the collection of the Peabody Museum of Harvard University. The canoe was purchased by Henry Gillman, then working for the U.S. Lighthouse Service, in 1873 and likely in the Minong Mine/McCargoe Cove area. It is in museum storage and in tip-top condition. Its short length, ten feet, raises the question of whether it was used only for intra-island travel, as it is small for a lake crossing. If it was used only within the island, there is a strong possibility it was made on Isle Royale. "Birch Bark Canoe," 76-45-10/10212, Peabody Museum of Archaeology and Ethnology, Harvard University, Cambridge, Mass.

61. Warner Wirta, personal communication with author, July 24, 2001, Duluth, Minn.; "Linklater Canoe," Vernacular Boat Archive, June 12, 1990, Isle Royale National Park.

62. Edwin Tappan Adney and Howard I. Chappelle, *Bark Canoes and Skin Boats of North America* (Washington, D.C.: Smithsonian, 1964), 125–26. Tchi-Ki-Wis also made miniature canoes for sale in the same "long-nose Ojibwe" shape.

63. Ellen Hanson, personal communication with author, October 17, 1988, Floodwood, Minn.

64. Carl Gawboy, letter to author, November 3, 2019, Duluth, Minn.

65. Carl Gawboy, personal communication with author, October 25, 2019, Duluth, Minn.

66. Murat Vardar, personal communication with author, October 22, 2019, Toronto, Ontario; Gawboy, personal communication. Vardar runs an informative blog devoted to canoe paddles, including historical ones. See www.paddlemaking.blogspot.com.

67. A similar-shaped paddle is in the National Museum of the American Indian in Washington, D.C. It has no handle, a thick throat, and a similar-shaped

blade. It was collected prior to 1877 from the Pic River Reserve, east of Thunder Bay, Ontario. Catalog 10/3531, National Museum of the American Indian, Washington, D.C.; Murat Vardar, personal communication; Albert E. Jenks, "The Wild Rice Gatherers of the Upper Lakes," 1056 in *Annual Report of the Bureau of American Ethnology*, 19, part 2 (1897–98), plate 70, "Indian Woman on Her Way to the Rice Bed to Tie the Stalks."

68. Scott Rumely, personal communication with Carol Maass, July 26, 1981, Rock Harbor, Isle Royale, Isle Royale National Park.

69. The primary function for the large kettle was as a vessel to hold a liquid preservative (copper sulfate) so nets could be dipped in it to extend their life. Also, at this time some Isle Royale fishermen were experimenting with dying their nets, which was thought would make them less visible and thus more effective fishing technology. Tchi-Ki-Wis was repurposing the use of the kettle from its normal fishery use. Timothy Cochrane and Hawk Tolson, *A Good Boat Speaks for Itself: Isle Royale Fishermen and Their Boats* (Minneapolis: University of Minnesota Press, 2002), 59.

70. Skinner, "Notes on the Eastern Cree and Northern Saulteaux," 44; see also William Richard's painting in this work. Gilbert White, personal communication with author, March 21 and 27, 2020, Grand Marais, Minn. For a diagram of a "horse collar style" harness, see http://oldschoolak.blogspot.com /2009/11/historical-sled-dog-harnesses-part-1.html.

71. Cory Carole Silverstein, "Clothed Encounters: The Power of Dress in Relations between Anishnaabe and British Peoples in the Great Lakes Region, 1760–2000" (PhD diss., McMaster University, 2000), 297.

72. Ibid., 303.

73. Ellen Hanson, interview, July 30, 1982.

74. David Sager, "Ojibwa Moccasins: Center Seam/Vamp," *Whispering Wind* 36, no. 6 (May–June 2007): 4–6.

75. I am assuming that these moccasins were made by Tchi-Ki-Wis, but that is not absolutely clear. They were part of the "Warren Collection" given to Isle Royale National Park by Alice Warren, and there are few Anishinaabeg objects in the park collection without provenance information. The Warrens and Frank's mother, Jennie, or Mrs. George Warren, were collectors of Indian objects, a number of which were made by Tchi-Ki-Wis. Unfortunately, the Warrens did not provide information on who made most of the Indian objects they collected, other than in a few letters or notes given to the park when they donated the objects. The design of these beaded moccasins is similar to those Tchi-Ki-Wis made, raising the likelihood she was the maker of them.

76. Silverstein, "Clothed Encounters," 306.

77. Ibid., 278, 287, 289, 293, 304.
78. An earlier family photograph has Clara and her sister, Margaret, or Maggie, each wearing a bandolier bag and the ceremonial dress (mostly off camera). The grainy photograph was taken outside their home at Jackfish Bay. As Margaret died circa 1911 at the age of twenty and both sisters appear to be teenagers in the photograph, we can date the bandolier bags and black floral dress as made no later than 1908 and perhaps earlier. This means that Clara was relatively young when she made these and raises the likelihood that Tchi-Ki-Wis helped her significantly.
79. Josephine and Annie Sloan, photograph, White Earth Reservation, National Museum of the American Indian, photograph object # 26/6690, Washington, D.C.
80. We know that Tchi-Ki-Wis was beading purses like this one, as she gave one to Ellen Hanson. Ellen Hanson, interview, July 30, 1982.
81. Carrie A. Lyford, *Ojibwa Crafts* (Washington, D.C.: Bureau of Indian Affairs, 1953), 147; Marcia G. Anderson, *A Bag Worth a Pony: The Art of the Ojibwe Bandolier Bag* (St. Paul: Minnesota Historical Society Press, 2017), 13.
82. Mrs. Mary Anderson with Mr. and Mrs. Arthur Johnson, interview by Sister Noemi Weygant, undated, Hoyt Lakes, Minn., Wirta Collection.
83. Anderson, *A Bag Worth a Pony*, 13.
84. Tchi-Ki-Wis was weaving beads on a loom, as she gave a "wampum belt" to Ellen Hanson. It is about six inches wide and a yard long. Ellen Hanson interview, July 30, 1982.
85. Anderson, *A Bag Worth a Pony*, 50.
86. I am surmising that Tchi-Ki-Wis must have had a substantial role in the making of these bags, as she gave one to an Anishinaabe woman who assisted her after John died. By that time, Clara was living in Embarrass, Minnesota, and likely had those she made with her. Ellen Hanson, interview, July 30, 1982. Alternately, the robe was at Jackfish Bay in 1933 because Clara felt it was safer there or it was the proper place for it. Why Tchi-Ki-Wis might have given the robe away, if it was Clara's, is difficult to fathom.
87. Anderson, *A Bag Worth a Pony*, 107, 101–3.
88. Marcia Anderson, personal communication with author, April 6, 2020, Minneapolis, Minn.
89. Only half of the mats made by Tchi-Ki-Wis have a strong provenance, that is, the accompanying record states that Tchi-Ki-Wis made them. In regard to the others, there is convincing evidence that she made those, too. For example, we have direct evidence she was making cedar mats on Birch Island in 1927 and 1929, and they were sold at Rock Harbor Lodge in 1930 and 1931.

Ellen Hanson witnessed Tchi-Ki-Wis weaving cedar mats in 1927 and watched Tchi-Ki-Wis go into the woods to collect roots for the natural dyes she preferred. The mats have atypical edging made of fishing line, strongly suggesting they were made at a fishery such as Birch Island. Tchi-Ki-Wis likely made them each year she was on Birch Island, 1927–30. We do know which island family they came from. The cedar mats (without provenance information identifying the maker) were found on Isle Royale when the park was being established or soon afterward. Tchi-Ki-Wis was the only Anishinaabe woman making mats on the island in that era. We know that Tchi-Ki-Wis sold mats directly to visitors, who would "commonly boat down McCargoe's Cove" to Birch Island to buy them. The "unattributed mats" ended up at the cottages of wealthy people who were friends with Frank and Alice Warren or who even knew John Linklater personally. Ellen Hanson, interview, November 11, 1988.

Summer cottagers acquired Tchi-Ki-Wis mats two ways: directly from John and Tchi-Ki-Wis or by purchasing them at the Rock Harbor Lodge. The Rock Harbor Lodge sold only mats made by Tchi-Ki-Wis. Theoretically, mats could have been purchased elsewhere and brought to the island, but the island custom of having "souvenirs" from Isle Royale makes it unlikely that someone would prefer another mat to those made by Tchi-Ki-Wis. There was "cachet" to having a mat made by Tchi-Ki-Wis displayed on cottage walls. Finally, to display a mat made by a different maker would mean going to the considerable effort of acquiring it elsewhere, packing it, and shipping it on an island ferry. Hence, I am confident that Tchi-Ki-Wis made all ten surviving mats. Ellen Hanson, personal communication, October 17, 1988; Dave Snyder, letter to author, August 20, 1987, Isle Royale National Park, Houghton, Mich.; Carol Maass, letter to Bruce Weber, August 28, 1984, Isle Royale National Park. On my copy of this letter, Dave Snyder, park historian, wrote on August 25, 1988, that Reuben Hill bought one mat from Mrs. Linklater in 1929 for $1.50.

90. Karen Daniels Petersen, "Chippewa Mat-Weaving Techniques," *Anthropological Papers* 67 (Washington, D.C.: Bureau of American Ethnology, Smithsonian, 1963), 217; Volney H. Jones, "Notes on the Manufacture of Cedar-Bark Mats by the Chippewa Indians," *Papers of the Michigan Academy of Science, Arts, and Letters* 32 (1946): 360.

91. A cedar mat made earlier and collected on Isle Royale in 1873 appears to have had a more utilitarian than decorative purpose, as evident by its simple checker weave. It is roughly the same size as Tchi-Ki-Wis's mats and is in superb condition despite its age. Cedar mat, 76-45-10/10219, Peabody

Museum of Archaeology and Ethnology, Harvard University, Cambridge, Mass.

92. "[Cedar bark] mat for Midewiwin rituals," National Museum of the American Indian, Smithsonian Institution, Washington, D.C.

93. Timothy G. Roufs, ed., *When Everybody Called Me Gah-bay-bi-nayass: "Forever-Flying Bird": An Ethnographic Biography of Paul Peter Buffalo* (Minneapolis: Wise Ink, 2019), 1:185.

94. *Minneapolis Tribune*, September 4, 1912.

95. *Cook County News Herald* (Grand Marais, Minn.), October 24, 1917; October 9, 1918; October 27, 1921; October 19, 1922; *The Pioneer* (Bemidji, Minn.), September 23, 1915; September 12, 1919. Two articles in *Red Lake News* encouraged the sale of cedar-bark bags and mats. *Red Lake (Minn.) News*, September 15, 1915; September 1, 1917.

96. Roufs, *When Everybody Called Me Gah-bay-bi-nayass*, 1:181–85.

97. Cornelius G. Shaw, diary, August 3, 1847, Rock Harbor, Isle Royale, Bentley Historical Library, Ann Arbor, Mich.

98. Cedar-bark mat made by Charlotte Connor Deschampe, July 11, 1947, USNM # E385734–0, Smithsonian, Washington, D.C.

99. Jones, "Notes on the Manufacture of Cedar-Bark Mats," 354. It is not known if Tchi-Ki-Wis or John sought permission to harvest the tree by making a tobacco offering prior to the harvesting, or if he left tobacco for the cedar tree spirits after the bark was removed. No one documented the harvesting or even the weaving process at Isle Royale. Given that Tchi-Ki-Wis was a traditionalist, there is a likelihood she did make tobacco offerings prior to harvesting tree bark. Frances Densmore, *How Indians Use Wild Plants for Food, Medicine, and Crafts* (New York: Dover, 1974), 386–87.

100. Ellen Hanson, "Mrs. Linklater and Her Talents," unpublished memoir, Wirta Collection.

101. Ellen Hanson, interview, July 30, 1982.

102. Ellen Hanson, personal communication, October 17, 1988.

103. Densmore, *How Indians Use Wild Plants*, 370–74. Grand Portage National Monument is a caretaker of a number of mats, including those made by Tchi-Ki-Wis. They are more conveniently located closer to their maker's descendants at Grand Portage rather than Isle Royale. Also at Grand Portage are cedar mats made by Grand Portage women. One mat made in Grand Portage in 1939 as a Works Progress Administration project also uses green cedar strips to define its geometric patterns. Clearly, Densmore's comment about green not being used by the Minnesota Chippewa is incorrect.

104. Petersen, "Chippewa Mat-Weaving Techniques," 226.

105. Jones, "Notes on the Manufacture of Cedar-Bark Mats," 362.
106. For readers who would like to know more about the process of making cedar-bark mats, I recommend two articles already cited: Peterson, "Chippewa Mat-Weaving Techniques," 217–84; and Jones, "Notes on the Manufacture of Cedar-Bark Mats," 341–63.
107. Aldrich, *Earth Never Tires*, 40.
108. Peterson, "Chippewa Mat-Weaving Techniques," 230.
109. Charlotte Deschampe mat, collected on Saganaga Lake, USN number E385734–0, Smithsonian, Washington, D.C. Another mat similar in design and color scheme was made by an anonymous Anishinaabe woman from Minnesota and is at the National Museum of the American Indian, Washington, D.C.
110. Paula Sundet, "Anishinabe Mat and Bag Weaving: Implications of Cultural Sophistication in Utilitarian Art" (master's thesis, Vermont College of Norwich University, 2002), 106.
111. The Northwest Coast mats are similar but different in that the cedar is split much finer and often the mats were and are made of cedar and wool. The weave is much tighter, giving it a different, smoother appearance, and the species of cedar used is different.
112. Tchi-Ki-Wis and John Linklater stayed in Minnesota from summer 1931 until his death in 1933 and hers in 1934. It is possible, but much less likely, that Tchi-Ki-Wis made cedar mats in Minnesota in 1931 and had them shipped to Isle Royale, particularly to Rock Harbor Lodge, to sell. This would have been quite inconvenient for her and John, as she lived most summers at Jackfish Bay, requiring extra effort to get the mats to a distant post office. How many cedar-bark mats Tchi-Ki-Wis made on Jackfish Bay or nearby is unknown. It is likely she made them early in the Linklaters' marriage and they then were rolled and carried when the family moved to new trapping, hunting, or gathering locations. Mats made at that location likely had a rougher, utilitarian use and did not survive.
113. John Linklater likely met George W. Warren, Frank M. Warren's father, first. John probably worked for him when George Warren was timber cruising in northern Minnesota. Their relationship appears to have been cordial but primarily based on the business of guiding and timber cruising. Linklater's relationship with Frank was a mix of friendship and business that included guiding and being a handyman. The Warrens paid Linklater an undisclosed amount for his efforts. It must have been "worth it" as he often set aside other jobs to assist the Warrens. Frank was only a few years younger than John, hence they were closer to being peers, while George and John were of

different generations. George H. Warren, *The Pioneer Woodsman as He Is Related to Lumbering in the Northwest* (Minneapolis: Hahn and Harmon, 1914), 155, 157.

114. Wood-and-canvas canoes were very common and were replacing birch-bark canoes by the 1920s when the Warrens purchased the canoe made by Tchi-Ki-Wis. See Mark Neuzil and Norman Sims, *Canoes: A Natural History in North America* (Minneapolis: University of Minnesota Press, 2016), 171–77.

115. Priscilla (Morse) Richardson, "Grandmother's Stories," no date, Isle Royale National Park, Mich.

116. Bertha Farmer, letter to John Linklater, Winton, Minn., circa summer 1931, Wirta Collection. The letter makes clear that while the Linklaters did not go out to Isle Royale during summer 1931, their grandson Frank Nelson did. Frank assumed a number of John's handyman responsibilities in Rock Harbor for the Warren, Morse, and Rockwell families. Twenty-year-old Frank also guided Frank Oastler and his wife that summer during their Isle Royale excursion.

117. Memorandum, Acting Superintendent, Isle Royale to Regional Director, Northeast Region, April 18, 1967, Isle Royale National Park. Isle Royale's first superintendent, George Baggley, was more positive about the Warren Collection and remarked, "I feel sure that it is a gift very well worth accepting." Baggley's boss, the regional director, thought that if Warren was a true friend of the park, perhaps he would not be offended if the collection was "culled" prior to acceptance. As is true in park management today, there is often a host of opinions among staff, though the hierarchy of the National Park Service means the regional director or superintendent makes a larger mark on what park priorities are. Memorandum, Midwest Regional Director to Superintendent, Isle Royale, December 17, 1941; Memorandum, Superintendent, Isle Royale, to Director, December 22, 1941, Isle Royale National Park.

118. The Warren Collection includes the Linklater canoe, formally acquired by the park in 1941. Memorandum, Isle Royale Superintendent to Director, Washington, July 22, 1941. The Warren Collection was one of the first donations made to the park, evidenced by their provisional catalog numbers of 1, 2, 3, 4. These numbers have been superseded. Accession Record, U.S. Department of the Interior, National Park Service, Frank M. Warren donor, June 19, 1941.

119. Jean Anderson, personal communication with author, March 27, 2020, Los Angeles, Calif.

120. For our purpose, the problem with the Warren Collection is its lack of explicit provenance information—specifically who made the objects and

where. It is difficult and sometimes impossible to identify who made what objects, especially those made by Tchi-Ki-Wis versus other Anishinaabeg craftspersons. There are dozens of Anishinaabeg-made objects in the collection, but we do not know who made them or where they were acquired. We know the Warrens traveled widely, often in the boundary waters, and thus could have purchased objects from anyone. Of the dozens of objects in the Warren Collection, there are likely quite a few more objects, such as birch-bark work, made by Tchi-Ki-Wis, but we cannot confidently say that they were. In some cases we can deduce that Tchi-Ki-Wis made a particular object, but for many more we cannot.

121. Tom Holm, *The Great Confusion in Indian Affairs: Native Americans and Whites in the Progressive Era* (Austin: University of Texas Press, 2005), 87, 123, 181.

122. Warner Wirta, personal communication with author, March 27, 2006, Duluth, Minn. Warner also gave me photographs of his grandmother in which he called her a "medicine person."

123. Gilbert Caribou, personal communication with author, March 1, 2007, Grand Portage, Minn. Gilbert used the term Breathing Life ceremony for the Midewiwin.

124. Basil Johnston, *The Manitous: The Spiritual World of the Ojibway* (New York: HarperCollins, 1995), 243.

125. "Minong Traditional Cultural Property," National Register of Historic Places, National Park Service, U.S. Department of the Interior, December 10, 2018, section 7, page 13. Some Anishinaabeg believe that the Minong, or Isle Royale, plants were particularly potent because they grew in a "marine climate," or close to the lakeshore where the cold waters of Lake Superior bathe the plants in humidity as well as test them with a harsh climate.

126. East, "Hunts Moose Only with His Camera."

127. Carl Gawboy, in "Rendezvous with History: A Grand Portage Story," film, 2011, Grand Portage National Park, Grand Portage, Minn.

3. Finding Their Way

1. "John Linklater," Alien Registration and Declaration of Holdings, February 27, 1918, Minnesota Commission of Public Safety, State of Minnesota, Iron Range Research Center, Chisholm, Minn.; 1930 Federal Census, Winton, Minn. The 1920 Federal Census lists their immigration date as 1899, but I am inclined to believe this was a transcription or mishearing error on the part of the census taker rather than a different date of immigration. 1930 Federal Census, Fall Lake, Minn.

2. William Linklater III served as a translator for Indian agent Albert McCraken's visit to Lac La Croix on September 2, 1889. He translated a contentious meeting in which John Blackstone was accused by the Indian agent of behaving illegally (giving or selling his ceremonial coat and medals to American Indians). The Lac La Croix people were reluctant to depose him. "Extract from Mr. Albert McCraken's Special Report for 1889," Indian Affairs, R.G. 10, vol. 3831, file 62, 842, Library and Archives Canada, Ottawa.

At this time, the whereabouts and health of John's mother, Ah-zhe-day-ge-she-gake, is not known. It is possible that she was with her husband, William, and could have potentially attended her son's marriage. She likely did attend her daughter Alice's marriage, ten months earlier in Rat Portage, or Kenora. I am more inclined to believe she had died prior to John and Tchi-Ki-Wis's marriage. William was paid her treaty annuity monies for 1889, but that was the last year.

Sister Alice's wedding and the death of John's mother may have freed John to marry Tchi-Ki-Wis, or alternately, "released" him from any physical or emotional caretaking he might have had for his mother. The mysterious life insurance "note" about the Linklater family lives, author unknown, records John's mother dying in 1887; it is inaccurate on a number of subjects, so the date is not definitive. The circumstances of Ah-zhe-day-ge-she-gake's death are not recorded. The scenarios presented here are conjectures on my part. Marriage of Alice Linklater and Daniel Morrisseau, Rat Portage, August 11, 1888, District of Rainy River, Rat Portage (Kenora), Ontario; "John Linklater," "Alien Registration," Iron Range Research Center, Chisholm, Minn.; "John Linklater," Frank M. and Alice Rockwell Warren Papers.

3. As their marriage record has not been found, it may, indeed, have not been recorded. Further, their marriage may not have been as I have depicted. An alternative scenario is that they were married in a traditional Anishinaabeg manner. If theirs was a traditional Anishinaabeg marriage, key elements would have been John gifting food (such as moose meat) or clothing to the Robinsons, thus substantiating he would be a good provider. Some marriages were "arranged" by parents at this time, but we do not know if this might have been the case for John and Tchi-Ki-Wis. The Robinsons would have hoped that or even asserted that their daughter's husband would provide economic stability for her and to a lesser degree the extended family. The Robinsons would have gauged John's behavior prior to courtship and from what they would have learned about his family. Courtship might have gone on for months, typically in the spring and summer months. Both Tchi-Ki-Wis and John would have sought out a spouse that they loved but also who

might better their lives. Tchi-Ki-Wis married while relatively young, customary among many Anishinaabeg. A feast might have accompanied the acknowledgment of the "marriage," and they might have set up their own home, their own *wiigwaasigamig*, near her parents. Months later they might have moved away from John and Susan Robinson. The actual marriage rite was informal, much less likely to be noted. Johann Georg Kohl, *Kitchi-Gami: Life among the Lake Superior Ojibway* (St. Paul: Minnesota Historical Society Press, 1985), 252–53, 395–97; Roufs, *When Everybody Called Me Gah-bay-bi-nayass*, 2:162–71.

4. William Linklater (e) Biographical Sheet, HBCA.

5. David I. Bushnell, "An Account of a Trip to Hunter's Island, Canada: Made during the Autumn of 1899," Library and Archives Canada, Ottawa. Of the decorated canoes Bushnell wrote: "Seldom are their bark canoes decorated. Only two have I ever seen, both on Basswood Lake. One of them had a row of dots extending from end to end. They were perhaps three inches in diameter of red pigment, seven on either side. The other had four crosses, in blue, one on either side of each other."

6. "Extract from Mr. Albert McCraken's Special Report of 1889"; photograph of John Blackstone on Basswood Lake, Lac La Croix photograph album, Ridley Library, Quetico Provincial Park, Atikokan, Ontario.

7. Sophie Connors Powell, interview by Warner Wirta, September 27, 1982, Grand Marais, Minn., Wirta Collection.

8. "Lac La Croix Family Clans," Ridley Library, Quetico Provincial Park, one page. It states "Blackstone—Caribou clan–Atik."

9. There were several Anishinaabeg settlements on Basswood Lake: on Washington Island and the mainland north of the island, Prairie Portage, and the "village" on Jackfish Bay. In Linklaters' day, the "village" at Jackfish Bay was smaller than the Washington Island and nearby mainland settlement, which even had a dance hall. We do not know whether the Linklaters may have "started" at Jackfish Bay or moved there after a few years elsewhere.

10. Robert Wells, interview by Shirley Peruniak, May 1, 1978, Ridley Library, Quetico Provincial Park. Wells thought he overheard John say he was born at Baptism Creek, but the dates are way off, not to mention Linklater's own legal admission in his "alien registration" that he was born at Fort Alexander, Manitoba. I am speculating that one of John and Tchi-Ki-Wis's daughters, likely Margaret, may have been the person John mentioned and Wells misheard or his memory of more than seventy-five years earlier was slightly off.

11. Lac La Croix, Treaty Paylist for 1893, 1895, 1898 through 1910, Library and Archives Canada, Ottawa. The Robinson-Linklater family regularly attended

every other treaty payment. The treaty payment was usually done at Lac La Croix, but sometimes in the early 1880s at Savanne, the Indian Department Agency Office. By 1884, Lac La Croix was no longer within the jurisdiction of the Savanne Agency.

12. Bushnell, "An Account of a Trip to Hunter's Island, Canada."

13. Lee Johnson, archaeologist, personal communication with author, December 4, 2019, Superior National Forest, Duluth, Minn.

14. Bushnell, "An Account of a Trip to Hunter's Island, Canada."

15. Frank M. Warren, letter to Mrs. Joseph Pecore, July 11, 1933, Frank M. and Alice Rockwell Warren Papers.

16. Aldrich, *Earth Never Tires*, 37.

17. Robert Maki, personal communication with author, November 18, 2019, Ely, Minn.

18. Carol Maass, "Notes from an interview with Scott Rumely," July 26, 1981, Isle Royale National Park, Houghton, Mich. Scott was nine years old when he lived with the Linklaters in 1927 at Birch Island, Isle Royale. Rumely mentioned the Linklaters put up a "teepee" and sweat lodge despite having four log buildings at the fishery. I am assuming they may have done much the same at their Jackfish Bay place, particularly if they had fewer buildings to use. One photograph of Tchi-Ki-Wis at their place with a team of dogs shows their dog "huts."

19. Mary Anderson, interview by Joan Najbar, March 27, 1983, Ely–Winton Historical Society, Minnesota Reflections, Minnesota Digital Library.

20. Jon Nelson, *Quetico: Near to Nature's Heart* (Toronto: Dundurn, 2009), 138; "Piscatorial Railway," *St. Paul Daily Globe*, August 4, 1895; Fifth Annual Report, Board of Game and Fish Commissioners of Minnesota, December 1, 1895, State of Minnesota, 10. Pound nets, in addition to gillnets, were used. The scale of the fishery is suggested by one later record in which 39,569 pounds of fish were caught in the "Winton District," chiefly Basswood Lake. *Transactions of the American Fisheries Society* 48 (December 1918): 58. Sweet, *Winton*, 21.

Bill Hanson, as a young man, fished for Leo Chosa on Basswood Lake. Bill Hanson file, Ridley Library, Quetico Provincial Park.

21. Lee Johnson, personal communication, December 4, 2019.

22. *Duluth Evening Herald*, January 18, 1906; *Two Harbors (Minn.) Iron News*, February 9, 16, and 23, 1906.

23. *Duluth Evening Herald*, February 13, 1907.

24. *Duluth Evening Herald*, February 14, 1907; *Duluth Evening Herald*, February 18, 1908; *Duluth Evening Herald*, April 28, 1908; *Duluth Evening Herald*, March 15,

1909; *Biannual Report of the State Game and Fish Commissioner of Minnesota* (Minneapolis: Syndicate Printing, 1918), 29.

25. Tripp, "Hunting Moose with a Camera."

26. Powell, *It Happened,* 68–69.

27. Aldrich, *Earth Never Tires,* 117.

28. Ibid., 190–91, 296, 329.

29. John Linklater, "Warden's Daily Report," May 29, 30, and 31, 1933, Wirta Collection. Linklater walked the sixteen-mile path in four and a half hours. He was sixty-three years old at the time.

30. Aldrich, *Earth Never Tires,* 79, 115, 122, 144.

31. Ellen Hanson, interview by Sister Noemi Weygant, August 30, 1982; Ellen Hanson, interview, July 9, 2008, Wirta Collection.

32. Grocery receipts from Winton Trading Co., April, October, November, 1930, Wirta Collection.

33. Ellen Hanson, interview by author, Floodwood, Minn., November 11, 1988.

34. Aldrich, *Earth Never Tires,* 296; Ellen Hanson, interview, July 30, 1982.

35. Ibid.

36. Maass, "Notes from an interview with Scott Rumely"; Cochrane and Tolson, *A Good Boat Speaks for Itself,* 35–36.

37. "LaPoste," Lac La Croix Treaty Paylist for 1893 and 1895, Library and Archives Canada. In the paylist entry for each year, the Indian agent noted one more "girl," never naming them (or Tchi-Ki-Wis or Susan Robinson).

38. Frank H. Nelson, December 1936, Social Security Applications and Claims Index, online.

39. Mrs. Helen Woods (granddaughter of the Linklaters), personal communication with author, December 15, 2014, Tower, Minn.; Arthur Johnson, interview by Sister Noemi Weygant, no date, Hoyt Lakes, Minn., Wirta Collection. Tchi-Ki-Wis and her parents evidently considered Margaret to be married to Arthur E. Nelson. 1911 Canadian Census for Lac La Croix. The reason for Arthur E. Nelson's abrupt departure for Canada troubled Linklater family members. Few knew of his marriage to a White Canadian woman, only weeks after Frank's birth. Exactly what happened to cause Margaret's death remains unknown. Additionally, there is no evidence that Arthur Nelson acknowledged or provided assistance for his son. It is likely he did not want to acknowledge a son—an "Indian son"—and marriage with a non-Native wife.

40. 1920 and 1930 U.S. Federal Census; Canadian consular registration certificate for Arthur Elmer Nelson, January 14, 1911, at Rainy River, Ontario; October 4, 1911, Registration of Marriages, Province of Ontario, Archives of Ontario, Toronto.

41. Mrs. Helen Woods, personal communication with author, December 15, 2014; Milt and Alice Powell, personal communication with author, May 17, 2013, Grand Marais, Minn.; Sophie Connors Powell, interview, September 27, 1982.

42. Martha Greene Phillips, *Border Country: The Northwoods Canoe Journals of Howard Greene, 1906–1916* (Minneapolis: University of Minnesota Press, 2017), 224–25, 237. Apparently desecrating graves was such a problem that in 1912 early Quetico Provincial Park rangers were charged "with protecting Indian graves from pilfering." *Quetico Provincial Park, Lac La Croix Amendment Proposal*, January 1992, Atikokan, Ontario Ministry of Natural Resources, Toronto.

43. Brenda J. Child, *My Grandfather's Knocking Sticks: Ojibwe Family Life and Labor on the Reservation* (St. Paul: Minnesota Historical Society Press, 2014), 50.

44. Mrs. Ellen Hanson, Ridley Library, Quetico Provincial Park. Translation of the Anishinaabemowin by Dr. John Nichols, personal communication with author, March 21, 2017, University of Minnesota, Minneapolis.

45. Margaret Bemister, *Thirty Indian Legends* (Toronto: Macmillian, 1912), 62; Johann Georg Kohl, *Kitchi-Gami: Life among the Lake Superior Ojibway* (St. Paul: Minnesota Historical Society Press, 1985), 434–37.

46. Sophie Connors Powell, interview, September 27, 1982.

47. Aslakson, "Jack Linklater." Some Anishinaabeg "altered" their names after a marriage. Thus, John "giving" Tchi-Ki-Wis a new name might be a reflection more of an accepted custom than a novelty as it was reported. Kohl, *Kitchi-Gami*, 275.

48. Warner often annotated his grandmother's name, Tchi-Ki-Wis, as meaning "spirit woman"; Wirta family photographs; Frank M. Warren, December 9, 1941, letter to Superintendent George Baggley, Isle Royale National Park, Houghton, Mich. A similar meaning was offered in Linklater's obituary in the *Minneapolis Tribune*, August 13, 1933, illustrating that Frank Warren was likely one of the main contributors to that full-page memorial.

49. Ellen Hanson, interview, July 9, 2008; Tauno Maki, oral history tape, January 3, 1996, Ely, Minn., Iron Range Research Center, Chisholm, Minn.

50. Dr. John D. Nichols, personal communication with author, April 7, 2018, University of Minnesota, Minneapolis.

51. Johnston, "Maudjee-kawiss: The First Son," in *The Manitous*, 17–20; J. Randolph Valentine, "The Majikikwewisag in Ojibwe Oral Tradition," *Papers of the 39th Algonquian Conference*, ed. Regina Darnell and Karl S. Hele (London: University of Western Ontario, 2008), 614–16, 625; Arden C. Ogg,

"Ojibwa Tales of the Foolish Maidens," *Actes du 20e Congres des Algonquinistes*, ed. William Cowan (Ottawa: Carleton University, 1989), 279, 286.

52. Sister Bernard Coleman, Ellen Frogner, and Estelle Eich, *Ojibwa Myths and Legends* (Minneapolis: Ross and Haines, 1962), 66, 105; these authors state that the meaning of "Mudjikiwis" is confused; some informants thought Mudjikiwis was a powerful thunderbird, or associated with the west wind, and others thought it was associated with spring and rain. This exercise is even harder given that these legendary figures' names (and their meaning) are now fading in memory in some Anishinaabeg communities. Valentine, "The Majikikwewisag in Ojibwe Oral Tradition," 615.

53. July 28, 1855, entry in Dominique du Ranquet, S.J., Mission Journal: 1853–1856, Fort William, Ontario, translation by William Lonc, S.J. (privately printed, 2011), 186. A leader named Kepechtotewe recorded seven generations of his paternal ancestors with Jesuit father Ranquet, stating that Madjikiwis was his oldest in a succession of Bois Forte leaders.

There was also a celebrated war chief, "Matchekewis," whose name, minus the first syllable comes close to matching Tch-Ki-Wis in pronunciation. Matchekewis was the Anishinaabeg leader who used trickery to seize Michilimackinaw from the British in 1763.

54. Lawrence Barkwell, compiler, "Treaty Three Métis"; "Halfbreeds of Fort Frances," 17 October 1871, Indian Affairs, Record Group 10, volume 3715, file 21, 809, Library and Archives Canada. In the payment to "Halfbreeds" for the Dawson Trail through their and Anishinaabeg territory, "John Linklater" is paid thirty dollars for ten people: himself, one "woman," seven boys, and one girl. This John Linklater appears to be "Linklater, John 'A,'" in the Biographical Sheets devised by the Hudson's Bay Company archivists. If so, he had been in the Rainy Lake area as early as 1848.

55. If the older Tchi-Ki-Wis was the Anishinaabeg namesake for the younger, or Helen Robinson, there may have been a relationship between the women that I have been unable to uncover. If they had an Anishinaabeg namesake relationship, the older woman would have agreed to look out for the younger one and even share some of her power with the younger one if need be. Upon the older Tchi-Ki-Wis's death, her spirit might be transferred to her namesake and the name live on. Roufs, *When Everybody Called Me Gah-bay-binayass*, 1:23–24.

56. Ahlgren and Ahlgren, *Lob Trees in the Wilderness*, 46, 95.

57. Ibid., 95.

58. J. William Trygg, "Swallow & Hopkins Lumber Company of Winton, Minnesota," 1952, 1, Minnesota Historical Society, St. Paul.

59. There are no employee records for the Swallow & Hopkin's Lumber Company. Hence, I am guessing when Linklater started working for them based on a photograph in the Ely–Winton Historical Society that identifies Linklater and Vincent Defoe (Defauld), "Hoisting Logs on Basswood Lake, 1902." A print of the same photograph at Packsack Canoe Trips (Outfitters), located on Fall Lake, identifies the photograph as taken in 1901. The accompanying text says: "The man in the white shirt, center, with a pike pole in the air, is John Linklater, famous game warden, skilled woodsman, and dog team pilot. He was known for his many exploits in tracking down and capturing outlaw fur trappers."

60. Herb Good, "Fall-Basswood Lake Logging Railroad," 1953, 3, appendix to Trygg's "Swallow & Hopkins," paper, Minnesota Historical Society, St. Paul; J. C. Ryan, "Indians in the Camps," *Timber Producers Bulletin* 44 (August–September 1989): 34.

61. Ahlgren and Ahlgren, *Lob Trees in the Wilderness*, 96.

62. Good, "Fall-Basswood Lake Logging Railroad," 3–4. Good further detailed that the "Russell" railroad cars "were approximately one half the length of the present day standard railroad flat cars."

   Calling Anishinaabeg women "squaws" was then commonplace. Its meaning was loathsome then and more so now. Some users were relatively ignorant of its connotations, while others were aggressive in their contempt of Indian women, using the term to imply drudgery, sexual looseness, alcoholism, and degradation. Lucy Eldersveld Murphy, *Great Lakes Creoles: A French-Indian Community on the Northern Borderlands, Prairie Du Chien, 1750–1860* (Cambridge: Cambridge University Press, 2014), 159.

   Default was spelled a number of different ways in the historical record, including Defauld, Default, and Defoe. To standardize spelling, I am using "Defauld."

63. Lee Johnson, personal communication, December 7, 2018.

64. Warner Wirta family photograph circa 1915 and 1920; U.S. Federal Census, Winton, Fall Lake, Minn.

65. Exactly when this might have occurred is not documented. Since the installation and use of telephones would make a "fast express" obsolete, it must have been before then. Phones were installed at the Winton sawmills in 1912 and at the mines probably soon afterward. Hence, Linklater's sled dog express was likely before 1912 and was no later than 1917. Margaret Sweet, personal communication with author, January 30, 2020, Ely–Winton Historical Society, Minn.

66. Aslakson, "Jack Linklater."

67. John Linklater file, Quetico Provincial Park, Atikokan, Ontario.
68. William Linklater, January 2, 1862, letter to Alexander McDonald at Albany, B.3/c/3, HBCA.
69. Egerton Ryerson Young, *By Canoe and Dog-Train among the Cree and Saulteaux Indians* (London: C. H. Kelly, 1890), 92–93.
70. Arthur Johnson, interview.
71. Brickner, "Jack Linklater as I Knew Him," 39.
72. Chilson D. (Studge) Aldrich, letter to Mac Martin, winter 1927, Ridley Library, Quetico Provincial Park.
73. Mrs. Arthur Johnson, interview by Sister Noemi Weygant, Hoyt Lakes, Minn., Wirta Collection.
74. John Linklater, Game Warden Report, December 23, 1931, Wirta Collection.
75. Aldrich, letter to Mac Martin.
76. Charles L. Gilman, "Whitey," *Minneapolis Star*, June 5, 1926. Whitey's adjustment to city life went well, even when briefly indoors. He was a big dog. When he was once challenged to a fight by a city dog, one smash of his paw sent the other dog away. Or as either Linklater or Hanson said, "Whitey never started a fight in his life—and he never failed to finish any fight forced on him." Whitey was originally from La Pas, Manitoba.
77. Al Evans, "Hitting the Snowshoe Trail," *Fins, Feathers, and Fur* 37 (March 1924): 146–51; Donald Hough, "Winter Vacations Minnesota's Latest: Snowshoe Campers Find Sunburn Is Chief Annoyance in Trip in Forest," *St. Paul Daily News*, March 30, 1924.
78. George Muchvich, interview by Warner Wirta, December 17, 1982, Ely, Minn., Wirta Collection.
79. Lee Brownell, interview by Warner Wirta, no date, Ely, Minn., Wirta Collection.
80. Dr. C. F. Hardy, "Trials and Big Trout," *Outdoor Recreation* 63 (October 1920): 285.
81. Gilman, "Going In by Gasoline," 308.
82. Charles L. Gilman, Forest, Stream, and Target (column), *Minneapolis Star*, September 17, 1927.
83. Darragh Aldrich, "When You Strike It Lucky: XIV. Over the Line with Jack Linklater," *Recreation* 57, no. 5 (November 1917): 263–64.
84. Bushnell, "An Account of a Trip to Hunter's Island."
85. William H. Richardson, "A Honeymoon in a Birch Bark Canoe: Being a Brief Account of the Wedding Journey of William H. and Jennie S. S. Richardson, 1897," "Historical Sketches of the Quetico-Superior," vol. 11 (1974), ed. J. Wesley White, Superior National Forest, Duluth, Minn. (no pagination).

86. "Over the Long Portage," an unattributed newspaper clipping from July or August 1933, John Linklater file, Ridley Library, Quetico. The caretaker of the just-established Camp Widjiwagan on the north arm of Burntside Lake recounted years later: "One of the game wardens [visitors] was an Indian, possibly a full-blooded Chippewa. His name was Linklater, a strange name for an Indian, but he was obviously an Indian and a particular attraction to the boys in camp and the rest of us too for that matter." C. Gordon Fredine, oral history, September 4, 1980, Kautz Family YMCA Collection, Archives, University of Minnesota, Minneapolis.

87. Ernest Oberholtzer, letter to Frank M. Warren, July 15, 1930, Quetico-Superior Council Papers, Minnesota Historical Society, St. Paul. Oberholtzer, with Frank Warren's help, was trying to provide an informational and pleasurable trip for members of the Special Senate Committee on Wild Life Resources to see Isle Royale and the boundary waters.

88. *The Tomahawk* (White Earth, Minn.), July 6, 1922. Mrs. Frank (Alice) Warren was also a Minnesota delegate to the 1928 Republican National Convention. "Warren, Mrs. Frank M." in www.politicalgraveyard.com.

89. Frank M. Warren, letter, January 16, 1932, to John Linklater, Winton, Minn., Frank M. and Alice Rockwell Warren Papers. Sheesheep Lake and indeed Linklater Lake on Isle Royale were named to recognize John, or in the case of Sheesheeb Lake to likely honor his Indian heritage and presence on the island. It is unclear if Sheesheeb Lake was named by Linklater to recognize Alice Warren. Smitty Parratt and Doug Welker, *The Place Names of Isle Royale* (Houghton, Mich.: Isle Royale National History Association, 1999), 45, 68.

90. Jean Anderson (Frank and Alice Warren's niece), personal communication with author, March 27, 2020, Los Angeles, Calif.

91. S. A. Macaulay, Northern Pacific Railway Company, St. Paul, letter, to John Linklater, October 9, 1929, Wirta Collection. Macaulay concluded his letter: "The hike across Isle Royale was a great experience and one which I will never forget."

92. Mrs. Matt Farmer, Madison, Wis., letter to John Linklater, March 19, 1931, Wirta Collection. Mrs. Farmer was referring to a lodge brochure she produced in 1930 that featured a trip from Rock Harbor Lodge to "John's Camp," on Birch Island, McCargoe Cove, and then a hike led by the Linklaters across the spine of the island, including a canoe "trip" across Sargent Lake and then onto Daisy Farm and a return boat ride to Rock Harbor Lodge. Word of the trip spread quickly as few trips across the island were even covered by a Northern Pacific Railroad promotion brochure.

The Rock Harbor Lodge brochure sings with praise for the trip: "The boat trip is around the end of the island to John's picturesque camp at McCargoe's Cove. The charm of this camp on lovely Birch Island will linger long in your memory. You spend the night sleeping on beds of soft spicy balsam boughs and woolly blankets. Your meals are served outdoors under silver birch trees—whitefish and lake trout hauled from the cold waters of Lake Superior and cooked over the campfire in John's inimitable way. On the following morning you go by blazed trail through the heart of the forest, reaching the shores of Sargent Lake by noon. After lunch your trip across Sargent Lake in canoes is begun. Then you hike through virgin forests again to Daisy Farm where you enter a commodious launch which takes you back to Rock Harbor Lodge." A copy of this brochure is at Bentley Historical Library, University of Michigan, Ann Arbor.

93. Frank M. Warren, Minneapolis, letter to John Linklater, April 15, 1931, Wirta Collection.

94. Cornelia O'Neill (niece of Frank and Alice Warren), letter to author, January 8, 1989, Greens Farms, Conn.

95. Warren, *The Pioneer Woodsman as He Is Related to Lumbering in the Northwest*, 155.

96. Frank M. Warren, Minneapolis, letter to Frank Nelson, March 24, 1937, Frank M. and Alice Rockwell Warren Papers.

97. Frank M. Warren folders (3), Quetico–Superior Council files, Minnesota Historical Society, St. Paul. R. Newell Searle, *Saving Quetico-Superior: A Land Set Apart* (St. Paul: Minnesota Historical Society, 1977), 36, 96, 99. Warren was on the executive committee of the Minneapolis chapter of the Izaak Walton League. Warren was a mining engineer and financier very active on the Iron Range, but he was also a conservationist working to protect the boundary waters and establish Isle Royale National Park.

98. Frank M. and Alice Rockwell Warren Papers.

99. "Veteran of North Woods Arrives in City with Dog Team to Greet MacMillan," *Minneapolis Tribune*, February 5, 1929; "Musher, Aged 67, Drives Dogs Here to See MacMillan," *Minneapolis Star*, February 4, 1929; "Igloo Pal Fails to 'Spot' MacMillan for his Hosts," *Minneapolis Star*, February 5, 1929. One article stated that Linklater was too "late" to greet MacMillan, but in reality he and the team did not appear in the publicity event because the dogs were "trainsick." Thus, despite the pressure for Linklater to have the dog team present for the publicity stunt of MacMillan's arrival, he declined to do so, as he was concerned for their well-being.

100. "Department Sled Dogs at the Minnesota State Fair," *Fins, Feathers, and Fur* 39 (September 1924): 36.

101. Allen Shoenfield, "Isle Royale Expedition Sails for Unnamed Port," *Great Falls (Mont.) Tribune*, August 3, 1928; Allen Shoenfield, "Expedition Seeking Secret Ancient Copper Workers Sets Sail for Old Isle Royale," *Weekly Kansas City Star*, August 8, 1928. The "expedition" gave frequent updates, which were syndicated throughout the United States as part of the North American Newspaper Alliance. While in route, a water spout broke the mast of a third yacht, the *Swastika*, that belatedly joined the expedition at McCargoe Cove and thus was near the Linklater fishery. "U. J. Hermann's Long Lost Yacht Joins Expedition," *Chicago Tribune*, August 11, 1928.

102. William P. F. Ferguson, *News-Herald* (Franklin, Penn.), August 29, 1928. A newspaper man, Isle Royale enthusiast, and amateur archaeologist, Ferguson was the main proponent of the idea of Norsemen, or a "Race of Men Known to Have Inhabited Lake Superior Island Long before the Indians," that provoked the expedition. Shoenfield, "Isle Royale Is to be Explored," *Lincoln (Neb.) Journal*, August 2, 1928.

103. It is unclear to what sites Linklater guided the expedition. He clearly was with them at McCargoe Cove and Birch Island, where he showed them a number of his finds. He was also with them "inland" at Siskiwit Lake, so he likely was with them at Chickenbone and Livermore Lakes, and perhaps Chippewa Harbor. George R. Fox, "Isle Royale Expedition," *Michigan History* 13, no. 2 (1929): 317, 319.

104. This "expedition" was the source of the top hat, given to John in 1928, that I first saw in the park slide file fifty years later. While giving a used top hat to "an Indian" was patronizing, John and later his father-in-law, John Robinson, clearly had fun wearing the hat.

105. Shoenfield, "Isle Royale Expedition Sails for Unnamed Port." In a virtually identical article, Linklater is named "Jan Lindlaker," showing how careless publicist Shoenfield was in getting John's name or characterization precise. Shoenfield, "Key to Mystery of Lost Race Is Sought," *Charlotte (N.C.) Observer*, August 14, 1928.

106. Expedition leaders were influential and brazen enough that they invited President Calvin Coolidge, then in the upper Midwest, to accompany them. It was only after the yachts were en route from Chicago that it was decided to "wire" their invitation to the president. President Coolidge responded, saying in remarks to the national press, in effect, that Isle Royale was unfortunately too far away. "Coolidge Invited to Visit Isle Royale Party Seeking

Trace of Prehistoric Man," *La Crosse (Wis.) Tribune*, July 31, 1928; "Exploring Party Asks Coolidge to Visit Isle Royale," *Wausau (Wis.) Daily Herald*, July 31, 1928; Calvin Coolidge, "Remarks by the President to Newspaper Correspondents" July 31, 1929, www.coolidgefoundation.org/wp-content/uploads/2016/11copy-of-VII-compressed.pdf.

    The McDonald–Massee Expedition's other goal was to advocate for the creation of Isle Royale as a national park.

107. George R. Fox, Chicago, letters to John Linklater, June 7 and July 6, 1931, Wirta Collection.

108. "The Lac La Croix Story: Grievances with Ontario," in *Quetico Provincial Park, Lac La Croix Amendment Proposal*, January 1992.

109. Leo G. Waisberg, Joan A. Lovisek, and Tim E. Holzkamm, "Ojibwa Reservations as 'An Incubus upon the Territory': The Indian Removal Policy of Ontario, 1874–1982," in *Papers of the 27th Algonquian Conference*, ed. David H. Pentland (Winnipeg: University of Manitoba, 1997), 347.

110. Department of Indian Affairs Circular, December 25, 1921, Ottawa, Canada. Copy held at Centre for Northern Studies, Lakehead University Library, Thunder Bay, Ontario.

111. Walter Caribou, interview, by Jerre Pete, February 4, 1997, Grand Portage, Minn. This oral history interview is part of the Vermilion Lake Bois Forte Oral History Project, Minnesota Historical Society, St. Paul. Walter Caribou, interview by Warner Wirta, no date, Grand Portage, Minn., Wirta Collection. Lynn Laitala, personal communication with author, November 11, 2018, Lake Linden, Mich.

112. Swallow and Hopkins sold their mill and holdings in 1921 to Weyerhaeuser. The St. Croix Lumber Company was sold in 1925. Jeff Forester, *The Forest for the Trees: How Humans Shaped the North Woods* (St. Paul: Minnesota Historical Society Press, 2004), 142.

4. "Talk to John"

1. The title of this chapter is inspired by Sigurd Olson's notes for his master's thesis on the timber wolf, which are sprinkled with "ask Jack," "Jack Linklater told me," and "Jack Linklater states."

    Stories about the legendary lynx persisted for some time. To assemble this vignette, I used a number of accounts: Charles L. Gilman, "Brule Lake Lynx Trails Tenderfoot Party through Superior Game Refuge," *Minneapolis Star*, February 27, 1926; "Rangers Leave to Lead Snowshoe Trek into Forest," *Minneapolis Tribune*, February 7, 1926; *Minneapolis Star*, March 10, 1928; Joseph Brickner, "Pioneer Game Warden," *Minnesota Conservation Volunteer*

24, no. 138 (November–December 1960): 54. The subheadings to the article by Gilman capture the spirit of the hoax: "Ghost Haunts Camps after Red-Eyed Monster Is Slain," and "Members of Gould Party Sleep with Cooks' Knives under Pillows."

2. John Linklater, game warden reports, May–June 1931, Warner Wirta Collection.

3. William Hanson, interview by Ellen Hanson, September 7, 1976, Floodwood, Minn. This is a "homemade tape" of Ellen Hanson questioning her husband about topics.

4. Hilary W. (Woody) Schermann, *Minnesota Game Warden* (privately published, 1987), 124; "The First Century in Review," *Minnesota Volunteer* 50, no. 295 (November–December 1987): 7.

5. Schermann, *Minnesota Game Warden*, 114, 122, 128–31.

6. Aslakson, "Jack Linklater."

7. Schermann, *Minnesota Game Warden*, 110.

8. Shepard Krech III, *The Ecological Indian: Myth and History* (New York: Norton, 1999), 177.

9. William H. Longley and John B. Moyle, "The Beaver in Minnesota," Technical Bulletin 4, August 1963, Division of Game and Fish, Minnesota Department of Conservation, St. Paul, 41. During the next twenty years, otter, fisher, and marten—all furbearers—were added to the state protected list.

10. "Rice Harvesting and Wild Fowl Food Supply," *Fins, Feathers, and Fur* 41 (March 1925): 7; C. E. Lucas, "A Viewpoint on the Disappearance of Rice Beds," *Fins, Feathers, and Fur* 36 (December 1923): 123; Leo Chosa, "Muskrats vs. Wild Rice," *Fins, Feathers, and Fur* 37 (March 1924): 165.

11. Weygant, *John (Jack) Linklater*, 9. Other wardens were planting wild rice. *St. Cloud Times*, April 22, 1930. Even clubs such as the Ely Commercial Club planted up to five hundred pounds of wild rice. *Minneapolis Tribune*, September 5, 1927.

12. At the time, a "lesser" category of "injurious species of wildlife," or vermin, included gophers, stray cats, vagrant dogs, crows, screech owls, long-eared owls, short-eared owls, sharp-shinned hawks, goshawks, broadwing hawks, marsh hawks, blackbirds, great horned owls, kingfishers, barred owls, English sparrows, blue herons, and, of course, wolves, coyotes, foxes, mink, weasels, and skunks. Game wardens were "instructed to study approved methods of destroying these creatures." Schermann, *Minnesota Game Warden*, 99–100.

13. "Superior Refuge Predator Animal Control," *Fins, Feathers, and Fur* 42 (June 1925): 31; J. Stokley Ligon, "Investigations, Experiment and Demonstration

in Predatory Animal Control in Northeastern Minnesota," Special Report No. 122 (Winter 1924–25) Bureau of Biological Survey, U.S. Department of Agriculture, copy at National Wildlife Research Center, Fort Collins, Colo.

14. J. Stokley Ligon, Monthly Narrative Report, October 1–31, 1924; Monthly Narrative Report, January 1–31, 1925; Monthly Narrative Report February 1–28, 1925, Predator Animal Control, Bureau of Biological Survey, National Wildlife Research Center, Fort Collins, Colo. The overall effort was handicapped by a number of factors: immigration of wolves from Canada, weather conditions, and surprisingly Ligon's conclusion that "wolves [are] scarce in the game refuge." The method of poisoning was somewhat limited; horse fat was used, rather than carcasses. "In an endeavor to keep the killing of fur-bearing animals down to a minimum, the policy of confining the use of poison to the ice of the larger lakes has been followed."

15. Sigurd F. Olson, "The Life History of the Timber Wolf and Coyote: A Study in Predatory Animal Control," (master's thesis, University of Illinois, 1932), 47.

16. "Statement of the Department's Policies in Relation to Superior National Forest and State Game Refuge," Fins, Feathers, and Fur 59 (May 1928): 88.

17. John Linklater, game warden report, January 28, 1932, Wirta Collection.

18. Sigurd Olson, thesis notes, Sigurd F. Olson Papers, Minnesota Historical Society, St. Paul.

19. Scott Richard Lyons, X-Marks: Native Signatures of Assent (Minneapolis: University of Minnesota Press, 2010), 86; Ojibwe People's Dictionary, s.v. "nitaage," https://ojibwe.lib.umn.edu/search?utf8=%E2%9C%93&q=to+kill &commit=Search&type=english.

20. "Izaak Walton League to Make Exhaustive Survey on Game," Minneapolis Tribune, August 1, 1923; "Average Value of Pelts of Fur-Bear Animals Taken in Canada," Fur-Fish-Game: Harding's Magazine, September 1929, 66.

21. Willis Raff, "Outlaw Trappers of the North Shore: Their Rationale Reviewed," unpublished, September 1981, Cook County Historical Society, Grand Marais, Minn., 9.

22. Julius F. Wolff Jr., "Our Pioneer Wardens," Minnesota Volunteer 50, no. 295 (November–December 1987): 18.

23. Aslakson, "Jack Linklater." The details of this account strongly suggest that Bill Hanson was the source, and they were massaged by the author. If Bill Hanson was the source, I am strongly inclined to believe it was true at its core, even if it appears to be too good to be true.

24. Bob Cary, "Citizen of the Northland," Ely (Minn.) Echo, October 18, 1984.

25. Art and Phyllis Johnson, interview by Warner Wirta, July 30, 1982, Babbitt, Minn., Wirta Collection.

26. Al Brownell, interview by Warner Wirta, undated, Ely, Minn., Wirta Collection.
27. Tauno Maki, interview, January 3, 1996, Ely, Minn., Iron Range Research Center, Chisholm, Minn.
28. Ted Pennala, letter to Tauno Maki, circa 1995, Ely, Minn. Letter in the possession of Robert Maki, Ely, Minn.
29. Ellen Hanson, interview, July 30, 1982.
30. Robert Hill, interview by Sister Noemi Weygant, undated, Ely, Minn., Wirta Collection.
31. Ted Pennala, letter. Pennala attributed the "slowness" and ineffectiveness of two wardens to the fact that they were political appointees and were ill suited to be wardens.
32. Ellen Hanson, interview by Warner Wirta, Floodwood, Minn., March 23, 1984. A copy of the tape is at the Iron Range Research Center, Chisholm, Minn.
33. Ibid.
34. Brickner, "Jack Linklater as I Knew Him," 39.
35. Bill Hanson, Linklater file notes by Shirley Peruniak, Ridley Library, Quetico Provincial Park.
36. "Former State Warden Jailed in West," *Minneapolis Tribune*, December 24, 1927; "Former Game Warden Pleads Not Guilty," *Cook County News-Herald*, January 5, 1928; Schermann, *Minnesota Game Warden*, 121; Ellen Hanson, interview by Sister Noemi Weygant and Julius F. Wolff Jr., undated, Ely, Minn.; "Hot Fur," in *Rendezvous: Selected Papers of the Fourth North American Fur Trade Conference, 1981*, ed. Thomas C. Buckley (St. Paul: North American Fur Trade Conference, 1984), 219.
37. Aldrich, letter to Mac Martin.
38. The Linklaters separation for work was only magnified in the summers when John regularly traveled to Isle Royale as a handyman and guide for Frank and Alice Warren. More commonly, Tchi-Ki-Wis stayed home, until later in the 1920s, when they purchased the Birch Island commercial fishery. Tchi-Ki-Wis, her father, and grandson Frankie went with John to Isle Royale, but she more often stayed at their fishery, rather than accompanied him guiding the Warrens and others.
39. George W. Warren, letter to Mrs. H. C. Hauser, Marquette, Mich., October 10, 1916. A copy of the letter was provided to me by Jody Borer, Atlanta, Ga.
40. *Duluth Herald*, February 17, 1917; *Fins, Feathers, and Furs* 10 (June 1917): 14; *Cook County News-Herald*, May 25, 1922; State of Minnesota v. Leo Chosa, Cook County Court Records, May 23, 1922, Grand Marais, Minn.

41. A newspaper article addressed the ironic hiring of Chosa: "Last fall an emergency force of 10 men, under the leadership of Leo Chosa, self-confessed outlaw who came over to the side of the law and order and offered to lead the war against the outlaws, set out to patrol the last wilderness of the northwest." *Minneapolis Star*, March 31, 1924.
42. Schermann, *Minnesota Game Warden*, 111; "2 Minnesotans Caught with 29 Beaver Hides," *Winona (Minn.) Daily News*, May 19, 1925.
43. "Halfbreed Warden Goes on Trail of His Own Brother," *Minneapolis Star*, November 10, 1923.
44. *Duluth Herald*, February 22 and 24, 1917. Warden Wood's comments signaled that he was White, and Chosa Indian, thus invoking stereotypes and a power differential to reinforce his view.
45. Tauno Maki, *Winton: From Boom to Bust* (privately printed, 1999), no pagination.
46. Ellen Hanson, interview by author.
47. Joe Brickner, a supervisory warden, wrote laudatory reminiscences of Linklater after his death. Brickner maintained Linklater's "mother [was] a full blood Sioux." That Brickner thought and said this meant that quite a number of men in the Game and Fish Department likely thought it as well. Brickner, "Jack Linklater as I Knew Him," 37.

    Ellen Hanson believed that Tchi-Ki-Wis "had also been raised in the Dakotas." Ellen Hanson, interview, November 11, 1988. One plausible explanation of this confusion is that if John spoke to his friends about being in the Red River area in his youth (for John meaning the Winnipeg area), Minnesotans hearing this might have assumed he was referring to North Dakota. And if his mother's family was from North Dakota, then they might assume she was Dakota.
48. Wolff, "Hot Fur," 218–19.
49. Ellen Hanson, interview, March 23, 1984.
50. Wolff, "Our Pioneer Wardens," 16.
51. *Bemidji (Minn.) Daily Pioneer*, September 22, 1905; "Believes Decision Would Be Upheld," *Bemidji (Minn.) Daily Pioneer*, January 17, 1911. Two subtitles to this article are revealing: "Indians Have Too Many Rights" and "Probable That Game Commission Will Request Wardens to Keep Close 'Tabs' on Red Men."
52. *The Tomahawk* (White Earth, Minn.), August 27, 1903; *Cook County News-Herald*, October 27, 1920. The newspaper account is illustrative of the situation: "Chas. Drouillard was arrested and fined $50 and costs for killing a deer on the reservation. He was brought in by the local game warden Saturday,

and taken before Justice Matt Johnson, where he pleaded guilty to the charge. Charlie was of the opinion that, being an Indian, he had a right to kill deer on the reservation at any time. He has not been alone in this opinion."

53. Erik M. Redix, *The Murder of Joe White, Ojibwe Leadership and Colonialism in Wisconsin* (East Lansing: Michigan State University Press, 2014).

54. *Minneapolis Tribune*, March 14, 1909; *Bemidji (Minn.) Daily Pioneer*, October 8, 1909; "Superior Game Refuge," *Fins, Feathers, and Furs* 10 (June 1917): 3; *Cook County News-Herald*, February 10, 1916, January 24, 1917.

55. Benjamin Heber Johnson, "Conservation, Subsistence, and Class at the Birth of the Superior National Forest," *Environmental History* 4, no. 1 (January 1999): 15–16.

56. Ellen Hanson, interview, July 9, 2008.

57. One event at Isle Royale illustrates Linklater's composed yet commanding presence. When the yacht *Alladin* with twenty passengers aboard went aground on the rocks at the entrance to McCargoe Cove, Linklater quietly led efforts to pull the vessel off the reef, even though all three other captains at the task were White. Fred Dustin, Field Journal, 1929, University of Michigan Museum of Anthropology, Ann Arbor.

58. Linklater's game warden reports—those that survive—are helpful in sleuthing out his actions. They are to the point, for example, for October 19, 1930: "Went to Babit Road and found part of deer in possession of Jos. Rustedt and arrested him. Took gun and told him to appear in court Monday and went back to Winton." His entry for Sunday, January 3, 1932: "Me and warden Krall walked down Portage River, we found some small traps near Nina Moose Lake and found two trapers at 66N, R14W and brought them to Portage River Ranger's Cabin. And called up Carlson and got back to Winton and we turned the prisoners to the Chief Warden Hanson." Wirta Collection. Linklater had limited schooling, so his spelling was sometimes in error, but overall his writing conveyed his points well.

59. Whether intentional or not, Linklater did not drink publicly or get a reputation "as liking to drink." He did drink a beer or two with Bill Hanson, and perhaps he drank in private with Joe Hoffman, his next-door neighbor on Jackfish Bay, who had a reputation as a moonshiner. But no stories link John with excessive alcohol. While speculative, he may have heard the stories and innuendoes about his grandmother's or other Indians' drinking problems and decided to avoid any such events that might impugn his character.

60. The letters and Christmas cards written to Linklater by former commissioner Gould, and Warden Brickner's laudatory comments about him contradict any easy conclusion that he was marginalized as an Indian kept on the force

just for show. Similarly, Linklater's friendships with Bill Hanson, various academics, Frank and Alice Warren, Studge and Darragh Aldrich, and Anishinaabeg in the area testify to his ability to successfully make friends of different backgrounds.

61. Aldrich, *Earth Never Tires*, 78; Aslakson, "Jack Linklater."

62. G. I. Wallace, Alvin R. Cahn, and Lyell J. Thomas, "Klebsiella Paralytica: A New Pathogenic Bacterium from 'Moose Disease,'" *Journal of Infectious Diseases* 53, no. 3 (November–December 1933): 407.

63. Olson, thesis notes, Sigurd F. Olson Papers.

64. Ellen Hanson, interview, November 11, 1988.

65. The location of the *Kamloops* had eluded Canadian authorities for the intervening months until Linklater found the bodies, albeit accidentally. Milford Johnson, as quoted in Peter Oikarinen, *Island Folk: The People of Isle Royale* (Houghton, Mich.: Isle Royale Natural History Association, 1979; reprint, Minneapolis: University of Minnesota Press, 2008), 86; Milford Johnson, interview by Peter Oikarinen, fall 1978, Two Harbors, Minn.; Ed Holte, interview by Lawrence Rakestraw, September 10, 1965, Wright Island, Isle Royale, Isle Royale National Park Oral History Collection.

   Later, when guiding, Linklater told about finding the bodies, shorn-off pilot house, and the *Kamloops* wreck visible in sixty feet of water to George A. West, of the Milwaukee Public Museum. In summer 1928, Linklater took West by canoe to look at the scene, from which West wrote a lurid account of a story not yet told. Intentional or not, West published it after Linklater's death. George West, "Missing Ship in Fiord," *Milwaukee Journal*, June 9, 1935.

66. Timothy Cochrane, "Research the Influence of Jack Linklater on Sigurd Olson," Minnesota Historical and Cultural Heritage Program, May 2019, Cook County Historical Society, Grand Marais. Linklater is cited fifteen times in Olson's thesis, and the number is undoubtedly higher, as a number of statements in Olson's thesis are unattributed.

67. Olson, thesis notes, Sigurd F. Olson Papers; Olson, "The Life History of the Timber Wolf and Coyote."

68. Sigurd F. Olson, "Organization and Range of the Pack," *Ecology* 19, no. 1 (January 1938): 168–70; Sigurd F. Olson, "A Study in Predatory Relationship with Particular Reference to the Wolf," *Scientific Monthly* 46 (April 1938): 323–36.

69. Aldrich, *Earth Never Tires*, 216.

70. Vernon Hagelin, "Picture Stories of the Ojibway," *The Dispatch* (Moline, Ill.), December 17, 1935.

71. Aslakson, "Jack Linklater."
72. Walter Breckenridge, "Minnesota's Smaller Owls," *Minnesota Conservation Volunteer* (May–June 1946): 39.
73. Ben East, "The Dark Grouse of the North," *Nature Magazine* 22, no. 5 (November 1933): 206. Found in Aldo Leopold's papers online; he wrote on the article "spruce hen" in pencil: "Library of Aldo Leopold"; The Aldo Leopold Archives, http//digital.library.wisc.edu/1711.d/Aldo Leopold.
74. We know some years Linklater was on the island because he signed the Warrens' guest book. He may not, however, have signed it each year. The Warrens came to the island virtually every year from 1911 to 1930, except for 1928. They typically came in the late summer (August and into early September). Frank and Alice Warren, the "Birches" guest book, 1911 through 1930, Isle Royale National Park, Houghton, Mich.
75. Cochrane, *Minong*, 55, 89–90.
76. The Warren House was in Rock Harbor, but the Warrens and Linklater often took trips to various places on Isle Royale, including one as far away as the head of Siskiwit Bay.
77. Fred Dustin, "An Archaeological Reconnaissance of Isle Royale," *Michigan History* 41, no. 1 (March 1957): 20; Fred Dustin, "Isle Royale Place Names," *Michigan History* 30 (1946): 717.
78. Fred Dustin, "A Summary of the Archeology of Isle Royale, Michigan," sections from *Papers of the Michigan Academy of Science, Arts and Letters* 16, no. 1 (1932): 5. To find the botanical specimens collected at or near Birch Island, go to "Michiganflora.net" and use "Birch Island" as the locality; records for birds collected by John Linklater for Norman Wood are Nashville warbler, ovenbird. and black-throated green warbler, University of Michigan Museum of Zoology, Bird Division; Norman A. Wood Diary, June 11 and 12, 1930, University of Michigan Museum of Zoology, Bird Division. Norman Wood wrote a number of follow-up letters to Linklater underscoring how warmly he felt toward the family; Wirta Collection. George Stanley letter to John Linklater, March 24, 1930, Winton, Minn.; Adolph Murie, letter to John Linklater, March 24, 1930, Winton, Minn., Wirta Collection. To honor Linklater, a Michigan fishery biologist, Walter Koelz, named a nearby lake "Linklater Lake." Dustin, "Isle Royale Place Names," 707.
79. Norman Wood, diary, University Museum, University of Michigan; Norman Wood, letter to John Linklater, June 29, 1930, Wirta Collection.
80. "Department News Notes," *Fins, Feathers, and Fur* 37 (March 1924): 173. Chosa thought the "strange malady" was the cause of the "dwindling of Minnesota's moose herd." Brainworm is a parasite that can kill moose. "These

parasites live in the brains of white-tailed deer, now abundant in Minnesota's warming climate. Brainworm larvae are shed into deer feces, and from there the larvae are consumed by land snails. Brainworm develops through several larval stages in the snails, finally infecting other species that inadvertently eat the snails. Land snails live on the surfaces of browse plants favored by deer and moose. 'Deer appear to have no ill effects,' says [Rolf] Peterson, 'but it's another story for moose. They suffer from neurological disease, acting oddly and having trouble standing and moving around, and may quickly die. In some areas, brainworm causes numerous moose deaths.'" Cheryl Lyn Dybas, "Minnesota's Moose: Ghosts of the Northern Forest," *BioScience* 59, no. 10 (November 2009): 827.

81. Wallace, Cahn, and Thomas, "Klebsiella Paralytica," 407.

82. "Deer Has Worms," *Minneapolis Star*, July 17, 1926; "Vanishing Moose Herds Believed Dying of Malady," *Minneapolis Tribune*, September 11, 1926; Charles L. Gilman, "Sick Moose," *Minneapolis Star*, October 1, 1926. Linklater worked alongside a young Dr. Ruel Fenstermacher and colleagues on three research trips. Fenstermacher developed a close working relationship, even friendship, with Linklater. Perhaps most interesting are the efforts behind the science, the give-and-take of their relationship. Linklater was a scientific source on moose behavior and locating moose, and he helped autopsy the moose (and a few deer). But he also hosted the scientists at state and Forest Service cabins and fed them with special north-woods foods, instructed the vets on skinning animals (and then when they were done, got the hides), took them on a canoe trip in the summer and later with a dog team to Ensign Lake, and so on. Linklater instructed them on how best to butcher the deer, which became tasty steaks after the science was done. He found and returned Fenstermacher's checkbook that the vet had dropped at the Game and Fish cabin. The scientists asked and trusted Linklater to "do things," such as watch the dogs (feces) when they tried to infect them with tapeworms from the moose. This particular effort did not work, but Linklater kept at the "science" long after they returned to St. Paul. R. Fenstermacher, E. F. Waller, and F. G. Wallace, "Report on Studies Made of Minnesota Moose from April 20, 1931 to September 22, 1932," Division of Entomology and Economic Zoology, Veterinary Medicine, 1931–1946, University of Minnesota Archive, Minneapolis; R. Fenstermacher, University Farm, St. Paul, letter to John Linklater, November 28, 1932, Wirta Collection.

83. "Many Moose Found Dead Last Spring," *Minneapolis Tribune*, September 21, 1932. The newspaper article was alarmist: "But the disease wave is coming on according to the professor and the year 1933 is set for the great

disease. . . . in the course of the last winter and this spring hundreds of moose have died in northern Minnesota. In the spring one timber cruiser is said to have stumbled upon eight or nine dead moose during the course of a week's travel in the backwoods of Cook County."

84. R. Fenstermacher and W. L. Jellison, "Diseases Affecting Moose," *Minnesota Bulletin* 294, January 1933, Agricultural Experiment Station, University of Minnesota, 4.

85. Lee C. Bradford, "The Moose Problem," *Minnesota Conservationist* 13 (June 1934): 23–27. Linklater is quoted extensively, beginning with "In the opinion of John Linklater." Article found in "Library of Aldo Leopold," moose file, Aldo Leopold Archives, http//digital.library.wisc.edu/1711.d/Aldo Leopold. Linklater's answer to why brainworm began was partly correct, namely, habitat change. The cutting of the white and red pine forests created new habitat for deer, deer populations soared and overlapped with moose, and deer became the passive carriers of brainworm, which is debilitating and often fatal to moose.

86. Ben East, "How Many Moose Roam Isle Royale?" *Ironwood (Mich.) Times,* August 22, 1930. East was against a hunting season on Isle Royale as it would "turn Isle Royale into a wealthy man's private hunting ground."

87. "Believes Moose Herd on Isle Royale Faces Danger of Starvation," *Ludington (Mich.) Daily News,* October 30, 1930; "Moose Herds Decrease," *Decatur (Ill.) Evening Herald,* November 22, 1930; Albert Stoll Jr. "Isle Royale Moose," *Ironwood (Mich.) Daily Globe,* March 11, 1925. Advocates for hunting had a few champions in the Michigan Department of Conservation. "Isle Royale Moose to Be Taken to Mainland," *Ironwood (Mich.) Daily Globe,* October 9, 1925; "Promises Untold Hunting Advantages on Isle Royale," *Ironwood (Mich.) Daily Globe,* April 1926; "Isle Royale Moose," *Fins, Feathers, and Fur* 96 (April 1931): 16.

One park advocate who developed a unique (and early) worry about "too many moose" was Albert Stoll. He expressed the fear "that the herd of moose is growing too large and that they may attempt to migrate across the ice to Canada." In the ensuing years, Stoll became more knowledgeable about moose and changed his opinion on moose numbers and behavior; *Lansing State Journal,* August 15, 1923.

88. Tripp, "Hunting Moose with a Camera."

89. Adolph Murie, letter to Dr. Dice, May 22, 1930, at the University of Michigan Museum, Zoology Division, University of Michigan Museum, Ann Arbor. Murie wrote: "The moose apparently came thru the winter in good shape. I have found no carcasses. Last year's calves seem to be about as numerous

as last fall. This indicated that the moose were not depleted by starvation during the winter."

90. Linklater's technique of "driving" a moose to get close to it was an adaptation of a common canoe guide technique. Indeed, he used this same method ten years earlier when he guided George, Frank, and Alice Warren on a 210-mile canoe trip along the boundary waters. There were three canoes used on the trip, one owned by George Warren and named "Nitchie, Jr.," or friend. This was also the first canoe trip Alice Warren made in the boundary waters and thus an opportunity for her to befriend Linklater, as her husband already had. George W. Warren, letter to Mrs. H. C. Hauser, October 10, 1916.

91. Diary entries, August 20, 1924; September 6, 1926; June 23, 1927; August 30, 1927; Frank M. and Alice Rockwell Warren Papers.

92. Frank M. Warren, "The Wildlife of Isle Royale," *American Game* 15, no. 1 (1926): 17; Frank M. Warren, letter to George R. Hogarth, Director of Conservation, September 10, 1929, Frank M. and Alice Rockwell Warren Papers; Frank M. Warren, letter to Albert Stoll, October 24, 1929, Isle Royale Collection, Bentley Historical Library, Ann Arbor; Frank M. Warren, letter to John Linklater, November 30, 1930, Wirta Collection.

93. Ben East, "How Many Moose on Isle Royale?" *Saginaw (Mich.) Daily News,* August 10, 1930.

94. "War on Wolves Urged to Preserve Home of Moose: Frank M. Warren Makes Plea for Isle Royale Resort," *Minneapolis Star,* October 29, 1929; "Believes Coyotes Are Killing Moose," *Escanaba (Mich.) Daily Press,* August 5, 1931.

95. Adolph Murie, *The Moose of Isle Royale* (Ann Arbor: University of Michigan Press, 1934), 41.

96. As part of creating the national park, private property was purchased in the late 1930s, or if the seller held out, their property was condemned and purchased. The purchase prices were notoriously low, even for the Depression. Many families struggled to get a fair price for their property. Many sold their property but received a life lease to last the lifetime of the seller's family members. Unlike many property owners, the Warrens, strong proponents of the park, sold their structures and land for one dollar and did not take a life lease.

97. Ben East, "Great Moose Herd Roams Isle Royale," *Saginaw (Mich.) News,* August 3; Ben East, "Just an Affair between Ladies," *Saginaw (Mich.) News,* August 10, 1930. Many of East's articles were syndicated to newspapers in Saginaw, Muskegon, Grand Rapids, and Ironwood, Michigan.

98. Ben East, "Are Bull Moose Likely to Charge?" *Saginaw (Mich.) Sunday News,* August 24, 1930; Ben East, "Unwounded Moose Will Attack Man," *Saginaw (Mich.) Sunday News,* August 24, 1930.

99. Ben East, "Hunts Moose Only with His Camera," *Saginaw (Mich.) Sunday News*, September 14, 1930. The article is accompanied by photographs of Linklater's home, Linklater calling moose with a birch-bark call, and Tchi-Ki-Wis Linklater with "a small model of the birch bark canoes of the Chippewa Indians. These little craft follow the pattern of the larger canoes in every detail, including ribs and planking." In another article, East observed: "I watched John Linklater bring a hopeful bull moose out of the birches and halfway across the open mud wallow at the mouth of the Chickenbone River, with soft, low grunts from a cone of the birchbark, and I marveled that a man could speak moose language so artfully." Ben East, "Black Pirates from a Snow Blind," *Esquire*, February 1, 1943, 142.

100. East, "Hunts Moose Only with his Camera."

101. Ben East, "Six in One Hole," *Saginaw (Mich.) News*, September 14, 1931.

102. William Lehr Koffel, letter to his mother, July 22, 1930, Bentley Historical Library, Ann Arbor, Michigan. Koffel, part Indian, addressed Linklater in the Potawatomi language, and Linklater replied in Anishinaabemowin. Koffel wrote of the event at Monument Rock: "Ben East tried to scale this rock a week ago and gave it up. A half breed Indian went up before him and tried to help East up. . . . Finally they lowered the baby ospreys by rope." Ben East, "They're Not Much to Look At," *Saginaw (Mich.) Sunday News*, August 17, 1930; Ben East, "A Hat Makes an Ample Nest," *Saginaw (Mich.) Sunday News*, August 24, 1930.

103. Fanny Scott Rumely, "Isle Royale," Easter 1974, Indiana University Archives, Bloomington, Ind.

104. East, "Six in One Hole."

105. Ellen Hanson, interview, November 11, 1988.

106. For example, Frank Warren "inspected" the Birch Island fishery for the Linklaters in late summer 1926. He carefully noted the boats, fishing gear, buildings, and miscellaneous equipment at the site. Frank M. Warren diary, August 1926, Frank M. and Alice Rockwell Warren Papers. Ed Holte, interview by Dr. Lawrence Rakestraw, September 10, 1965, Wright Island, Isle Royale Oral History Collection; transcript of Milford Johnson interview by Peter Oikarinen, fall 1978, Two Harbors, Minn.; copy of the transcript is in author's possession.

107. The price Hanson and Linklater paid for Birch Island fishery is not known. Captain Robert Francis was asking $4,500 to $5,000 for the fishery, but the deed of sale is for only $1. Francis needed the money for his and his wife's retirement. It is also not known if Linklater was a "silent partner." Hanson was the legal owner on the deed, although Linklater witnessed the sale.

Linklater and Warren first learned that Francis wanted to sell in summer 1926 and "inspected" the operation. Linklater was obviously very positive about it, given Francis was asserting that $3,000 could be made each year. After the Linklaters could not return for the 1931 fishing season, the buildings were sporadically used for a few years by park enthusiasts; then they were abandoned and moldered. When the park commission bought the property, it only bought the buildings and 3.23 acres, and the investment in fishing equipment was lost.

George G. Barnum, Duluth, letter to Thomas Cole, Island Cooper Company, July 3, 1926, Albert Stoll file, Isle Royale Collection, Bentley Library, Ann Arbor; Frank Warren diary, September 7, and back page of diary, 1926, Frank M. and Alice Rockwell Warren Papers; "William Hanson Location," Isle Royale Property Ownership Book, 1935, Isle Royale National Park files; Robert L. Francis and Sarah Francis to William A. Hanson, 3 December 1926, Record of Deeds 2, Keweenaw County, Isle Royal [sic], Eagle River, Mich.

108. Robert Maki, personal communication with author, November 26, 2019, Ely, Minn. Bob is Ellen Hanson's nephew.

109. "Report of Accident to State Employee," State of Minnesota, July 13, 1933, Wirta Papers. The report was completed by Bill Hanson, who would have known Linklater's salary at the time. For the conversion of 1933 currency to today, I used https://www.in2013dollars.com/us/inflation/1933?amount =150.

110. "Game Wardens Aid Makes Trip from Winton to See Explorer," *Minneapolis Tribune*, February 5, 1929.

111. Frank Warren diary, 1929, Frank M. and Alice Rockwell Warren Papers.

112. Riding a moose while it was swimming in the water, like you might ride a horse, was a daredevil's task and might win you legendary status. Linklater also got Warren close enough to get on a moose, but Warren did not. Apparently, Linklater did not think it appropriate to do so.

113. Milford and Myrtle Johnson, interview by Ivan Tolley, Crystal Cove, Isle Royale, September 17, 1974, Isle Royale National Park.

114. Dr. Frank R. Oastler, "Isle Royale—A National Park," *Outdoor America* 9 (1931): 11, 41; Frank R. Oastler, "A Survey of Isle Royale—Lake Superior," *American Planning and Civic Annual* 3 (1931): 29–34; Frank R. Oastler, "Isle Royale Measures Up to Standards for National Park," *Ironwood (Mich.) Times*, October 16, 1931.

115. The same essay in which Linklater is the key subject was also published in a *National Parks Magazine* teaser. Sigurd Olson, "Wilderness Music," *National Parks Magazine* 30, no. 125 (April–June 1956): 63, 64, 80, 81.

116. Sigurd Olson, *Reflections from the North County* (New York: Knopf, 1976; reprint, Minneapolis: University of Minnesota Press, 1998), 157.

117. Sigurd Olson, *Runes of the North* (New York: Knopf, 1973; reprint, Minneapolis: University of Minnesota Press, 1997), 95–96.

118. Sigurd Olson, *Open Horizons* (New York: Knopf, 1969; reprint, Minneapolis: University of Minnesota Press, 1998), 161.

119. Olson, "Wilderness Music," in *The Singing Wilderness*, 197–99. Tchi-Ki-Wis also spoke of hearing spirits. Mary Anderson, interview by Joan Najbar, March 27, 1983, Ely–Winton Historical Society, Ely, Minn.

120. The Lac La Croix First Nation Anishinaabemowin name for Twin Falls, Gaabaswe wejiwang, recognizes it as a focal point for unusual experience and story. "The falls that has an echo. The location in a bay amongst very tall pines provides a chamber as the water rumbles over the rocks. The place holds many stories and legends of the many people who used this route." Kalvin Ottertail and Margaret Ottertail, "Lac La Croix First Nation Quetico's Traditional Lake Names," March 2000, Ridley Library, Quetico Provincial Park, Atikokan, Ontario, 10.

121. David Backes, *The Wilderness Within: The Life of Sigurd F. Olson* (Minneapolis: University of Minnesota Press, 1997), 60–61.

122. Tchi-Ki-Wis told Mary Anderson, who stayed with her after John died, that "when the wind is blowing hard, when you are in bed. When the winds were blowing hard at night, it would be the spirits talking. A lot of times, when you pass on, they come back here. There is something unfinished. They want to tell you something." Mrs. Mary Anderson with Mr. and Mrs. Arthur Johnson, interview by Sister Noemi Weygant, undated, Hoyt Lakes, Minn., Wirta Collection.

123. For example, Linklater would have known winds were highly respected as the creator of music and life breath. The four winds were connected to the four directions and to the sky creator Manitou. The four winds were critical to Anishinaabeg belief, as after the deluge that flooded the earth, the winds helped dry and re-create the earth. Or the spirits talking may have been his own protector spirit associated with his Anishinaabeg name Great Muskrat, which helped restore land after the great flood. Or, for example, Linklater could have been hearing the spirits residing in the waters, in trees, and in the sacred plant *manoomin*, or wild rice.

124. A better representation of the Anishinaabemowin word would be *Memegwesi*. Erik Redix, personal communication with author, June 14, 2020, Grand Portage, Minn.; Sigurd Olson, *Listening Point* (New York: Knopf, 1958; reprint, Minneapolis: University of Minnesota Press, 1997), 169–70.

125. Olson, *Reflections from the North Country*, 23.
126. Olson, *Listening Point*, 73.
127. Considering "the Linklater effect" on Olson is shaped by one obvious fact, namely, Linklater would never read what Olson wrote about him. In effect, Olson had full license to shape his interactions with Linklater for his reading audience. Olson was (consciously and unconsciously) free to craft his experiences with Linklater to suit the purpose of his narratives as well as the fickleness of memory.
128. Sigurd Olson, *The Lonely Land* (New York: Knopf, 1961; reprint, Minneapolis: University of Minnesota Press, 1997), 210. Olson seemed to have kept a look out for "Linklaters" on his long canoe trips. He would have been frustrated in his effort to find the right Linklaters, as it is a common Métis and Indian name. Thus, there are Linklaters in Winnipeg, Kenora, Moose Factory, Fort Albany, Berens River, Pine Falls, and so on. The Linklaters regularly married Indigenous women and dispersed widely throughout Canada.
129. Robert Hill, interview by Sister Noemi Weygant, August 20, 1982, Ely, Minn., Wirta Collection; "Quetico Superior Files," Sigurd Olson Papers. Robert Hill related a story about when Olson and Linklater were traveling together in winter circa 1930 and stopped by a cabin his family used as a small logging camp. Robert, the youngest, was given the task of cooking for his father and brothers. One day Sig and John came by, smelled the stew he was making, were invited to eat, and they ate all of his stew. In the telling, the story was funny to Robert now, but his father was not pleased that he "let them eat it all."
130. John Linklater, "An Old Indian Prophecy," *Fins, Feathers, and Fur* 36 (March 1924): 155–56. That Linklater was a writer at all is remarkable given his fleeting schooling. His warden logs, in his fluid penmanship, make clear he was very capable at expressing himself and describing his warden activities.
131. When Linklater was told this prophecy is hard to pinpoint. A fellow game warden remembered Linklater talking about this prophecy and that he heard it "as a boy." Since Linklater did not live on Basswood Lake until he was a young man, he must have heard the prophecy no earlier than 1889 and after he befriended this elder. Brickner, "Jack Linklater as I Knew Him," 38.
132. "50 Per Cent Decrease of the Moose in Superior Forest Is Reported to Preus," *St. Paul Daily News*, March 30, 1924; "Looking Over the Beaver Country," *Fins, Feathers and Fur* 41 (March 1925): 13; "Statement of the Department's Policies in Relation to Superior National Forest and State Game Refuge," *Fins, Feathers, and Fur* 59 (May 1928): 101.
   Apparently, John's friend made another prophecy that was not included in this vignette, that "they would live . . . to hear people's voices come to them

from all parts of the world. . . . The forecast of hearing people's voices coming from all parts of the world is, of course, our radio of today." Brickner, "Jack Linklater as I Knew Him," 38.

133. An Anishinaabeg traditionalist might add that they departed or vanished because something has gone wrong. It is not simply because moose were killed, particularly if that killing gave life to others. Killing in itself was not viewed as an act of harm against moose, if conducted with respect. But if the spirits of moose are injured or insulted, moose might disappear by returning to whence they came. Christopher Vecsey, *Traditional Ojibwa Religion and Its Historical Changes* (Philadelphia: American Philosophical Society, 1983), 76.

134. Tripp, "Hunting Moose with a Camera."

135. William P. Ferguson, "The Franklin Isle Royale Expedition," *Michigan History* 8 (1924): 463–64.

136. "Isle Royale Is Described by State Game Warden in Radio Address from WBEO," *Marquette (Mich.) Mining Journal*, March 15, 1932; A. A. Webster, "Minong—The Floating Island," *American Forests* 38 (August 1932): 439–41. A. A. Webster, Detroit, letter to John Linklater, April 14, 1931, Wirta Collection. It begins "My Dear John: One of the outdoor magazines has written me relative to the caribou on Isle Royale. . . . I would like your opinion before I make reply, and would appreciate the favor if you will write me as soon as possible telling the caribou history for the past several years, applying to those animals once on the island. Tell me, please, when they were most abundant, the greatest possible numbers, and when the last was seen."

137. Webster, "Minong," 439; Cochrane, *Minong*, 45–46.

138. "The Pictured Rocks," *Fins, Feathers, and Fur* 98 (June 1931): 25.

139. Fikret Berkes, *Sacred Ecology* (New York: Routledge, 2008), 7.

140. George A. West, "Copper: Its Mining and Use by the Aborigines of the Lake Superior Region: Report of the McDonald–Massee Isle Royale Expedition, 1928," *Bulletin of the Public Museum of the City of Milwaukee* 10, no. 1 (1929): 26–27.

141. Melvin Gagnon, personal communication with author, Grand Portage, Minn. December 1, 2021. Mel learned this from his mother, Emma Montferrand Gagnon, who in turn learned it from her father.

142. Tripp, "Hunting Moose with a Camera."

143. Linklater knew how to call other animals toward him by mimicking their sounds, as this diary note makes clear: "John saw a mink along the shore, he called it and it came to the edge of the water and nearly swam out." Frank Warren diary, 1927, Frank M. and Alice Rockwell Warren Papers.

144. Brickner, "Jack Linklater as I Knew Him," 40.

145. Aslakson, "Jack Linklater."
146. Aldrich, *Earth Never Tires*, 194–95.
147. Tom Holm, *The Great Confusion in Indian Affairs: Native Americans and Whites in the Progressive Era* (Austin: University of Texas Press, 2005), 118.
148. Aslakson, "Jack Linklater."
149. Donald Chosa, interview with Warner Wirta, September 11, 1982, Wirta Collection; Weygant, *John (Jack) Linklater*, 10.

5. Making the Carry

1. Robert Cary, "Spirit of Basswood Lake," *Boundary Waters Journal* (Winter 1999): 23–24. Cary wrote another, earlier piece about Linklater, with his pencil sketch of John as a centerpiece. Robert Cary, "Citizen of the Northland," *Ely Echo*, October 15, 1984. The earlier piece recapped some of Linklater's history, including that he was "a superb woodsman, and could 'live off the land' if it was required." It concludes: "Some say the spirit of John Linklater still walks and talks on the canoe trails of the border lakes," a similar conclusion to his article in the *Boundary Waters Journal*.
2. "John James Linklater," death record, 1933, Lake County, Two Harbors, Minn. The death record also stated that he was an "Indian," born in North Dakota, and the birthplace of his parents was unknown. Sadly, drowning was common in the lake country. Less than two months after Linklater drowned, four other people drowned on Basswood Lake, despite that three were said to be "expert swimmers." One of the group was a well-to-do man, H. H. Bigelow, from the Twin Cities. *Minneapolis Star*, September 18 and 20, 1933.
3. Robert Page Lincoln, "Some Canoe Facts," *Minneapolis Tribune*, August 13, 1933. The author places a good deal of the blame on the fact that "few if any Indians are swimmers. Linklater, the warden who drowned, was part Indian, and did not know how to swim a stroke." In this account, Linklater's deficiency in knowing how to swim is cited as a key reason for his death. Only a month later in the same body of water, when four Whites drowned, it was reported as a "pure" tragedy and little fault of the victims.
4. Merwin W. Peterson, one of Sigurd Olson's partners at Border Lakes Outfitting Company, said Linklater died of a heart attack. John Sansted, interview by Warner Wirta, August 21, 1982, Winton, Minn., Wirta Collection. A noted guide, Sansted also mentioned that when they found Linklater's body, "his watch had stopped at 2:30." Most commentators assumed Jack did not know how to swim. Sansted added a detail that others did not: after Tchi-Ki-Wis made it to shore, she waited for John, then slowly, reluctantly she realized he was gone. She then started walking the shoreline for home, arriving at the Hoffmans' place hours later with her clothes in tatters.

5. Mary Anderson with Mr. and Mrs. Arthur Johnson, interview by Sister Noemi Weygant, Hoyt Lakes, Minn., no date, Wirta Collection.

6. Brickner, "Jack Linklater as I Knew Him," 40. Brickner also reported he and Linklater had had a close call in the same canoe and motor only two days earlier. Brickner further stated he was not sure what exactly happened then and why they did not get injured. According to a friend of Brickner, Dr. Julius Wolff, "Brickner never got over Jack's drowning, sort of blamed himself." Linklater file, Ridley Library, Quetico Provincial Park, Atikokan, Ontario.

7. Warner Wirta speaking in his interview with Ellen Hanson, Ely, Minn., July 9, 2008, Wirta Collection.

8. Linklater file, Shirley Peruniak notes, Ridley Library, Quetico Provincial Park, Atikokan, Ontario; William Hanson, interview, September 7, 1976.

9. Linklater was agile well into his late fifties. For example, photographs show him leading a climbing group (he is the only one carrying a rope) of Rock Harbor cottagers to Monument Rock, and another shows him on top of a sea stack at Isle Royale that Dr. Oastler had asked him to climb for a picture-taking opportunity. Frank M. Warren and Dr. Frank R. Oastler, photograph albums, Isle Royale National Park.

10. Brickner, "Jack Linklater as I Knew Him," 40.

11. Aslakson, "Jack Linklater," *Minneapolis Sunday Tribune*, August 18, 1933. Tchi-Ki-Wis also "always paddled close to shore, or the shoreline." Ellen Hanson interview, November 11, 1988.

12. Roufs, *When Everybody Called Me Gah-bay-bi-nayass*, 2:233–38; Jennifer S. H. Brown and Robert Brightman, eds., *"The Orders of the Dreamed": George Nelson on Cree and Northern Ojibwa Religion and Myth, 1823* (St. Paul: Minnesota Historical Society, 1988), 139, 144.

13. It is not known how devoted an Anglican Linklater was. He spoke little of it, or of his church going. He had little opportunity to attend an Anglican church as an adult.

14. On July 11, 1933, the following newspapers carried the story on John Link-later's death: *Oakland (Calif.) Tribune, Fort Lauderdale (Fla.) News, Victoria (British Columbia) Daily Times, Fort Worth Star-Telegram, Birmingham (Ala.) News, Bristol (Tenn.) Bulletin, Windsor (Ontario) Star; Calgary Herald; Lansing (Mich.) State Journal, Salt Lake Telegram, Virginia (Minn.) Daily Enterprise, Pittsburgh Sun Telegraph,* and *York (Pa.) Dispatch.* On July 12, 1933, the following newspapers carried the story: *Atlanta Constitution, Pensacola (Fla.) News Journal,* and *Orlando Evening Star.* Follow-up articles on July 13 and 14 were carried in the *Minneapolis Tribune* (both days), *St. Cloud (Minn.) Times* (both days), *Ely (Minn.) Miner,* and *Tower (Minn.) Weekly News.*

15. "Famous Guide Dies," *Birmingham (Ala.) News*, July 11, 1933. Most print articles were very similar to this version. The contrast between the nationally memorialized death of John Linklater and his parents could not be starker. The deaths—where and exactly when—of Linklater's parents, William and Ah-zhe-day-ge-she-gake, were not recorded and are a mystery. My best hypothesis is that both died in remote locations, that is, not on a reserve, in a town, or at a HBC post but in the vast "bush" of northwestern Ontario.

16. Aslakson, "Jack Linklater"; Sam G. Anderson, Hutchinson, Minn., letter to John Linklater, January 27, 1933, Wirta Collection.

17. "Jack Linklater, Wilderness Guide and Warden, Drowns," *Minneapolis Journal*, July 10, 1933.

18. Jack Linklater, game warden report, January 16, 1932, included this note: "folks called me on account of sickness." Mayme Wirta, Embarrass, Minn., letter, January 31, 1932, to John Linklater, Winton; "Dear Tana, Will you send some of that medicine for itch? The Sulphur and the soap, they left it up Jack Fish and would like you to get some at Ely, if possible," Wirta Collection; "[Tchi-Ki-Wis] needs salve, can't sleep," undated message in Wirta Collection; Frank M. Warren, letter to John Linklater, January 16, 1932, Wirta Collection.

19. John Robinson—"the old man—sick in bed"—in a John Linklater letter to Hilma J. Nelson (his granddaughter-in-law), September 10, 1932, Winton, Minn., Wirta Collection. John Robinson died May 29, 1935, in the Cook Home, Duluth. Certificate of Death, State of Minnesota, Division of Vital Statistics, (for St. Louis County). Little information was recorded on his death certificate. The doctor guessed he was "about 80." Clara Linklater Wirta died November 30, 1936, in Biwabik, Minn. Certificate of Death 14602, Division of Vital Statistics, State of Minnesota, Biwabik, St. Louis County.

20. John Boatman, *My Elders Taught Me: Aspects of Western Great Lakes American Indian Philosophy* (Lanham, Md.: University Press of America, 1992), 39.

21. John and Vi Sansted, interview, Winton, Minn., August 21, 1982, Wirta Collection; Mary Anderson with Mr. and Mrs. Arthur Johnson, interview.

22. Lake County Death Certificate, 1934, Two Harbors, Minn. Tchi-Ki-Wis's exact date of death was November 12, 1934.

23. A different example of how an information vacuum about the Linklaters created a need for an answer was the rumor, among a few Isle Royale visitors, that John had more than one wife. The rumor recorded years after his death is far-fetched, especially as Tchi-Ki-Wis was the only Indigenous woman who came and worked on Birch Island. Ruth Spencer, letter to Clifford Wellington, Champion, Mich., December 20, 1941, Chynoweth Collection,

University Archives and Copper Country Historical Collection, Michigan Technological University, Houghton.

24. "Drowning Victim Buried Monday," *Cook County News Herald*, May 3, 1933. Adam Roach LaPlante had worked for Holger Johnson at Chippewa Harbor for three years. He drowned at Wright Island, Isle Royale. Having spent the past winter on Isle Royale, he had not "been home for a year and half." One summer Adam Roach was joined by his grandmother Mary LaPlante, and they both worked for Holger Johnson at his homespun resort. Mrs. LaPlante taught some of the Johnson kids birch-bark techniques, such as making baskets and miniature canoes and doing quill work on the baskets. Mrs. Violet Miller, interview by author, October 12, 1988, Ahmeek, Mich.

25. Ben East, "Isle Royale Moose Fat and Contented," *Saginaw (Mich.) Daily News*, August 24, 1930.

26. Ben East, "Winter Sky Roads to Isle Royal," *National Geographic Magazine*, December 1931, 773.

27. Memorandum, Regional Director to Acting Superintendent, Isle Royale National Park, October 10, 1967, Isle Royale National Park files.

28. Memorandum, Isle Royale Superintendent to Regional Director, January 27, 1961; Memorandum, Regional Director to Isle Royale Superintendent, June 19, 1961; John Linklater Cabin, Birch Island, Historical American Building Survey Inventory, September 29, 1965; Memorandum, Regional Director to Director, August 16, 1967; Memorandum, Chief, Office of Archeology and Historic Preservation to Regional Director, September 18, 1967, Isle Royale National Park files.

The demise of the Linklater cabins fits into a larger pattern of neglect of historic structures on Isle Royale that became dilapidated for lack of maintenance and funding, were proclaimed a safety hazard, and then after some give-and-take between historic preservation–minded personnel, were finally determined to be a safety hazard to tourists or not of significant historical importance to warrant maintaining them. The key to this pattern is the years of neglect (making stabilization or repair impracticable later), then asking the question of the buildings' historical importance once they are rundown.

Fortunately, Isle Royale and the National Park Service have changed their course on affirming and interpreting an Anishinaabeg past on Isle Royale. The most significant evidence of this is the 2019 "Minong" Traditional Cultural Property (TCP) nomination on the National Register of Historic Places. The Minong TCP affirms the historic and contemporary importance of Isle Royale to the people of the Grand Portage Band of Minnesota Chippewa Tribe. The park and the Grand Portage Band celebrated their relationship twice. The first event was to recognize the Minong Traditional Cultural Property designation with a feast and comments by VIPs, such as the tribal chairwoman Beth Drost and Superintendent Phyllis Green, on July 23, 2019, at Windigo. The second celebration was to honor the raising of the Grand Portage tribal flag and their deepening relationship at Windigo on August 17, 2021.

29. Robert Maki, personal communication with author, Fall Lake, Minn., October 25, 2020.

30. In contrast, in the 1920s, Yosemite National Park managers came to the exact opposite conclusion. "Yosemite Indian Field Days suggest that at least some NPS officials and many American tourists imagined these places of 'wilderness' as, in fact, the last bastion of an authentic Indianness." Boyd Cothran, "Working the Indian Field Days: The Economy of Authenticity and the Question of Agency in Yosemite Valley," *American Indian Quarterly* 34, no. 2 (Spring 2010): 197.

31. The erasure of the Linklaters' place is, on the surface, the same as the "erasure" of Dorothy Moltor's and Benny Ambrose's homes in the Boundary Waters Canoe Area Wilderness. But Moltor and Ambrose were White, and both lived on later in their respective Boundary Waters homes than the Linklaters. They are much celebrated today, especially Moltor, with a museum established in her honor, while the Linklaters and Jackfish Bay and Basswood Lake Anishinaabeg are comparatively hardly remembered.

32. There are quite a number of these "maybe stories," such as (1) he was a U.S. Marshall in Tower, Minnesota, in the early 1890s; "Jack Linklater: Drowning Victim," *Ely (Minn.) Miner*, July 14, 1933. (2) Linklater hauled annuity payments to Indian villages for the Canadian government; Aslakson, "Jack Linklater." (3) He was attacked on the trail while making a portage in northern Ontario, but he stood off a group of "thieving Indians" that wanted his goods; ibid.

33. Temporary (really seasonal) work for the HBC was often not well documented. So it is possible he did work for the HBC in his young adulthood.

34. Ben East, "Indian Guide on Isle Royale Lived Thru Trap Evolution," *Herald Press* (St. Joseph, Mich.), September 18, 1930; East, "Hunts Moose Only with His Camera."

35. "Surveyor's Report of Exploration Survey Report No. 10," January 2, 1900, in *Report of the Survey and Exploration of Northern Ontario*, Legislative Assembly of Ontario, 1901. If Jack Linklater was the "J. J. Linklater" on this survey, he would have revisited Lac Seul and much of the country of his youth.

36. Tchi-Ki-Wis's reticence to speak with Whites was a common Anishinaabeg coping mechanism in addition to being customary. Or as one Anishinaabe

put it, "You shouldn't tell a white man nothing! . . . You know what they've done. . . . They've taken everything—blueberries, game, wild life, flowers, even the land. We haven't any of that now. They're even trying to take away our religion." Roufs, *When Everybody Called Me Gah-bay-bi-nayass*, 2:332.

37. Mary Anderson with Mr. and Mrs. Arthur Johnson, interview.

38. Frank M. Warren, letter to Albert Stoll, *Detroit News*, October 24, 1929, "Isle Royale Collection," Bentley Library, Ann Arbor, Mich. In the letter, Warren wrote about the photographs that were presumed to be his that were published by the *Detroit News*. Warren noted: "The cow moose in the picture you published with your article in *The Detroit News*, October 20, 1929, was taken with my camera by my friend, John Linklater, in 1925. . . . I sent the picture to the *News* through Mr. A. A. Webster, October 10, 1925." Webster was also a conservation-minded author. The key point here is that some photographs credited to Warren were taken by Linklater. Privately, Warren repeatedly noted in his diary when Linklater took photos and, beginning in 1926, shot movie footage. Frank Warren diary, August 23, 1924; August 29, 1926, and September 6, 1926, Frank M. and Alice Rockwell Warren Papers.

39. Lodge owner Fred Schoenfield of Belle Isle, Isle Royale, preferred Linklater, rather than himself, to pilot his vessel around Blake Point en route to Rock Harbor, despite Linklater having few summers of navigating the big lake. Fred Dustin, Field Journal, 1929, University of Michigan Museum of Anthropology, Ann Arbor.

40. Cothran, "Working the Indian Field Days," 195.

41. Frank M. Warren, letter to John Linklater, September 25, 1928, Isle Royale, Wirta Collection.

42. Alice Warren's niece Jean Anderson noted: "They [Frank and Alice Warren] very much liked to talk about Jack. . . . Uncle Frank considered Jack the best friend he ever had." Jean Anderson, personal communication with author, March 27, 2020, Los Angeles, Calif.

43. Mrs. Cornelia O'Neil (also a niece of the Warrens), letter, December 2, 1988, Green Farms, Connecticut, to author. Frank and Alice Warren's friendship with Linklater budged but did not transcend their social, economic, and racially prescribed roles and differences. Since Linklater never voiced his feelings about the Warrens that we are privy to, it is difficult to judge what he thought about them. Linklater regularly wrote and received letters from them, and worked and camped with them. They were "friends" for thirty years. Ultimately, though, Linklater was expected to live in their world of elites as a guide.

298 ◆ NOTES TO CHAPTER 5

44. "John Linklater," "Alien Registration and Declaration of Holdings," Minnesota Commission of Public Safety, State of Minnesota, Iron Range Research Center, Chisholm; Frank Nelson, 1920, U.S. Census, Winton, Minn. There is only one account of Clara Linklater attending boarding school at Lake Vermilion. No one remembered if Margaret went there. Mrs. John Landgen Klug, interview by Warner Wirta, no date, Two Harbors, Wirta Collection. A number of Chosa children went to Vermilion Lake Indian School, so perhaps both Linklater daughters did, but if they did, it was probably for a short period of time, otherwise there likely would be more records or memories of their presence at the boarding school.

45. Minnesota Department of State, Motor Vehicle Department, letter to Mr. John Linklater, March 29, 1932, Winton, Minn.

46. Jean M. O'Brien, *Firsting and Lasting: Writing Indians Out of Existence in New England* (Minneapolis: University of Minnesota Press, 2010), 134–35; Cothran, "Working the Indian Field Days," 195, 208.

47. After Linklater's death, in a private letter, Warren wrote: "John was the only man I have ever known outside of my father who would gladly have laid down his life for me if it would have saved mine. In over thirty-six years, I have never knew him to do or heard of his having done any act that was unkind to someone else. He was honest, loyal and true." Frank Warren, letter to Mrs. Joseph Pecore, July 11, 1933, Schroeder, Minn., Frank M. and Alice Rockwell Warren Papers.

48. Aldrich, *Earth Never Tires*, 76.

49. John Linklater file, Ridley Library, Quetico Provincial Park, Atikokan, Ontario.

50. Linklater, "An Old Indian Prophecy," 155–56.

51. For example, Linklater would learn from elders that the nadir of rabbit and sturgeon populations (because of heavy fishing pressure on the Rainy River) preceded Treaty 3 making in 1870, putting the Anishinaabeg ogimaag in even a more difficult position, as the bands were hungry. Simon J. Dawson, "Memorandum in Reference to the Indians on the Line of Route between Lake Superior and the Red River Settlement," December 19, 1870, Library and Archives Canada, MG 11, C.O. 42, vol. 698, 141–42.

52. Fikret Berkes, "Traditional Ecological Knowledge in Perspective," in *Traditional Ecological Knowledge: Concepts and Cases*, ed. J. T. Inglis (Ottawa: Canadian Museum of Nature and the International Development Research Centre, 1993): 1–2.

53. East, "How Many Moose on Isle Royale?"

54. "Controversy Is Now Ended," *St. Cloud (Minn.) Times*, June 3, 1933.

55. David McNabb, "Wilderness and Extinction: The Lac La Croix and Sturgeon

Lake First Nations," in *Circles of Time: Aboriginal Land Rights and Resistance in Ontario* (Waterloo, Ont.: Wilfrid Laurier University Press, 1999), 89–100.

56. Lynn Marie Laitala, "Jackfish Pete: Pete LaPrairie's Story," in *The Wilderness Debate Rages On*, ed. Michael P. Nelson and J. Baird Callicott (Athens: University of Georgia Press, 2008), 218–30; Carl Gawboy, personal communication with author, December 9, 2014, Duluth, Minn.

57. Sigurd Olson's positive view of predators such as wolves and stopping the campaign to poison them was likely learned from his mentors at the University of Illinois. Professors Victor Shelford and Alvin Cahn were strong advocates for the role of wolves in keeping a balance of nature. David Backes, personal communication with author, April 14, 2019.

58. "Club Notes," *Sunday Minneapolis Tribune*, November 30, 1947.

59. Ben Chynoweth, letter to John Smith, August 4, 1966; A. A. Webster, untitled note, after an August 1937 visit to Birch Island, Chynoweth Collection, University Archives and Copper Country Historical Collections, Michigan Technological University, Houghton.

60. Linklater sketched specific "wolf trails" on a 1928 map of Superior National Forest with annotations. Sigurd Olson wrote on the map, "wolf trails that Jack knew." The trails wind throughout the forest from lake to lake and overland. That Linklater could remember and chart these many and long trails testifies to his observational skills that were linked with a geographic mastery. Sigurd Olson Papers, Minnesota Historical Society.

61. Milton H. Stenlund, *A Wildlife Biologist Recalls Fifty Years with Wolves in Minnesota* (Grand Rapids, Minn.: Northprint, 1985), 11.

62. Brickner, "John Linklater," 39.

63. For example, Linklater's account of Tchi-Ki-Wis and her grandmother paddling across Gichi Gami to Isle Royale and his grandfather observing such an event is differentially captured in three accounts. The accounts are retold by archaeologists George West and George Fox, and the third by an unnamed person (Fred Dustin is most likely) and in a note in *Michigan History*. Linklater would have related this narrative in 1928 and perhaps in 1930. The three accounts are consistent in some elements, such as (1) Tchi-Ki-Wis and her grandmother paddled to Minong, (2) they left from the Canadian shore (likely Fort William area), and (3) they all conclude with Linklater's comment about where Anishinaabeg people camped once they made it to Minong (implicit reaction to spurious stories that they left the island without camping overnight there, supposedly being scared to do so).

The accounts differ on two key elements: (1) whether Linklater's grandfather (likely Great-Uncle Thomas Richards) just observed the party leaving for Isle Royale, or whether he went with them, and (2) the explanation of the spiritual nature of the trip. West's rendering talks of evil spirits dwelling on the island making it a less attractive place to visit. Fox recounts the need to appease spirits, but the spirits are unnamed and not located; for example, they could be of the lake or of the island or both. The spirit is not necessarily depicted as evil. The *Michigan History* account talks more of Indians' "awe" of going to the island, and the mystery of why there was such a reluctance to go, although it offers guesses about why there was this reluctance. Perhaps the widest gulf in the three narratives is the feeling of "awe" expressed in one account versus the fear of an evil spirit in another. Important to note, both authors likely heard Linklater tell the story at the same time, August 1928, during the McDonald–Massee Expedition to Isle Royale. For more on the difference between "being scared" and being reverential about spirits related to lake crossings, see Cochrane, *Minong*, 61–69.

Which account best captured Linklater's oral history, or did Linklater vary his telling? Linklater's grandfather (really, great-uncle) would not have made the trip, as he was both elderly and an HBC employee at the time. And since Linklater would be respectful in explicating a narrative about important Anishinaabeg beliefs and customs, I doubt he would significantly vary his telling. I am inclined to believe it was the chroniclers' biases (and inattentiveness in one) that are reflected in the differences in the accounts, rather than Linklater significantly changing his story. George A. West, "Copper: Its Mining and Use by the Aborigines of the Lake Superior Region, Report of the McDonald–Massee Isle Royale Expedition," *Bulletin of the Public Museum of the City of Milwaukee* 10 (1929), 31; Fox, "The Isle Royale Expedition," 317, 319; "Centennial Notes," *Michigan History Magazine* 19 (1935), 454–55.

Tacked on to all three accounts is another example of how Linklater's "teachings" may have been distorted. And because his account of Anishinaabeg going to Minong is one of the rarest of observations, readers have accentuated his supposed words. Some have taken his comments literally, such as "the Indians did not remain on the coast but made their camps on the inland lakes." "Centennial Notes," 455. This became conventional wisdom among the few interested archaeologists at the time. However, it is quite possible Linklater is speaking of the few instances of which he knew firsthand and is largely making a general comment about attractive camp locations. Always attentive to good camp sites, he could be simply suggesting that a sheltered, warmer place (south facing?), like his residence on Jackfish Bay or Birch Island, would be a more comfortable camp to make rather than the colder, windy lakeshore. If this is correct, a "general comment" morphed into a hard-and-fast "rule." The authors' interests and biases likely "warped" their telling, perhaps overemphasizing what Linklater had originally suggested. Since archaeologists were actively searching for Anishinaabeg camps, this statement became a "road map" for them.

The key point is that three authors left us different accounts of what Linklater said to them about the same event. Linklater was experienced enough to know that his listeners might misunderstand his "teachings." Still he persisted in teaching these archaeologists about Anishinaabeg history, beliefs, and custom.

64. John and Tchi-Ki-Wis continued to have a team at their place on Jackfish Bay as late as the winter of 1932–33, when grandson Frank Nelson used the team at the Crawford Lodge on Basswood Lake. John Linklater, letter to Mrs. Frank Nelson, September 10, 1932, Duluth, Wirta Collection.

65. There was an eventual relaxation of the July 15, 1870, deadline for applying for Métis scrip in Canada. The new deadline was extended to 1885; thus, it made John Linklater eligible for Métis scrip. However, he likely learned of this after some delay. Years later, the Canadian government rejected any Métis scrip claims that came from the United States, eliminating the possibility that Linklater could receive Métis scrip. He never was formally recognized as Métis, unlike his father, sister, and a host of uncles and aunts and cousins.

66. "John Linklater," "Alien Registration."

67. Copies of the "Isle Royale: Wilderness Unspoiled," Northern Pacific brochure are found both in the Bentley Historical Library, Ann Arbor, and in the Cheynoweth Collection, University Archive and Historical Collections, Michigan Technological University Archive, Houghton.

68. Martha Harrouin Foster, *We Know Who We Are: Métis Identity in a Montana Community* (Norman: University of Oklahoma Press, 2006), 10. Linklater's unshakeable comfortableness in his indigeneity is contrasted with some Métis who became American citizens. Often Métis were forced to "guard and preserve [their American citizenry] by denying their indigeneity." Michael Witgen, *An Infinity of Nations: How the Native New World Shaped Early North America* (Philadelphia: University of Pennsylvania Press, 2012), 344.

69. "History of Lac Seul Communities," Lac Seul First Nation, http://lacseulfn .org/about/history.

70. O'Brien, *Firsting and Lasting*, 141.

71. The Linklaters' "strategy" about where they lived paralleled that of "Métis road communities" in the Canadian Prairie Provinces. Initially fleeing retribution from the Métis Rebellions, blatant discrimination, and the ineffectualness of Métis scrip to enable them to become landowners, many Métis

ended up living on unused, unclaimed land between road rights-of-way and homesteads. They were landless. This strategy of living on the road edges in remote, northern locations has some similarities to what John and Tchi-Ki-Wis Linklater did, finding places where settlement was light and the presence of government authority was insubstantial.

The relocation of William III (and his children Alice and John) east and southeast of the Red River area was uncommon for the Métis diaspora. Most Métis moved west and northwest from the Red River area, essentially the opposite direction. A comparatively few eventually made their way to North Dakota (like uncle John Linklater) and Montana. But very few headed east into Ontario, such as the Linklaters. "Dispersal of the Métis," map in "Red River Insurgence," Gabriel DuMont Institute, Regina, Saskatchewan, 1985.

72. Aslakson, "Jack Linklater."

73. Scott Richard Lyons, *X-Marks: Native Signatures of Assent* (Minneapolis: University of Minnesota Press, 2010), 157.

74. Métis scholar Brenda Macdougall wrote, "lay people and scholars alike have found it problematic to reconcile the Métis with existing social, cultural, economic, or political reference points because of their implicit and explicit defiance of those basic systematic categories [Indian or White] that define our understanding of the world." Brenda Macdougall, "The Myth of Métis Cultural Ambivalence," in *Contours of a People: Metis Family, Mobility, and History*, ed. Nicole St-Onge, Carolyn Podruchny, and Brenda Macdougall (Norman: University of Oklahoma Press, 2012), 430.

75. Jennifer S. H. Brown, "Metis, Halfbreeds, and Other Real People: Challenging Cultures and Categories," *History Teacher* 27, no. 1 (November 1993): 21.

76. O'Brien, *Firsting and Lasting*, 151.

77. Witgen, *An Infinity of Nations*, 368.

78. This paragraph stems from the idea put forth by Anishinaabe scholar Scott Lyons, who notes Indians were always interested in "modernity," not plodding along as unadaptable traditionalists. Lyons, *X-Marks*, 11, 99.

79. Ellen Hanson, interview, July 20, 1982, Wirta Collection.

80. William Hanson, interview, September 7, 1976.

"An Old Indian Prophecy"

1. John Linklater file, Shirley Peruniak notes, Ridley Library, Quetico Provincial Park.

2. Chilson Aldrich, letter, winter 1927, Quetico Provincial Park.

INDEX

TIMOTHY COCHRANE is the author of *A Good Boat Speaks for Itself: Isle Royale Fishermen and Their Boats* (Minnesota, 2002), *Minong—the Good Place: Ojibwe and Isle Royale,* and *Gichi Bitobig, Grand Marais: Early Accounts of the Anishinaabeg and the North Shore Fur Trade* (Minnesota, 2018). He has worked as a fire lookout, backcountry ranger, historian, and anthropologist, and for many years was superintendent for the National Park Service in Minnesota, Alaska, and Isle Royale, Michigan. Throughout his career he has had the good fortune to work extensively with Native American tribes, most recently with the Grand Portage Band of Lake Superior Chippewa.